SEX AND LOVE
IN THE BIBLE

By WILLIAM GRAHAM COLE

❧❦❧

ASSOCIATION PRESS
NEW YORK

SEX

AND

LOVE

IN

THE BIBLE

SEX AND LOVE IN THE BIBLE

Copyright © 1959 by
National Board of Young Men's Christian Associations

Association Press, 291 Broadway, New York 7, N.Y.

Library of Congress catalog card number: 59–12108

Printed in the United States of America

For
   Graham and Ted and Steve

ACKNOWLEDGMENTS

THE INDEBTEDNESS of an author is beyond calculation. Not the most skillful certified public accountant could possibly list and audit the total liabilities; for even while the books are being balanced, new bills present themselves for notice if not for payment. No one can ever repay in full. All of us are in a perennial state of bankruptcy, in need of deficit financing. One's personal ledger can carry only the larger, more obvious loans.

Most of the Scripture quotations in this volume are from the Revised Standard Version of the Bible, copyrighted 1946 and 1952 by the Division of Christian Education, National Council of Churches, and they are used by permission. I am indebted to the Abingdon Press for permission to quote from two articles in Volume I of *The Interpreter's Bible,* and to the Oxford University Press for allowing me to use excerpts from *A Companion to the Bible,* edited by J. J. von Allmen, from Paul Tillich's *Love, Power, and Justice,* from *Israel,* by Johannes Pedersen, and from my own earlier work, *Sex in Christianity and Psychoanalysis.* I am deeply in the debt of

Paul Tillich, my former teacher and present friend, for many insights and interpretations. Rudolph Bultmann, Frederick C. Grant, and C. H. Dodd have enriched my understanding of the New Testament, as Johannes Pedersen, George Ernest Wright, and James Muilenburg have added to my knowledge of the Old Testament. Drs. Sandor Rado and Aaron Karush have provided me with much of whatever feeling for depth psychology I may possess. My friends and colleagues on the faculty of Williams College have made regular deposits in the vaults of my ongoing education, and their erudition continually augments my resources. To them and to all my intellectual benefactors past and present I express my grateful indebtedness.

It is customary for an author to pay tribute to his wife, and I would conform to this happy tradition. But more than mere custom is involved here. My pen gropes for words unsullied by common usage to express a gratitude so clearly merited. Not only has she typed the manuscript, a labor whose magnitude only those familiar with my illegible scrawl can properly appreciate, but also she has in every chapter provided an insight, understanding, and wisdom without which this volume would be much the poorer. She is indeed "flesh of my flesh and bone of my bones," the incarnation of all that is best in biblical woman: a Sarah, a Rachel, a Shulammite, a Martha, and a Mary. She joins me in dedicating this work to our three sons.

W.G.C.

CONTENTS

Introduction   15

1. Divine Love in the Old Testament   xi

2. Human Love in the Old Testament   53

3. Divine Love in the New Testament   89

4. Human Love in the New Testament   128

5. Sex Attitudes and Practices: Israel against
   Her Neighbors   161

6. Sex Attitudes and Practices: the Early
   Church against the Graeco-Roman
   World   193

7. Premarital Sex Relations in the Bible   230

8. Sex in Marriage   268

9. Prostitution, Adultery, and Divorce   306

10. Homosexuality in the Bible   342

11. Other Sexual Deviations: Masturbation,
    Immodesty, Rape, Incest, Bestiality   373

12. The Bible and the World of Dr. Kinsey   403

Index   438

Biblical References   444

INTRODUCTION

ONE OF THE MORE crucial problems of our modern society is in the area of sex and love. Not only has the United States been stirred by the Kinsey Reports, by an increase in the output of near-pornography in magazines and movies, by a growing sexual precocity in the young, but England also has been preoccupied with the Wolfenden Report on homosexuality and prostitution, alarmed by a recent outbreak of brutal sex crimes, and interested in Eustace Chesser's studies of the sexual relationships of English women. Scandinavia is the focus of considerable attention with its legalized abortion for unwed mothers and state-supported institutions for illegitimate children. All over the world, family patterns are changing as women in the underdeveloped countries begin to demand equality and dignity.

The church has stepped up the tempo of its concern for family life. Most of the major Protestant denominations have established departments of study and action in this area, as has the National Council of Churches in the United States of America. The 1958 Lambeth Conference of Anglican Bishops issued a highly significant report on "The Family in Contemporary Society"; and the officers of the World Council of Churches and the International Missionary Council called an international consultative conference on the population explosion and responsible parenthood at Oxford, England, in April of 1959. The flow of books and pamphlets written from a Christian perspective on sex and family life has increased markedly in the last decade.

Some attention has been given to the Bible in these writings, conferences, and departments. But this attention has for the most part been spotty and confined to particular passages. Against the background of growing concern it seems important to have available a somewhat more systematic treatment of sex and love in the Bible. That is precisely what the present volume is intended to do. Such a treatment, if it is to be helpful, must place bifocal spectacles on the nose of the biblical reader. Through one half of the lens he must be able to see the treatment of sex and love in the Old and New Testaments without bias or distortion, and in such a way that it can be properly understood and profitably used. But this means that the various passages must be seen in the context of their times. The Bible is woven on the loom of history, and none of it can be really understood if the reader is ignorant of the events and circumstances surrounding it, of the changing conditions of the ancient Hebrews as they interacted with their Canaanite neighbors and with the mighty empires of antiquity, of the Jews after the Babylonian exile and the special problems they faced in their efforts to rebuild their national life, of the early church and its place in the Graeco-Roman world. The first concern, therefore, must be to understand what the Bible has to say in its own terms to its own times.

But that alone will not suffice. We have learned a great deal about sex and love in the centuries since the biblical canon was closed, more particularly in the last seventy-five years. Sigmund Freud and his colleagues, successors, and dissenters in the psychoanalytic movement have subjected the human libido and its vicissitudes to microscopic scrutiny. The clinical psychologists have amassed an impressive array of data on the sexual behavior of all mammals, of whom man is only one—at least from their standpoint. The late Dr. Kinsey and his associates studied in considerable detail the sex habits and foibles of Americans, both male and female, and produced a series of statistical tables and charts which cannot be ignored, however they may annoy and embarrass. Anthropologists are gathering incredibly complete information about the love life of primitive societies in all parts of the world, information which simply must be taken into account by any sexual theories or ethics which lay claim to universality. Beside this collection of scientific and semi-scientific facts, how does the Bible stand up? Does it have anything to say to Western man in the last half of

the twentieth century? Or is it hopelessly outdated and
limited, coming as it does from circumstances entirely
different from our own? The second half of the lens
must provide this kind of vision if we are to see the
whole of the pattern, if a full and usable view of the
Bible is to be obtained.

This bifocal approach to the Bible is what the present volume seeks to provide. Its success or failure in
this enterprise must, in the final analysis, be judged by
the reader. But the task, if one may shift the metaphor
and borrow a figure from the comic strip *Alley Oop,*
is to begin by stepping into Dr. Wonmug's Time Machine for a journey backward through the centuries.
We want to know what the biblical peoples thought,
how they felt and acted, and what were the economic,
political, social, and religious factors influencing them.
Then, returning to the present—hopefully rich with
raw materials—we want to subject them to the scrutiny
of our modern laboratories, to appraise our findings
and discover what relevance, if any, they may have for
our own era and the difficult problems we face today in
the relations between the sexes. We may return from
the past empty-handed, or we may uncover a new
source of power, revolutionary in its implications. The
results of the journey cannot be predicted. The expe-
dition may prove to be many things. One thing it will
not be, however, is dull!

WILLIAM GRAHAM COLE

1

DIVINE LOVE

IN THE

OLD

TESTAMENT

Any discussion of love in the Old Testament must
begin with Hosea, the prophet who married a whore.
This is not because there is little or no mention of love
before Hosea, who lived and preached in the northern
kingdom of Israel in the middle of the eighth century
B.C., but because all the developments in early Hebrew
thought are in some sense preparatory to and gathered

up in the career and the message of this wronged husband.

The book which bears his name opens with a cryptic autobiographical account (a kind of biblical *Of Human Bondage*) of his curious relationship with Gomer, the woman who became his wife. There are several theories which seek to interpret the enigmatic references to Hosea's marriage. Some see it as pure allegory, not to be taken literally at all, while others insist that a genuine historical experience is at least referred to, if not actually recorded here. But allegory or fact, the story is filled with pathos. At the command of God the prophet married "a wife of harlotry" (Hosea 1:2), perhaps a sacred prostitute at one of the temples dedicated to the local gods of fertility. Such an act doubtless shocked the good people of Israel, who were unaware of the symbolic nature of this divinely directed union, pointing to the fact that "the land commits great harlotry by forsaking the Lord" (Hosea 1:2). Three children were born to Hosea and Gomer, and each was given a name scolding Israel for its faithlessness to its God. Perhaps Hosea hoped to redeem his wife from her wantonness, believing that she needed the love of a good man. He would not be the last romantic to entertain such a hope, nor would he be the last to have his hope desert him. The hussy apparently continued to ply her trade, unable to break with her past. The betrayed husband determined to end this farce and he sold his wife into slavery. But the poor unfortunate discovered that he was himself a slave; he loved her in spite of her perfidy. And so he ransomed her, buying her back from her captors. This time, however, he would not allow himself to be deceived. He would carry her into the wilderness where she could not take other lovers. He alone would woo her, he alone would sate her hunger. And gradually, slowly, he would win her loyalty and her love so that her need to stray would abate and vanish.

A tender and moving love story. But Hosea had an enormous temerity. He compared himself to God! He saw in his own tragic experience a parable illustrating the relationship between the Lord God of Israel and his chosen people. The covenant sealed between them centuries earlier had been a marriage bond. And was Israel not already a harlot? Did she not at the very nuptial feast at the foot of Sinai cast herself before another lover, the golden calf, while Moses sealed the pact with God on Sinai's misty height? Like Hosea with Gomer, God had been incredibly long-suffering with Israel and her repeated infidelities. Carried across the threshold of her new home, Canaan, by her indulgent spouse, Israel settled down not to a life of domestic fidelity but to a career of whoredom with the pagan gods of her Canaanite neighbors. Significantly, these gods were fertility deities, and they were called Baals, a Canaanite term which meant also "husband." A man was the *baal* of his wife. The Hebrews forsook the God of their fathers, the God who rescued them from Egyp-

tian bondage, the God of the sacred covenant at Mount
Sinai, and worshiped the gods of the soil.

It is not difficult to understand this apostasy. The
Hebrews had been a people of the desert, wandering
nomads whose economy rested on their flocks. They
knew nothing of agriculture, of seedtime and harvest,
of furrow and ploughshare. Their early attempts at
farming were doubtless abortive. The crops of the first
season simply did not grow. Then their Canaanite
neighbors, in the obliging fashion of all good neighbors from time immemorial, offered advice and counsel.
"See here," they said, "if you want to raise fruits and
vegetables, you must pray to the Baals who control
these things. Your God may know about flocks and
herds. He may be very good out in the desert, but he
has no power here. These lands are controlled by the
Baals." (*Baal* also meant lord, owner. A man was the
baal of his land.) So the Canaanites showed the newcomers how to offer sacrifices and perform the prescribed ritual to the gods who guaranteed the fertility
of the fields, and incidentally also showed them how to
hoe and plant. The results the next season were star-
tling: a good crop, a bounteous harvest. Obviously, the
Canaanites were quite right. To insure agricultural
success, one must worship the gods of agriculture.
Hence, Israelite idolatry, Israelite infidelity to her God
of Sinai.

So God became a wife-beater. He punished Israel

for her infidelity. This is the whole story of the book of Judges, which tells a sorry cycle of apostasy followed by punishment, which begets repentance leading to deliverance. Nor is there great difficulty in understanding that process. The Canaanite Baals were all local deities, intimately associated with a particular village or section. Once the Israelites forsook their national God for these provincial divinities, they lost all sense of unity as a tribe, a people, a *volk*. Hence, invading clans, driven into fertile Canaan by the droughts of Arabia Deserta to seek fodder for their flocks, could easily defeat the local inhabitants, divided as were these latter, lacking any unifying principle. Then, there would arise a judge in Israel, a Gideon, a Deborah, a Jephthah, who saw the triumph of the nomadic marauders as divine judgment and called Israel to penitence for her sins and renewal of her loyalty to God. The foxhole religion awakened the national self-consciousness, which aroused the sleeping unity. In union there is strength, and the nomadic interlopers were easily repelled, driven back into the desert where they belonged. But once the danger was past, complacency lulled the unity back into the sleep of local loyalties, and the cycle began anew.

All of this Hosea saw as evidence of a divine forbearance strangely akin to his own patience with the meanderings of the fickle Gomer. She had been unfaithful. Of that there could be no doubt. But so had Israel been faithless to God. And not once, but repeatedly. Tears, recriminations, threats, promises, bribes—all in vain. But one thing remained—the severance of the sacred bond, a sale, slavery for the willful wench! As Hosea cast off Gomer, so would God do to Israel, and deliver her to captors who would make her yearn for her rightful and loving husband. But not forever. As Hosea could not forsake Gomer, could not leave her to a fate she richly deserved, God could not forsake his beloved Israel, however false and wicked she may have proven herself. Out of his own broken but still loving heart, Hosea found the broken heart of God and penned the most poignant lines of Scripture:

> *How can I give you up, O Ephraim!*
> *How can I hand you over, O Israel! . . .*
> *My heart recoils within me,*
> *my compassion grows warm and tender.*
> *I will not execute my fierce anger,*
> *I will not again destroy Ephraim;*
> *for I am God and not man,*
> *the Holy One in your midst,*
> *and I will not come to destroy.*
>
> (Hosea 11:8–9)

As Hosea would quarantine Gomer from temptation, taking her to the wilderness where none save himself could quench the thirst of her desire, God would return his people to the scenes of their honeymoon days, renewing their first love, their early rapture:

> *Therefore, behold, I will allure her,*
>   *and bring her into the wilderness,*
>   *and speak tenderly to her.*
> *And there I will give her her vineyards, . . .*
> *And there she shall answer as in the days*
>   *of her youth,*
>   *as at the time when she came out of the*
>   *land of Egypt.*
>
> (Hosea: 2:14–15)

It may come as something of a shock to the reader unversed in the Bible to learn that Hosea used but one word for love, both his own obviously sensual love for Gomer and the presumably unsensual love of God for his people. That word, in Hebrew, is *aheb*. How can such a thing be possible? How can one use the same word to describe the purely spiritual love of God for his children and the highly carnal love of a man for a maid, even if such a love is purified by the sanctity of marriage? But our modern prudery and propriety have no passports to enter the biblical domain. William Temple, late Archbishop of Canterbury, once remarked that the Judeo-Christian tradition is the most materialistic of all world religions, and he was profoundly right. The Old Testament is a book totally lacking in abstractions, in speculation or philosophizing. It is concrete, particular, practical. When it talks about justice, it uses the term *mishpat*, which means in Hebrew a family, a clan, a community. Justice, in other words, is simply the kind of behavior one would expect people of one blood to display to one another. The love of God, then, is not some vague, ghostly quality, totally removed from human experience, unlike the love of man for woman.

The Hebrew was not afraid of talking about God in human terms. After all, those are the only terms any man really knows. The Greek might wander into realms beyond his ken, might soar up to the heavens and spin his clouds of theory. Not the Hebrew. Philosophy was alien to him; his forte was narrative. If he wanted to inform you about God, he told you a story: This is what God did once upon a time. And it was always what God did in an encounter with man. Sophisticated moderns scorn what they call the anthropomorphisms of the primitives, the tendency to ascribe human qualities to the divine. The Hebrews knew better; they understood perfectly well that God's thoughts are not man's thoughts, that the divine way is not the human way. The one is as high above the other as the heaven is above the earth. But the Hebrew knew, too, that man simply cannot think about anything unless he does it "anthropomorphically," in terms of his own experience and understanding. The love of God, then, is like the love of man. It is even like the love of man for woman, so that the highly sensual Song of Songs, obviously a poem originally celebrating sexual love, is included in the Hebrew Scriptures as an allegory of the love of God for Israel. The book of Hosea serves as a kind of Rosetta Stone for our study of love in the Old Testament.

With its key, we can decipher and understand the developments both before and after. These developments must be seen from two perspectives: God's love for his creation manifested uniquely to his chosen people; and the human love for God and for the neighbor, the fellow mortal.

The divine love, to begin where Israel began, is spontaneous and free. Nothing in Israel could account for the fact that God set his heart upon her as a people, loving them and leading them in the paths of his covenant law. They were no more righteous or religious than any of their neighbors. Abraham, the father of the race, was, significantly, the son of an idolater (Joshua 24:2). Why Israel should have been singled out from all the tribes who wandered across the face of the Fertile Crescent was as much a mystery to them as it is to us. They, too, thought, "How odd of God to choose the Jews!" Modern interpreters who have sought the explanation in some unique quality in the Hebrew people, variously described as "spiritual sensitivity" or "religious genius," make claims for the Hebrews they were unwilling to make for themselves. Every Jew is taught to say, "A wandering Aramean was my father" (Deuteronomy 26:5). The Old Testament can find no other reason for God's choice of Israel than his free, unmerited love. The prophet Amos placed Israel's deliverance from bondage in Egypt side by side with the divine rescue of the Philistines from Caphtor, and the Syrians from Kir (Amos 9:7), seeing God as moved with com-

passion for all captive peoples languishing under oppression; but neither Philistines nor Syrians were led to
Mount Sinai and wedded to God in holy covenant. "It
was not because you were more in number than any
other people that the Lord set his love upon you and
chose you, for you were the fewest of all peoples; but
it is because the Lord loves you, and is keeping the oath
that he swore to your fathers, that the Lord has brought
you out with a mighty hand, and redeemed you from
the house of bondage" (Deuteronomy 7:7–8).

The divine love was first of all spontaneous, and it
was manifested in the mighty acts of God. It was
neither a vague, spiritual force pervading the whole of
the cosmos, as in Oriental religions, nor was it a capricious emotion of the moment, as in much of Greek
mythology. God revealed his love in his irruption into
the historical process to bless or to curse, to build or to
destroy, to plant or to root up. And his love was for the
community, for the people. He spoke to individuals; he
called Abraham and Moses; he used Gideon and Saul,
but never for their own sake. They were his instruments, his mouthpieces, and their mission was always
seen in the larger context of Israel as a whole. God had
a plan and Israel had a destiny: the most inclusive and
incredibly arrogant view of manifest destiny ever
known. "I will indeed bless you," God said to Abraham,
"and I will multiply your descendants as the stars of
the heaven and as the sand which is on the seashore.
. . . and by your descendants shall all the nations of the

earth bless themselves" (Genesis 22:17–18). Israel was to be a light to lighten the Gentiles, bringing all nations to share the covenant relationship with God which she had known. It was arrogant in one sense, and yet it was magnificently unselfish, marvelously universal in scope. For Israel was not to hoard this treasure she had found, or rather had been given. She was to share it with the whole community of mankind. The dismemberment of humanity wrought at the Tower of Babel was to be undone. "Earth shall be fair and all her folk be one, nor till that hour shall God's whole will be done." To use Hosea's metaphor, it is as though a maiden finding the answer to her prayer in a youth of matchless beauty, virtue, and wisdom, instead of jealously binding him to herself in exclusive wedlock should call out to all others of her sex, inviting them to share her beloved. To be sure, many of the visions of the coming Messianic Age in the Old Testament saw Israel as occupying the place of the favorite wife, with the Gentiles as Mary-come-latelies, as concubines. But side by side with these are to be found prophecies which were entirely universalistic, welcoming all to the covenant on terms of absolute equality. Amos heard God asking Israel, "Are you not like the Ethiopians to me?" (Amos 9:7). "You only have I known of all the families of the earth; therefore I will punish you for all your iniquities" (3:2). Israel's special relationship to God brought with it special responsibilities and special peril.

THE COVENANT

This marriage, in which God chose his bride not for
her comeliness or virtue but solely because he loved
her, was consummated first at Mount Sinai in the covenant relationship inaugurated there. Again and again
the prophets referred to the ransom from bondage, the
rescue from Egypt, the bond sealed at Sinai. The most
characteristic word in the mouth of God was "I am
Yahweh,[1] your God, who brought you up out of the
land of Egypt." Here Israel became conscious of herself
as a people with a history and a destiny. As she looked
to her past, it became clear that this relationship with
Yahweh had antecedents, and the legendary folk epics
of Genesis are filled with covenants between God and
his people; through Abraham, Isaac, Jacob, and Joseph.
But these legends are not history as we understand that
term today. They are rather on the order of the story
of Washington and the cherry tree ("Father, I cannot
tell a lie") or of Lincoln and his twelve-mile walk to
return money to a customer who had overpaid him.
Such tales have a mythical quality about them. It is
dubious whether they portray the strict truth, but that

---

[1] The name of God revealed to Moses from the burning bush (Exodus 3) is in the ancient Hebrew simply JHWH, since the early form
of the language had no vowels. Early English translators of the Old
Testament misread the Hebrew text and translated *Jehovah*, a hybrid.
Modern scholars are agreed that the name was probably Yahweh. The
initial letter of the sacred Tetragrammaton is J but it is pronounced
in Hebrew, as in German, as Y.

is not their purpose. They convey something more fundamental than mere fact; they are purveyors of vision and dream, of the aspirations and ideals of a people. So Israel saw the divine love already at work among her forefathers, even as modern Americans find a divinity shaping the ends of the Pilgrims at Plymouth and the Puritans at Massachusetts Bay. Sinai was a height commanding vistas both of past and future, and whichever direction one looked, he saw the love of God for Israel. Behind lay the election of Abraham, the promise to Isaac, the bond with Jacob, the liberating plagues in Egypt, the wonder of the waters: "Sing to Yahweh gloriously! The horse and rider has he cast into the sea!" Still visible were the guiding pillars of cloud by day and fire by night, the merciful manna from on high. Ahead lay the wilderness wanderings, the conquest of Canaan, the battles with Moabites and Canaanites, with Edomites and Philistines. And over all, before and behind, arched the spontaneous and dynamic love of the Most High.

The documents which describe the history of Israel, from its beginnings in Abraham and even before—in the stories of creation, fall, flood, and Babel, which are stories of mankind and not solely of the Hebrews—down to the establishment of the monarchy in Saul and David, date initially from the tenth and ninth centuries before Christ. The authors of these documents were the Toynbees of antiquity, writing not simply a universal history but a philosophical theology of history as well. One of the documents is known to Old Testament scholars as J because it makes use of the term JHWH for God from the beginning, starting with the creation story found in Genesis 2. Another is called E, from its careful restriction of the Hebrew word *Elohim* for God until the revelation of the sacred name JHWH to Moses in Exodus 3. The J document is earlier, probably compiled by a group of historians associated with the court of King David at Jerusalem in the tenth century B.C. The E document seems to stem from the court of the northern kingdom after the division of the Hebrew peoples into two separate entities following the death of Solomon in 922 B.C., with Rehoboam, the son of Solomon and grandson of David, on the throne of the kingdom of Judah in the south, and with Jeroboam I the monarch of the newly created nation of Israel in the north. Both the J and the E documents were edited and worked together by a group of priestly editors after the return from exile in Babylon in the fifth and fourth centuries B.C. But all three—the J document, the E document, and the contributions of the priestly editors (known to Old Testament scholars simply as P)—reveal the same underlying conviction of the love of God as the central principle which renders all past history intelligible.

The teeth of literary criticism of the literature of antiquity were cut in the Renaissance on the verbal monuments of Greece and Rome—the epic poems of Homer and Virgil, the dialogues of Plato, the dramas of

Aeschylus, Sophocles, Terence, and Plautus. It was no far step from these foundation stones to the rocks of Scripture, though the latter were surrounded by powerful and pious taboos. The so-called "higher criticism" of the Bible, which applied the techniques derived from the study of pagan classics, encountered in its infancy and still encounters strong opposition from those who would place Holy Writ in a sacred grove, shielded from the profaning scrutiny of mere mortals.

These self-appointed guardians of Scripture have no quarrel with "lower criticism," the attempt to find the most accurate Greek and Hebrew texts of the books of the Bible by comparing and studying ancient manuscripts. They do sound the alarm, however, at the efforts of the higher critics to discern the dates, human authorship, and historical circumstances giving rise to the various writings collected in the canon. They are distressed at what they regard as a degradation of the Bible from its previous lofty pedestal as the Word of God, inerrant and infallible in every respect. What they overlook is the valuable historical data which higher criticism has made available, data which can be used by all, regardless of their doctrine of the Bible. To be able to arrange the prophecies of Isaiah, for example, in chronological order and to relate them to the relevant events in ancient history, does not make them any less the Word of God than they were before. Nor does the tracing of separate documents through the early legal and historical books of the Old Testament necessarily

imply that the Holy Spirit had no hand in their composition. The fact is that even nonfundamentalist biblical scholars are now transcending the earlier dissect-
ing of the manuscripts and finding a unity binding all
the separate parts together. Some scholars find this
unity in the *Heilsgeschicte* or history of salvation,
some in the theme of the covenant; but whatever the
language used, the idea is the same. From beginning
to end the Old Testament testifies to the love of God
for Israel, a spontaneous and uncaused love which expressed itself in history.

We have looked back from Sinai to the covenants between God and the patriarchs, to the deliverance from
Egypt, to the documents which tell these tales and sing
these songs. It remains now to look forward, where, for
a time at least, we shall be dealing with the same documents, which carry us to the establishment of the monarchy and perhaps beyond. The religious leaders of Israel had a habit of renewing the covenant at decisive
moments in the nation's history, looking back over the
former evidences of the divine love and favor and calling for grateful recollection and dedication. After the
long years of the wilderness wandering, the tribes under
the leadership of Joshua finally made their entrance into
the Promised Land, crossing the river Jordan. Joshua
erected an altar at Gilgal, built of twelve stones taken
from the miraculously dry river bed, saying, "When
your children ask their fathers in time to come, 'What
do these stones mean?' then you shall let your children

know, 'Israel passed over this Jordan on dry ground.'
For JHWH your God dried up the waters of the Jordan
for you until you passed over, as JHWH your God did
to the Red Sea, which he dried up for us until we passed
over" (Joshua 4:21–23). At the end of Joshua's life, after
the successful establishment of a firm foothold in the
land of Canaan, all Israel was summoned to a solemn
conclave at Shechem, where Joshua rehearsed for the
people all that Yahweh had done for them from the call
of Abraham down to that moment, and then called
upon them to renew their covenant oaths and obligations (Joshua 24).

This theme of recollection and renewal is repeated
over and again throughout the Old Testament. The
point is that the divine love manifests itself in history,
in the collective experience of Israel. So convinced of
the power of that love were the Hebrews that throughout all their career of warfare, they never interpreted
their defeats as God's defeats. When, after the mysterious collapse of the walls of Jericho and the destruction
of the city, the tribes moved up from the Jordan valley
to attack the town of Ai on the heights of the central
hills, they were at first repulsed. Their first thought was
to discover how they had displeased Yahweh, and the
casting of the sacred lot revealed the sin of Achan, who
had secreted a share of the spoils of Jericho for his own
personal use. The prompt execution of Achan plus a
clever military stratagem delivered the city of Ai swiftly
into their hands (Joshua 7–8). A reverse in the fortunes

of the nation was always seen as a mark of divine displeasure. So all of the judges read the signs of their times, the victories of the Moabites and Midianites, the Amorites and the Philistines. As soon as Israel repented of her apostasy and returned to the covenant, the nation was speedily delivered from the hands of her enemies. The unity which the covenant consciousness rescued from the divisiveness of loyalties to local Baals always provided the necessary strength to throw off the yoke of oppression, as long as the oppressors were simply primitive nomadic tribes.

THE MONARCHY

With the coming of the Philistines, however, the situation radically changed. This people, who gave their name to the land (Palestine means the land of the Philistines), represented a level of culture far superior to that of the Israelites and their neighbors. The Philistines came from the north, probably driven from their own homes by the widespread migrations of the first millennium before Christ, to which the Trojan war celebrated by Homer was perhaps related. These newcomers brought with them an Iron Age civilization; while Israel still dwelt in the shadow of the Late Stone Age. Chariots and metal spears and swords gave the Philistines a marked advantage in combat with stone axes and wooden spears. It is one of the ironies of history that their name has become a symbol of crudity and lack of appreciation for culture, when the fact is that they occupied a level of development far superior to the Israelites who bequeathed to posterity their contempt for their conquerors. Against such a foe, even a unified Israel was powerless, though the close of the book of Judges suggests that unity was a questionable commodity. "In those days there was no king in Israel; every man did what was right in his own eyes" (Judges 21:25).

This produced the demand for a monarch over Israel, a more permanent executive than the former judges who had responded to emergency situations with emergency measures, and then, when the danger was passed, returned to their homes. There are two documents describing the foundation of the monarchy in the first book of Samuel, one of them closely related to the J document of earlier acquaintance, the other bearing a strong family resemblance to the editorial writing of the priestly authors in P. According to the first source it was Yahweh himself who commanded Samuel, the last of the judges, to anoint Saul as king over Israel (1 Samuel 9:1–10:16). The second source makes it appear that Yahweh was displeased with the popular demand for a king, since he alone was the rightful king of his people. Samuel, as Yahweh's spokesman, pleaded with Israel to forsake their blasphemous desire, warning them of the dire consequences which the future held. When the people persisted, Yahweh instructed Samuel to let them have their way (1 Samuel 8). Whatever the facts, Samuel anointed Saul king and the war of inde-

pendence from the Philistines began. Saul seemed to
have possessed marked capacities as a soldier and as a
leader. Men would follow him with devotion, fighting
fiercely for their freedom. At first, all went well. Several
important victories crowned the shields of the new king
and his attractive young son, Jonathan. But then, something happened. Again, there are two accounts given in
First Samuel. The first tells of Saul's failure to follow
the divine command in his sparing the life of Agag, king
of the Amalekites (1 Samuel 15). The second attributes
the rupture between Saul and Samuel to Saul's impatient insistence on officiating at a pre-battle sacrifice
himself instead of waiting for the arrival of the old
priest-seer whose rightful duty the king had usurped
(1 Samuel 13). The mists of antiquity cloud our vision of
the events, but one thing is clear. A deep melancholy
now gripped Saul and he felt himself deserted by Yahweh. Yet he was compelled by circumstance to continue to act his part as king and commander-in-chief.
Saul is a tragic hero whose stature does not suffer beside
any of the protagonists of Greek drama. His grandeur
and greatness survive even the treatment of a group
of court historians so eager to please King David that
they painted the conflict between the first two kings of
Israel in colors as favorable as possible to the second.

Once more, two narratives celebrate the first en-
counter between Saul and David. One brings the young
David to the royal tent as a musician sought out by
Saul's attendants to soothe the king's melancholy and

ease his anguish (1 Samuel 16:14 ff.). The other story is
the famous battle with Goliath (1 Samuel 17). David
rose swiftly to prominence in the Israelite army and implanted himself deeply in the affections of all: of the
king, of his son Jonathan and his daughter Michal, and
of the soldiers and their families. Then one day, returning from a fight with the Philistines, Saul and David
were greeted by the Israelite women with garlands and
with a song: "Saul has slain his thousands, but David
his tens of thousands." Doubtless the women meant
well but they could not have hurt the king more had
they struck him in the face. Already convinced of his
own rejection by Yahweh, Saul began to watch this
winsome young man at his side.

David, for his part, did not help. His actions were
calculated to arouse the older man's suspicions, not to
allay them. To begin with, he asked for the hand of
Michal, Saul's daughter, an act innocent enough except
that David's subsequent attitude toward this young lady
indicated that he was not overly fond of her, and to ally
one's self by marriage to the royal house was to place
one's foot on the first rung of a ladder that might lead
to the throne itself. David's friendship with Jonathan
appears to have been perfectly genuine. Indeed so
genuine was it that many have made of it a homosexual
relationship, though this seems to be pouring more into
David's phrase, "Your love to me surpasses that of
women," than it can actually carry. But Saul saw the
intimate relationship with the heir apparent, saw the

effort to enter the family, saw the popularity with troops and people, and knew that David had more than one eye on the crown. And this David could not in honesty deny.

So Saul's "evil spirit" turned him from his main responsibility, the fight against the Philistines, to the futile pursuit of the exiled David and the band of outlaws who rallied to the youth's side. The divine favor was no longer with the old king. When the Philistines gathered their forces for a pulverizing blow at the army of Israel, Saul did not know what to do. Samuel was dead, the oracle of Yahweh was silent, and no prophet appeared in the land. In a dramatic and moving story, Saul is described, in the closing chapters of First Samuel, crossing the plain late at night to visit the witch at Endor, asking her to raise the ghost of Samuel, pleading with the conjured spirit for advice, collapsing in shock when told of his impending defeat and death on the morrow. Saul roused himself, however, with the dawn and went back to his duty and his doom. Jonathan, the eldest son, perished with his father in the battle, which left the leadership of the scattered and vanquished Israelites to Ish-bosheth, a younger son who was a weakling. The nation would look to him in vain for deliverance from Philistine tyranny.

This provided David with the opportunity he sought, and in a shabby and shady "deal" with Abner, the captain of the remnants of Saul's host and the real power in Israel, he secured the throne he had coveted so long. His court historians depicted all of this as guided by the divine Providence, but their sanctimonious soapflakes cannot thoroughly cleanse from the linen the dirt which still shows through. Be it said of David, however, that Yahweh was obviously with him, for all his opportunism. He rallied the nation and in a series of brilliant campaigns broke the power of the Philistines forever, establishing Israel as a powerful and independent nation. He captured the city of Jerusalem and made it his capital, a stroke of masterful statesmanship, since it was identified neither with his own southern tribes of Judah and Benjamin nor with Saul's northern tribes of Israel. Like Washington, D.C., it stood midway between north and south, on neutral ground. Here David brought the Ark of the Covenant, the ancient palladium of war and the symbol of Yahweh, which had lain neglected since its capture by the Philistines at the battle of Shiloh. Jerusalem thus became the political *and* religious center of the nation.

The closing years of David's reign, though for the most part peaceful and prosperous, were marked by internal strife. The shameful affair with Bathsheba, involving the murder of her husband, Uriah the Hittite, brought prompt condemnation from Yahweh through the mouth of Nathan, the prophet (2 Samuel 11–12). This incident reveals, however, a striking difference between Israel and her neighbors, for in no other nation of the Fertile Crescent would it have been possible for a religious leader to rebuke a king and live. In Egypt, the

Pharaoh was a divine being, related to the sun god Aton or Ra. No one dared question the act of a god. In Mesopotamia, the king was not himself a deity but he was appointed by the gods to rule in their behalf as their personal representative. In Israel, throughout the course of the monarchy, conflict continually raged between the king who was, after all, Yahweh's anointed, and the prophets, who spoke in the name of Yahweh against the king. But though the monarch was annoyed and sometimes enraged by the presumption of the prophet, he did not execute the upstart. David crumpled before the condemnation of Nathan; Ahab accepted the epithets of Elijah; Zedekiah protected Jeremiah, though he hated him and feared him; Jezebel, Ahab's queen, who was the daughter of Ethbaal, king of Sidon, and accustomed to the divine rights of Oriental despotism, was utterly mystified by her husband's forbearance with Elijah and refused to accept Naboth's negative response to the offer to buy his vineyard. She simply had Naboth murdered and annexed the property (1 Kings 21). Thus acts royalty that is really royal! In Israel things were different. The king was always responsible to Yahweh who demanded justice, and even unjust monarchs carried an uneasy awareness of that responsibility. Though the days of constitutional monarchy lay far in the future, the nation nonetheless knew the meaning of a covenant monarchy, a covenant between ruler and subjects, a covenant solemnly sealed before Yahweh who would judge them both.

To return to the declining years of David the king, the most tragic episode of his reign was the revolt of his son Absalom. This whole drama, beginning with Absalom's murder of his half brother Amnon and ending with the brutal but necessary slaughter of Absalom by Joab, David's "hatchet man," highlights the weaknesses of the aging king. He was obviously a weak father, overly indulgent with his numerous offspring. When Amnon raped his half sister, Absalom's twin Tamar, and then turned from her in disgust, "King David," we read, "was very angry." But there the matter stopped. Absalom brooded over the infamy for two years and avenged his sister, killing her assaulter. David banished the fratricide, but he could not stand by his decision. He relented and allowed the hothead to return. Absalom was an ambitious young man and not troubled by scruples. He took advantage of his father's increasing remoteness from the people to stir up rebellion. "Oh that I were judge in the land!" he would say to those resentful of their inability to get their cases heard in the royal court. "Then every man with a suit or cause might come to me, and I would give him justice" (2 Samuel 15:4). It seems clear that the revolt would have died a-borning had there not been many who held just grievances against the king. But the king was old, and the malcontents flocked to the standard of Absalom, the young, the winsome, the promising. So successful was the cause that David was forced to flee from Jerusalem to save his life. Only the loyalty of the people outside the royal city averted the calamity and destroyed the rebellious army. Joab rightly saw that Absalom was an apple which would rot any barrel and disobeyed David's explicit instructions that no harm should come to the lad. With the cool dispatch which characterized his entire career, Joab did what had to be done. He sent Absalom to join his ancestors. Then in 2 Samuel 18 comes the narrative which moves any parent to tears, the description of David's uncontrollable grief at the news. "O my son Absalom, my son, my son Absalom! Would I had died instead of you, O Absalom, my son, my son!"

David's final weakness was his submission to the pleas of Nathan, the prophet, and Bathsheba, his favorite wife, and his proclamation of Solomon as his successor while he himself remained alive, though feeble. This meant that older sons, experienced in battle and in statecraft, were passed over for Bathsheba's young son who had grown up in a court increasingly luxurious and Oriental. It meant further that no covenant was entered between Solomon and his subjects. Both Saul and David had been chosen by the people. Not so with Solomon, who was seated on the throne by royal decree. The reputation of this monarch for wisdom is a little difficult to understand, since his policies bankrupted the kingdom and rent it in two. A certain wit he may have possessed, as evidenced in the famous judgment between two women laying claim to the same child (1 Kings 3:16–28); but wit and wisdom are very distant cousins and often dwell in separate houses.

Solomon gave to Israel a magnificent temple and adorned Jerusalem with splendid public buildings, but at what a cost! To the son of David the people remained loyal, in deed if not in heart, but his grandson must prove himself. On Solomon's death, representatives of the northern tribes, against whom the late king had blatantly discriminated in favor of his own southern kinsmen, came to Rehoboam, the son and successor, demanding to know whether the ruinous policies of the past were to be continued by the new administration. The wiser and older members of the cabinet advised conciliation and a covenant, but the young king preferred the bold front counseled by his contemporaries at court, and acted the part of potentate. To the delegates from the north, who were perfectly willing to serve a reasonable king under a covenant, he declared, "My father made your yoke heavy; but I will add to your yoke; my father chastised you with whips, but I will chastise you with scorpions" (1 Kings 12:14).

If Rehoboam had deliberately set out to split his kingdom, he could not have contrived an answer better designed to produce such a result. The response was swift. The northern tribes cried out: "What portion have we in David? We have no inheritance in the son of Jesse. To your tents, O Israel! Look now to your own house, David." From henceforth there were to be two kings, two capitals, two peoples, Israel in the north and Judah in the south. From 922 until 722 B.C. the divided kingdom worshiped one God, spoke one language, cherished one tradition, but lived under different rulers. The two centers of political loyalty fluctuated in their relationship—now hostile, engaging in petty border raids and territorial squabbles; now friendly, allied against a common foe, co-operating in commerce.

In Judah, the loyalty to "the house and lineage of David" burned brightly until the very end, when Babylon destroyed Jerusalem and led the inhabitants into captivity in 586 B.C. One dynasty occupied the throne, one house reigned in unbroken succession with only one small interlude between 845 and 829 B.C., when Queen Athaliah usurped the throne and held it. But at her death the power returned where it belonged. In Israel, to the north, nine different dynasties came to the throne in two centuries—most of them by assassination and revolution. In the final years of Israel's life as a nation, before Assyria led its people off into captivity and oblivion, five different kings reigned in twenty-five years and only one of the five succeeded his father. Each of the other four climbed to the throne over the bloody body of his predecessor. The year 722 B.C. is the date on the tombstone of Israel, when the so-called "lost tribes" scattered across the Fertile Crescent and were absorbed. "The Virgin of Israel is fallen. Prostrate she lies upon the ground. None raises her up." Judah had a happier fate. She, too, suffered exile, by the rivers of Babylon, from 586 to 538 B.C. But thanks to the triumph of Persia and a new policy toward conquered peoples, Judah was permitted to return home and rebuild her national life.

Ezra, the priest, and Nehemiah, the governor, led the people to a new birth of religious and political existence.

AFTER THE EXILE

In 332 B.C., Alexander the Great annexed the Persian Empire to his Macedonian and Greek conquests, and the chosen people passed under the Hellenistic yoke. This change of masters affected Jewish life only minimally until the cataclysmic struggle against Antiochus IV (called Epiphanes) in 168 B.C. Alexander's empire at his death was divided among his three leading generals. Palestine was originally included in the spoils falling to Ptolemy, who established his headquarters and his dynasty in Egypt, and it remained under Egyptian suzerainty for more than a century. The descendants of Seleucus, the general who fell heir to Asia Minor and the rest of the Persian Empire, were ambitious, and in the second century B.C. Antiochus III wrested Palestine from Egyptian control and attached it to his own holdings.

The Seleucids had always been more zealous missionaries for Hellenistic culture than the Ptolemies, and this fact gave rise to conflict with the Jews, who had, since the Babylonian exile, become increasingly determined to preserve their purity of race and life. Antiochus IV grew impatient with this stiff-necked race and resolved to enlighten them at any cost. He marched an army into Jerusalem, erected a statue of Zeus within the sacrosanct and numinously empty Holy of Holies in the Temple and sacrificed swine on the high altar. This "Abomination of Desolation" was a humiliation the proud people could not endure. A priest in a small village struck the first blow. Mattathias and his sons, Judas, Simon, and Jonathan, rose and killed the agents of Antiochus, and a full-scale war of independence began. Judas, soon called Maccabeus, "the Hammerer," assumed the leadership and by brilliant guerilla warfare defeated several armies sent by Antiochus against him. The book of Daniel celebrates the suffering and the passionately patriotic hope of the Jews during this early Maccabean period. Arbitration finally prevailed and a measure of national independence was secured, with full religious liberty. The freedom to worship after their own fashion endured, but political autonomy ceased in 63 B.C. when Pompey incorporated Palestine into the eastern provinces of Rome.

Throughout this long history, the religious leaders of the chosen people saw the love of God actively at work. Sometimes the divine love was punitive, as when Assyria served as a rod taken up in Yahweh's hand to chastise Israel for her sins, or when Babylon triumphed and destroyed Jerusalem. Sometimes that love was active to save, as when Yahweh rescued his holy city from the besieging hosts of Sennacherib, or when he raised up Cyrus the Persian to rescue Judah from Babylonian bondage. God could blaze with fierce anger; he could melt with tender affection. But always his love was above and beneath and within, and always it was to be seen in the events of history. The prophets never tired of rehearsing for the people the evidences of God's loving-kindness throughout their national existence. Isaiah sang of Israel as a vineyard, planted and tended with careful devotion by her owner and Lord (5:1–7). Jeremiah looked back to the very beginnings of the divine mercy and protection in the wilderness and contrasted the faithfulness of God with the perfidy of Israel (2:1–37). And always, though the prophets foresaw doom and disaster as the inevitable consequence of apostasy and disobedience, there was the promise of deliverance if only the people would return and repent. "If you return, O Israel. . . . If you remove your abominations from my presence, and do not waver, and if you swear, 'As Yahweh lives,' in truth, in justice, and in uprightness, then nations shall bless themselves in him, and in him shall they glory" (Jeremiah 4:1–2).

DEUTERONOMY

The book of Deuteronomy, which dates from the reign of King Josiah—who ruled in Jerusalem from 639 to 609 B.C.—and which reflected the strong influence of the prophetic insights, portrayed the love of God for his creation in marvelously concrete terms. The precepts of the Deuteronomic law are reminiscent of the story of the mother of twelve children who was asked which one she loved most. She thought for a moment and then answered, "The one who is sick until he gets well. The one who is away until he comes home. The one who is in trouble until he is safe." So God's love was seen as extended to all his children, but especially to those who needed it most, to the weak ones who were unable to protect their own rights: the widow and the orphan, the alien and the servant, the child and the unloved wife. Even beasts of burden, the trees of the forest, and the birds of the air were objects of his loving concern. No distinctions were to be made between rich and poor, noble and peasant, strong and weak. "Judge righteously between a man and his brother or the alien that is with him. You shall not be partial in judgment; you shall hear the small and the great alike," for God loves all (Deuteronomy 1:16–17). This again is something new under the sun, for the law codes of Israel's neighbors made precise distinctions between classes of men, exacting different penalties from privileged and underprivileged. This was not possible for the chosen people, since they were all chosen by God's love. Of course, many passages throughout the Old Testament suggest that God loved not only righteousness but those who were righteous and hated both the wicked and their wickedness. But always behind such words lay the all-embracing character of the divine being who was "a gracious God and merciful, slow to anger, and abounding in steadfast love, and repentest of evil" (Jonah 4:2). "Though your sins are like scarlet, they shall be as white as snow;

though they are red like crimson, they shall become like wool. If you are willing and obedient, you shall eat the good of the land" (Isaiah 1:18–19).

SECOND ISAIAH

This note of the forgiving character of God's love rises to its Old Testament climax in the visions of the great prophet of the Babylonian exile whose words are found in chapters 40–55 of the book of Isaiah. The Second Isaiah (so-called because the prophet of the exile probably thought of himself as a disciple of the first Isaiah) saw God's tender heart moved by the sufferings of Israel so that now the punishment was finished, and the chosen people could be allowed to return to their homeland. "I, I am He who blots out your transgressions . . . and I will not remember your sins" (Isaiah 43:25). "Behold, I have taken from your hand the cup of staggering; the bowl of my wrath you shall drink no more" (51:22). "For Yahweh has called you like a wife forsaken and grieved in spirit, like a wife of youth when she is cast off. . . . For a brief moment I forsook you, but with great compassion I will gather you. In overflowing wrath for a moment I hid my face from you, but with everlasting love I will have compassion on you" (54:6–8). And as in Yahweh's original choice of Israel, there was nothing on the human side to explain or justify the divine activity. Unlike his predecessors in the prophetic office, the Second Isaiah did not see deliverance and restoration as carrying the price tag of repentance and reformation. He did not find any evidence of a change of heart in his people. The sole reason for the rescue of Israel from Babylonian captivity was the compassionate love of the Most High, who was moved again, as he was long ago by the sufferings in Egypt, to deliver and to restore, to soothe and to heal. "Zion said, 'Yahweh has forsaken me, my Lord has forgotten me.' 'Can a woman forget her sucking child, that she should have no compassion on the son of her womb?' Even these may forget, yet I will not forget you" (49:14–15). Israel was to be comforted and tenderly told that her warfare was ended, her iniquity pardoned, for she had paid doubly for all her sins. Babylon had gone too far in punishment, and now the doors of the prison were to be thrown open and a highway across the desert would lead the wandering ones home. Every rough place was to be smoothed out, every mountain lowered, and every valley raised (chap. 40). Yahweh had pity upon his people. He heard their sighs and cries and would heed their afflictions, soothe their hurts, and restore them to their rightful homeland.

The Second Isaiah was the first prophet of the Old Testament who foretold history decisively, for whom there was no alternative of divine challenge and human response. Previous prophets had announced what Yahweh was about to do, but they were not seers proclaiming a plainly certain future. There was always the question as to Israel's response. *If* Israel would repent, then it might be that Yahweh would restrain his fierce anger and turn from his determination to judge. *If* Israel continued as a people fat of heart and blind of eye, then surely the doom would fall. But always there was the decisive "if." History was a blend of activity, God's and man's. Now the great prophet of the exile changed all of this. Yahweh would act without respect to human response. To be sure, Israel was invited to return in loving gratitude. "Return to me, for I have redeemed you" (Isaiah 44:22). "Incline your ear, and come to me; hear, that your soul may live; and I will make with you an everlasting covenant, my steadfast, sure love for David" (55:3). But deliverance was not made conditional upon the acceptance of the invitation. Yahweh's rescuing love was unconditional, without respect to Israel's response.

This was doubtless because of the overpowering monotheism which dominated the consciousness of the prophet. For him, as for the earlier Isaiah, Yahweh was everything. Beside God, all kingdoms, armies, horses, chariots, mighty men of war, faded into nothing. To the eyes of ordinary mortals, it might appear that history is determined by human machinations, by diplomacy and strategy, by rulers and soldiers, statesmen and leaders. To the eyes of faith it was clear that Yahweh directed all events. Sennacherib the Assyrian fancied himself master of the ancient world. He did not know that he was but a rod taken up in the hand of God, a rod to be cast down when he had served his purpose. Cyrus the

Persian was to be the human agent of Babylon's destruction and Israel's release. But he, too, was only a pawn moved across the chessboard of history by the One who controls all kings, queens, bishops, knights, and castles. Isaiah 40–55 contains the most unequivocal statement of absolute monotheism in the Old Testament.

Among the visions of this prophet are to be found the songs of the servant of Yahweh, who was to be the agent of salvation to the Gentiles. He was to suffer undeservedly and vicariously for the sins of other nations, who were to be brought to repentance by his uncomplaining bearing of their burden. They looked upon his agony and confessed, "Surely he has borne our griefs and carried our sorrows; yet we esteemed him stricken, smitten by God and afflicted. But he was wounded for our transgressions, he was bruised for our iniquities; upon him was the chastisement that made us whole, and with his stripes we are healed. All we like sheep have gone astray; we have turned every one to his own way; and Yahweh has laid on him the iniquity of us all" (53:4–6). He made himself "an offering for sin"; he "bore the sin of many, and made intercession for the transgressors." The identity of the suffering servant and the details of how his pain was to bring peace are shrouded in mystery. Biblical scholars offer various solutions to the problems involved here, and no one answer has yet emerged which is satisfactory to all. But two things are clear. In the first instance, we encounter here a magnificent conception of a love which suffers and redeems, a

conception which from a Christian perspective represents the summit of the lofty ranges of the Old Testament. And second, it is inescapably obvious that the
New Testament saw the death of Christ on the cross as
organically related to this vision of vicarious atonement.
It is doubtful to many whether the Second Isaiah actually looked forward to the Christ; and there are those
who raise numerous questions about Jesus' own view of
himself and his mission; but in the mind of the early
church there was no doubt whatever. As Jesus had fulfilled the messianic prophecies over and again in his
lifetime, he fulfilled this greatest of them all in his
death.

SUMMARY

The love of God for his creation, then, as seen in the
Old Testament, was first of all spontaneous and uncaused by its object. It was manifested primarily to a
covenanted people through the divine direction of her
history. And it was a love which redeemed and suffered
and saved. It was like the love of a man for his wife, like
the love of a parent for his children. It was not a sentimental love which shrunk from responsibility and from
correction. God's love could scorch and scald as well as
warm. Indeed, on occasion the love was obscured by
hate. It must be confessed that the Old Testament frequently limited the love of Yahweh narrowly and exclusively to his chosen people, seeing his attitude to-

ward all others as either indifference, as in Hosea or
Ezekiel, or as positively demonic, as in Habbakuk or
some of the Psalms. But always out of the ruins wrought
by petty provincialism and narrow nationalism rose the
limitless sweep of universalism, the love of God for all
that he had made, for the whole earth was full of his
glory.

2

HUMAN LOVE
IN THE
OLD
TESTAMENT

§

WE HAVE ALREADY OBSERVED that the Old Testament uses the same word, *aheb* (the verb is *aheb,* the noun *ahabah*), to denote the love of God and the love of man. A similar economy prevails in the realm of human love, where the one verb and its cognates refer not only to man's love for God but also to his love for neighbor, including sensual love for members of the opposite sex.

The Old Testament knows of no bifurcation of affection into sacred and profane, and it manifests such an ignorance for two reasons. To begin with, Hebrew life was throughout characterized by what is known in philosophical circles as "holism," the impetus to see life in terms of wholes rather than as parts, to unite rather than to divide. There was no separation of any aspect of existence into sacred and secular. All of life was lived under the demands and the promises of the covenant relationship with Yahweh, and no part of it was exempt. There were, to be sure, certain times, places, and persons who were especially "holy," but nowhere was man given free rein to direct his own affairs as he chose, apart from the claims of Yahweh. God refused to be shut off into a separate compartment, labeled "religious," leaving the rest of the world free to pursue its secular concerns. It is significant that the Hebrew language does not even contain a word meaning "religion." God cannot be escaped, though the men of the Bible tried to get away, as do the men of today and every day. The beginning of the biblical story contains the attempt of the first man to hide himself from Yahweh, and that theme is repeated throughout the long narrative. Moses sought to evade the dangerous and difficult mission delivered to him; Jeremiah cried out that he would not speak in the name of Yahweh any more; Jonah fled to a far country to escape the hand of the Almighty. Job complained that even in sleep God would not let him alone, and the Psalmist submitted to the ubiquity of the divine presence, the impossibility of flight, whether to heaven, into the depths of hell, or to the uttermost parts of the sea. As Paul Tillich has put it, in *The Shaking of the Foundations,* "God is inescapable. He is God only because He is inescapable, and that alone is God which is inescapable." Thus, all of life was seen as an essential unity, and love was no exception.

The second reason for the lack of differentiation between the various levels of love in the Hebrew language is the emphasis placed there upon the will and its actions rather than on the heart and its feelings or the mind and its thoughts. To love was not primarily to be caught up by a powerful and ephemeral passion (though this sense of the word sometimes appears, as in the story of Amnon's infatuation with Tamar or in the Song of Songs), but rather to point one's will in a given direction, to act in a certain fashion. Augustine was profoundly biblical when he wrote that all human societies are created by a common love and that the character of any society is determined by the object of its love. In these terms, the Old Testament understood all of life as driven by *ahabah,* by devotion and desire. No man is free to choose whether or not to love; he is free only to choose what he shall love. And that choice is decisive in determining what he shall become. This is why the whole Old Testament, from Genesis to Malachi, was preoccupied with the problem of idolatry, which is not essentially a bowing before images of wood or stone, but the investment of one's love in the wrong place. To love means to obey, to serve, to be grasped by concern for the welfare of another. It does not mean to feel giddy or ecstatic.

This particular journey in the time machine is perhaps the most difficult of all for us to take; for we are Greek rather than Hebrew in our orientation, and under the influence of romanticism we have so cheapened and sentimentalized the term "love" that it is only by the exertion of considerable effort that we can understand the Old Testament world. We pursue knowledge by the road of dissection rather than by the path of fusion. When we want to comprehend something we pull it apart; we break it up into its constituent parts and examine each particle microscopically. This is our habitual pattern—in philosophy, psychology, history, and in literary criticism no less than in the physical and biological sciences. The fate of Orpheus at the hands of the Thracian women is mild beside the mauling love has received in modern culture.

From Tin Pan Alley to Hollywood, from the sudsy studios which purvey the steady stream of soap operas across the waves of sight and sound to the publishing houses and their output of novels and slick magazine fiction, from the higher brows of Broadway to the even loftier foreheads of the European intelligentsia, poor old Eros has been beaten, bedraggled, and bedeviled until he is no long recognizable. Love is mawkish, emotional, sentimental, and is constantly coming and going. As one child recently observed concerning the current popular songs, "In all of them someone is either falling in love or out of love. No one ever seems to stay put!" Perhaps this is due to the fact that modern Western man is an adolescent, while the ancient Hebrew was grown-up, though such an idea will seem the quintessence of heresy to those who believe that a later arrival on the stage of history must always be superior to its predecessors. It is, however, a long journey from the frenetic and fragile love of today's heroes and heroines to the quiet and steadfast devotion of Abraham to Sarah, or to Jacob's fourteen-year servitude for the hand of Rachel. The landscape is strange, the language is alien to our ears, and adjustment to the environment is not easy.

THE DIVINE-HUMAN ENCOUNTER

The original outline for this chapter called for two major subheadings, one dealing with the love of man for God, the other with the love of man for man. The second part was then to be broken down into sections describing the ties between those of one blood: husband and wife, parents and children; between neighbors; and between strangers. But this pudding proved difficult in the eating, because it is simply not possible to discuss the Old Testament conception of man's love for God apart from man's love for man. God was never apprehended by Hebrew life in himself but always in the context of history, that is to say, in human existence.

The awful otherness of Yahweh called forth the oft-repeated assertion that "no man can see God and live." His majesty and his power were so terrible that they were dangerous as well as creative, like a high voltage dynamo or a nuclear reactor.

When Moses climbed to Sinai's heights, the children of Israel were warned not to approach or to touch the holy mountain lest they die. And even Moses himself, apparently immune to the destructive forces which filled the rock, could not see Yahweh face to face. He was granted a privilege unparalleled in Hebrew history: the sight of God's back passing by, but even this he could not endure without protection. God hid him in the cleft of a rock and covered him with his hand lest the mere mortal be shriveled to dust by the divine glory (Exodus 33:18–23). The Ark of the Covenant, which probably contained the two stone tablets of the Decalogue and which was therefore intimately associated with the power of the Presence, was likewise dangerous. When the priests were carrying the Ark into Jerusalem in a cart, the oxen stumbled, rocking the cart and the Ark. Uzzah, a layman without priestly insulation, instinctively reached to steady the sacred vessel and was instantly struck dead (2 Samuel 6:6–7). Isaiah's vision of Yahweh in the Temple made him cry out, "Woe is me, for I am undone!" (Isaiah 6).

This fear of seeing God face to face purged Old Testament religion of all traces of mysticism. There was no desire to be one with God, to be absorbed into his

divine Being, to lose one's individuality in his totality.
The love of God meant obedience, not communion or
identification, and obedience translated itself primarily
into loving one's neighbor. One can see this principle
dramatically illustrated in the prophets (*nebiim*) of Israel. They are first encountered in the Old Testament as
a group. After Saul had been secretly anointed king
over Israel by Samuel, he returned to his home and on
the way he met a band of prophets coming down from
a mountaintop, "with harp, tambourine, flute, and lyre
before them, prophesying" (1 Samuel 10:5). As Samuel
foretold, the spirit of Yahweh came mightily upon the
new king and he "prophesied among them." The verb
"to prophesy" in this context meant not to foretell the
future but to behave ecstatically, to babble incoherently
under the influence of the Spirit. The bizarre conduct
associated with prophesying is apparent when in a second burst of such activity, Saul stripped off his clothing
and lay naked all day and all night, causing the people
to ask, "Is Saul also among the prophets?" (1 Samuel
19:24).

This is a phenomenon frequently found in the history
of religions. In contemporary society it can be seen
among certain Pentecostal groups, popularly known as
"holy rollers" because of their propensity to leap about,
to fall to the ground and roll. These people are commonly referred to by the more respectable segments of
the churches as "the lunatic fringe." The mystical seizure, the spasm, the trance, the fleck of foam at the lips,

the wild roll of the eyes—all of these are common enough in religions of every age and every place. But they were unknown, apparently, to the nomadic Hebrews prior to their entrance into Canaan, just as the dervishes were unknown to the pre-Islamic Arabs and even to the early Moslems before their explosion out of the Arabian peninsula after the death of Mohammed and their ensuing contact with the cultures of Asia Minor and Persia. The term "prophet" occurs seldom in the Old Testament before the passages describing the establishment of the monarchy, and for the most part these references are embedded either in the P document which is post-exilic or in the Deuteronomy (the "second law") which dates from the reign of King Josiah late in the seventh century.

Prophetic activity associated with music, "the harp, tambourine, flute, or lyre," with dancing and leaping, was evidently a religious phenomenon of Canaanite origin, not indigenous to nomadic culture, either Hebrew or Arab. In the contest with the Canaanite priests of Baal on Mount Carmel, Elijah witnessed these holy men in frenzy. "They cried aloud, and cut themselves after their custom with swords and lances, until the blood gushed out upon them. And as midday passed, they raved on" (1 Kings 18:28–29). Historical and archeological studies of the religions of Asia Minor and Syria have shown that orgiastic cults of this type flourished in ancient times. The devotees of Bacchus, of Dionysus, of the Syrian Baals, participated in wild rites involving the use of fermented beverages and frequently culminating in the letting of blood and/or sacred sexual activity. In the preceding chapter we have seen that an Israel newly arrived in Canaan was influenced by the prevailing culture, and that culture apparently contained bands of prophets, who not only sought union with the deity but acted it out in dramatic and ecstatic ritual. The Israelites of the desert days had known what it meant to be possessed by the Spirit of Yahweh, to be whipped into frenzy before going into battle. That Spirit "came upon" Othniel (Judges 3:10), Gideon (6:34), Jephthah (11:29), and Samson (15:14), enabling them to do wondrous works and to lead the people to victory over their enemies. Samson in particular appears to have been mightily moved so that his supernatural rapture armed him with incredible strength and destructive power.

But this essentially nomadic seizure by the Spirit, oriented toward military activity, was quite different from the prophetism of Canaan. As Dean Fosbroke has pointed out,[1] there are three important contrasts to be observed:

First, the ecstatic state of prophetic rapture could in Canaan be induced by certain definitely prescribed techniques. The use of music, the beating of drums, the stirring of the blood by moving and dancing to the contagious rhythms of the simple percussion instru-

---

[1] *The Interpreter's Bible* (Nashville, Tenn.: Abingdon Press, 1952), Vol. I, pp. 201 ff.

ments, the repetition of certain magical formulae, perhaps the added assistance of fermented liquors or drugs
—all of these guaranteed the desired result. The visitation of the divine Spirit could be compelled by human activity. Among the Israelites, none knew when
the Spirit of Yahweh might appear. It was mysterious,
incalculable and unpredictable. Yahweh was a god of
the storm, and his presence came as suddenly and as
unexpectedly as the desert sirocco or the earthquake.
He and he alone knew when and where and how he
would appear. The initiative was always with him,
never with man.

In the second place, the center of focus for the pagan
prophet was the self, the inner emotional experience,
the frenzy and the rapture. The purpose was an intense
encounter with the divine, an encounter which would
stretch and expand the entire being of the one thus
possessed. The result of the flow of sacred energy was
meaningless, self-centered activity, whirling about the
axis of one's own excited consciousness, even on occasion gashing the body and letting the blood. The
Israelites on whom the Spirit of Yahweh laid hold were
always driven to concrete activity in the real world, to
fight, to do, to go forth in the name of the Lord. They
were instruments in the hands of a Power with purpose
and direction, with a task to be performed. Their attention was directed outside themselves, not within,
and they saw themselves not as passive containers of

divine energy but rather as conductors of that energy, as channels through which it could flow to fulfillment.

Finally, the Canaanite enthusiasts were seeking union with their god, a loss of their self-consciousness and an absorption into the deity. They called themselves the god-inhabited, or god-possessed, and took the name of their lord. The devotees of Bacchus, for example, called themselves the Bacchae, and they donned costumes and headdresses making them resemble as nearly as possible the form they believed their god to wear. But such an attitude was glaringly absent from the Old Testament. The Hebrew was never under any illusion that it was possible for man to share the divine life or to participate in the divine Being. Yahweh sent his power into men, driving them beyond themselves, but he never infused a mortal with his self. No man could stand such a visitation. He would be destroyed; he would explode.

Israel was influenced, then, by the prophetism of Canaan. Saul behaved ecstatically; Elisha used music to induce a state of exaltation; the prophets traveled in groups. This we should expect. It would be surprising if any people remained hermetically sealed off from its neighbors. What is notable is not the similarities but the differences. For Israel was not transformed by the customs of Canaan but rather transformed them, as she transformed the myths of Babylon and Egypt, making of them vehicles of Yahwism. "It is," as Dr. Fosbroke observes, "indeed a far cry from the bands of ecstatics to the great solitary figures of a Hosea, a Micah, or a Jeremiah; from the devotees who found a refuge from the actual in the vaporings of their own excited fantasy to the men who accepted fearlessly the dread impact of austere reality."[2] There is a striking change from the ecstatic prophetism of the groups around Samuel to the solitary prophets of the eighth and sixth centuries. So Amos, the first of the so-called "writing prophets," rejected the title altogether, saying to Amaziah, the high priest of Israel, "I am no prophet, nor a prophet's son; but I am a herdsman, and a dresser of sycamore trees, and Yahweh took me from following the flock, and Yahweh said to me, 'Go, prophesy to my people Israel' " (Amos 7:14–15). By this he meant to disclaim any status as a professional holy man, as one who "earned his bread" as Amaziah accused him of doing by serving as a *nabi* or seer.

Samuel had apparently done some of this, as when Saul's servant suggested consulting the old man as to the whereabouts of the missing asses, and Saul asked, "But if we go, what can we bring the man? For the bread in our sacks is gone, and there is no present to bring to the man of God. What have we?" Whereupon the servant produced a fourth part of a shekel of silver, to give to the man of God. And the narrative goes on, significantly, "Formerly in Israel, when a man went to inquire of God, he said, 'Come, let us go to the seer'; for he who is now called a prophet was formerly called

---

[2] *Ibid.*, p. 203.

a seer" (1 Samuel 9:7–9). Elisha rebuked Gehazi for soliciting and accepting two talents of silver from Naaman the Syrian as payment for his cure from leprosy, but it is clear that Naaman expected to pay for such services (2 Kings 5).

This is why all the early writing prophets had trouble with the title. They sought to dissociate themselves from the ecstatic bands of professionals who not only cultivated visions but also made a profit thereby. It was not, however, with their predecessors in prophecy that the great religious leaders of Israel had their chief difficulty in interpreting the love of man for God and its implications. Rather, the priests provided the primary stumbling block in their insistence upon the cult as the essence of God's requirements. What the priests said to king and people was, to be sure, "Love Yahweh and serve him," but how was that love to be manifested? Their response was, "By sacrifice." Man was to show his love for God through his religiosity, by going regularly to the altar and offering there his praise and his prayers, the fruits of his fields and his flocks. If he performed the prescribed ritual regularly and faithfully, he had fulfilled his obligations to God and might rest secure. Against this view the prophets of Israel, beginning even as early as Samuel, protested that "to obey is better than sacrifice, and to hearken than the fat of rams. Has Yahweh as great delight in burnt offerings and sacrifices, as in obeying the voice of Yahweh?" (1 Samuel 15:22).

LOVE AS JUSTICE

The prophetic struggle was carried out on two fronts. At first, they wrestled with their pagan neighbors, insisting that the love of God did not involve withdrawal from the world into unity with the divine. Then, they arrayed themselves against the priests, declaring that man does not express his love for Yahweh *primarily* by means of the cult, by sacrifice and ritual. How is God to be loved if not in personal ecstasy or at the community shrine? It is all very well to speak of obedience as better than sacrifice, but what does it mean to obey? Had not God commanded the erection of altars and the regular offering there of the best that man owned? To this question the great prophets answered with one voice: "You seek to love God? Then love your neighbor." This is why it is impossible to separate the Old Testament conception of human love into the two neat categories: the love of man for God and the love of man for man. The two are inextricably related to each other in both of the Testaments (or better Covenants) of the Bible. The First Epistle of John is a magnificent summation of the whole. "If any one says, 'I love God,' and hates his brother, he is a liar; for he who does not love his brother whom he has seen, cannot love God whom he has not seen. And this commandment we have from him, that he who loves God should love his brother also" (4:20–21).

In this connection, it is important to remember the meaning of love in the Hebrew, which was not ephemeral emotion but steadfast concern, involving the will rather than the feelings. Thus, to love one's neighbor did not mean to become romantically involved with him or to be overcome by sentiments of tenderness in his presence. That is a caricature which was no more appropriate to the neighbor than to God or the self who were also to be loved. Such feelings toward the divine were characteristic of the ecstatic, the enthusiast, but they had no place in the Hebrew scheme of things, where Yahweh was regarded with awe and with reverence. He was never "a livin' doll," as Jane Russell cloyingly and blasphemously referred to the Almighty. Such an attitude toward the self is regarded by psychologists as a pathological state called narcissism, the romantic attachment to one's own person. The Hebrew term *aheb* has as many shades of meaning as the English word *love*, and it is important to distinguish them in both languages. When a man says to his wife, "I love you," he does not mean the same thing that he means when he addresses those words to his parents or his children. We say, "I love good books," or "I love to ski," which carries still a different connotation. And the love of God and the love of the neighbor as the self, enjoined upon congregations by Scripture and sermon, are clearly something else again. Greek as a language is wealthier in vocabulary, where *agape* signifies the love of God for man and the love of the Christian for his neighbor, *philia* stands for the love between friends, and *eros* for romantic attachment with sexual overtones. But impoverished though Hebrew may be, it is perfectly possible to read in context and to understand what is meant.

The first and most important sense in which the Old Testament uses the term love in its human dimensions is as respect and service. God's love for his creation is portrayed in the speech out of the whirlwind in the closing chapters of the book of Job as giving to each creature its due, "To each its own," from the Pleiades and Orion to the crocodile and the hippopotamus. So man was commanded to act within creation; to give to every man what belongs to him. It is wrong to treat any man as though he were a beast. Even the slave and the stranger had their rights, and limits were set upon the owner and the host. Was a wife "unloved"?—which is to say that she had lost her attraction for her husband —she must still be "loved," or treated with respect and given her just portion. Love in this sense has little or nothing to do with affection. Man is commanded to love even those whom he dislikes.

Herein lies the clue to the anomalous biblical fiat of love. How can anyone be *commanded* to love? One either loves or does not love another. He cannot control his emotions, his feelings. He may want to love the girl who has everything: beauty, brains, money, family position, and a father who is president of the company; but efforts to force such love may be in vain, though it must be confessed that to love such a creature would appear a pleasure! Contrawise, a man may (like Hosea) find himself bound to a woman who mistreats him, abuses him, who may be ugly and hateful, so that all his friends wonder what he can possibly see in her. Nevertheless, in spite of all, in spite of his own better judgment, he continues to love her. One simply does not say, "Go to! Now I will love or not love." It happens or it does not. How, then, can the Bible tell us to love our neighbors, the stranger within the gates, even our enemies? The answer is that we are not commanded to direct our affections or our emotions at all, but our wills. We are not expected to "like" everybody. There is something very wrong and very undiscriminating about any human being who likes everyone. What we are forbidden to do is to act as though our individual tastes were divine decrees, permitting us to mistreat or misuse those unfortunate enough to lie beyond the warming rays of our affection and approval. The Bible asks simply that all men be viewed as children of God and therefore worthy of respect and even reverence. This is the first and most important way in which to love God—to emulate him in loving his children, even as he loves them, by giving to them what belongs to them.

The biblical equation of love for God and love for one's neighbor must be seen, like all biblical ideas, against the background of the history of the chosen people. Israel began her self-conscious career as a na-

tion in the desert. In the nomadic tribe, a radical egal-
itarianism prevailed. The members of the clan were all
of one blood, and if one of them was injured or killed,
they did not say, "The blood of so-and-so has been
shed," but rather, "Our blood has been shed." Nothing
was allowed to stand in the way of a swift and
terrible vengeance against the one who had attacked
the tribe. The individual was given powerful protection
by his belonging to the clan, the family, the *mish-
pahah*. Once cut off from this source of his security
and of his identity, he was fair game for anyone who
cared to rob or kill him. So Cain's punishment was ex-
pulsion from the clan, and he cried out in fear, "I shall
be a fugitive and a wanderer on the earth, and whoever finds me will slay me" (Genesis 4:14).

The injunction, "An eye for an eye and a tooth for a
tooth," is usually regarded as a primitive and blood-
thirsty rule, but its inception in biblical times represented a considerable ethical advance. What it was
saying, in effect, was, "You shall take no more than an
eye for an eye," curtailing the practice of killing the
offender who dared to gouge out an eye or knock out a
tooth. The tribe knew a binding solidarity, a "one for
all and all for one" psychology, and it did not know
private property in the sense of personal wealth. The
individual might own certain items of importance to
him: his spear, his knife, the nomadic equivalents of
toilet articles, toothbrush, etc. But the real economic
life of the clan was based upon its flocks, and no indi-

vidual owned these; they were the common property of all. Thus, the community prospered or hungered together. It was unthinkable that one tribesman should live in feast and another in famine. This togetherness, this sharing of blood and of property, was sanctioned by Yahweh and was strengthened by religious creed and custom.

The conquest of Canaan brought about a revolution in the life of Israel. A previously nomadic people now became an agricultural one, and as they developed, a commercial economy grew increasingly predominant. Pastoral life was a soil in which community and equality flourished, but these flowers rapidly withered and died when transplanted to locales where their roots had to draw their sustenance from a society which farmed and bought and sold. Inequality inevitably appeared at the very beginning in the division of the land. Some tracts were bound to be more fertile, more productive, than others. And as there was inequity in the land itself, there were diversities in those who tilled it, in skill, industry, and resourcefulness. As though this double indemnity did not in itself create enough dismemberment of a hitherto unified society, the selling of one's produce and the buying of more land, better seed, more efficient tools, had an even greater dismembering effect, for some were more shrewd as traders than others. The total result, gradual as it was, inescapably initiated and fostered a stratified society, with rich and poor, the successful and the unsuccessful, the haves and the have-nots. Failure frequently breeds further failure, while prosperity reproduces itself, and the clefts between classes widened year by year. With the establishment of the monarchy came further stratification. Those close to the court were rewarded by the royal favor with noble status, marking them off from the plebs. The whole picture is a marvelous illustration of the Marxist thesis, showing the devils which are loosed upon the world when the Pandora's box of private property is opened. So long as the lid of community ownership is kept tightly shut, all is a paradise of innocence and equality, but once lift that lid, and all is lost.

This was essentially the view of the early Nazirites and Rechabites who protested the vices of the new life in Canaan and sought by their personal example to recall Israel to the sterner days of the desert. It was also the view of the prophets who appeared with the inception of the monarchy. They saw all the evils and injustices of the nation as the result of whoring after the Baals, who encouraged such goings on, while Yahweh strenuously opposed the greed which lost sight of all one's responsibility to love the neighbor, to respect and to serve him, to give him what belonged to him: his dignity as a man and as a brother. The Baals were morally indifferent. It mattered little to them how their devotees behaved toward one another so long as they offered the proper sacrifices and observed the prescribed ritual. This was a contagious illusion, and

Israel rapidly contracted the disease, believing that her duty to Yahweh was fulfilled through the cult. The king and the priest *did* divide the national existence into two areas, sacred and secular. The sacred was the shrine, the sacrifice, the altar. Certain days were set aside for festival, for prayer, for thanksgiving. But the market place, the court, the thoroughfares on which men lived out their lives—these were secular. Here, so Israel tended to believe, a man could act as he pleased, could strike sharp bargains, give false measure, bribe judges. This was of no concern to Yahweh. Man showed his love for God by the generosity of his contributions to the priests, the frequency of his visitations to the shrine, the fervor with which he swore, "As Yahweh lives." His actions toward his neighbor were his own business, and after all, business is business. This is the picture provided by the prophets.

As we have seen, Samuel sounded the theme which was to be taken up by the later prophets and elaborated into sonatas and symphonies: "To obey is better than sacrifice." Nathan rebuked King David for his selfish and ruthless elimination of Uriah, husband of Bathsheba, and significantly a Hittite; Elijah denounced Jezebel for her despotic destruction of Naboth and seizure of the vineyard given to him by Yahweh. But it was Amos who gave the fiercest and most eloquent expression to the divine demand for love to the neighbor which means justice. To the northern kingdom in the middle of the eighth century B.C., flourishing with peace, prosperity, and progress under the reign of Jeroboam II, enjoying a revival of religion in the form of thronged temples and crowded cultic rituals, the prophet thundered forth the flaming words of Yahweh: "I hate, I despise your feasts, and I take no delight in your solemn assemblies. Even though you offer me your burnt offerings and cereal offerings, I will not accept them, and the peace offerings of your fatted beasts I will not look upon. Take away from me the noise of your songs; to the melody of your harps I will not listen. But let justice roll down like waters, and righteousness like an ever-flowing stream" (Amos 5:21–24). Worship without influence on behavior is an abomination in the sight of God. The nation felt secure in its religiosity, and not only turned deaf ears to those who sought to recall and remind Israel of the equality of the desert days, but also persecuted these apostles of austerity. "You made the Nazirites drink wine, and commanded the prophets, saying, 'You shall not prophesy'" (2:12). "They hate him who reproves in the gate, and they abhor him who speaks the truth" (5:10). Amos called the whole cult into question, pointing back: "Did you bring to me sacrifices and offerings the forty years in the wilderness, O house of Israel?" (5:25). It is especially heinous because the sacred festivals at the shrines were financed by money wrung from the poor and the weak.

Amos spoke the word which Yahweh put in the mouths of all the prophets. Hosea, Micah, Isaiah, Jere-

miah, all echoed the divine demand for obedience
rather than sacrifice, for just dealings with one's neighbors. And the prophetic insights were codified in the
laws of Deuteronomy. As Yahweh was passionately
ethical, he demanded that man be ethical, that man's
love for him be shown in man's love for man. This love
had both its positive and negative side. The negative
side may be called justice, refraining from murder,
adultery, thievery, dishonesty, filial impiety, etc. But
there was more than mere justice in Deuteronomy;
there was the positive aspect as well, which was love.
Not only were there provisions for the Sabbath rest of
servants, slaves, and beasts of burden, for loans without interest to the needy, but also for the sabbatical
year when the slaves were to be released and all debts
forgiven, for the newly married that they might enjoy
the pleasures of wedlock, for the slave, for the poor.
All of this is illustrative of the Hebrew understanding
of love as will in action rather than as feeling or emotion. *Ahabah* is not a sentiment of personal preference,
of individual taste, but an overpowering sense of responsibility, of community. Both the Law and prophets
reminded Israel of the solidarity and equality of the
days in the desert, and the continuing call to brotherhood sounded in the covenant. This took the form of
interest in the welfare of all, including the reproving
of the neighbor's sin. Silence implied assent, and therefore shared responsibility.

There are in the Old Testament numerous sugges-

tions that the love for the neighbor was limited to those
of one's own household, clan, or nation. Both the love
of God and the love of the Israelite sometimes were
seen as confined within the boundaries of the Hebrew
people. The law prohibiting the taking of interest on
loans, the selling of meat from animals stricken by
disease, the bearing of false witness, did not apply to
Gentiles, to the "lesser breeds without the law." The
enemies of Israel were the enemies of God and were
hated with a perfect hatred. The prophet Nahum rejoiced in the downfall of Nineveh, capital city of Assyria, attributing the bloody destruction, the "hosts of
slain and heaps of corpses," "her little ones dashed in
pieces at the head of every street," to the avenging
hand of Yahweh. Neither Hosea nor Ezekiel revealed
any divine interest in the larger families of nations,
and the leaders of post-exilic Israel set up the most
elaborate taboos against fraternization or intermarriage
with the Gentiles, a successful enterprise despite the
eloquent protest of the authors of Ruth and Jonah. The
former book is a charming little idyll of the devotion of
a daughter-in-law to her dead husband's mother, but
its major message is the foreign ancestry of the great
King David. His great-grandmother was a Moabitess.
The adventures of Jonah have served as the center of a
senseless controversy over whether the prophet was in
fact swallowed by a great fish. Such contention has obscured the genuine contribution the book has to make,
its conviction that God cares for all men—even Israel's

bitterest enemies—and will deliver any who will repent
and turn to him.

This is the more characteristic viewpoint of the Old
Testament, in what we, at least, regard as its loftiest
reaches, in its universalism, its conviction that love and
justice are not limited by the boundaries of family or
religions or national community. Love begins at home
but does not stop there. It is gradually to widen to include the whole of humanity. This was implicit from
the very beginning and was spelled out explicitly
through the centuries of Israel's historical vicissitudes.
Not that the spelling out represents an evolutionary
progression from primitive nationalism to sophisticated
universalism. Both attitudes are discernible from beginning to end in the Old Testament, with now one and
now the other in the ascendancy. But the heights are
represented by those spots which give perspective, a
view of all the nations, while the depths have their
vision blocked by a narrow parochialism which can see
no farther than Israel.

LOVE IN THE FAMILY

In the first instance, then, human love in the Old
Testament means that love of God and love of neighbor are like two sides of one coin, each implying and
demanding the other. And love of neighbor means
seeking his good in all areas of life. To move from the
wider sphere of general humanitarian love to the nar-

rower confines of love within the family, we turn our attention to the ties between parents and children. At first glance, it might appear that these relations carried little affectional content, so preoccupied were the legal codes with matters relating to authority and obedience. "Honor thy father and thy mother" conveys overtones of respect and reverence but scarcely approximates the deeper emotion expected by the modern West. The rights of the father were almost absolute with respect to his children. Any youth who either struck or cursed his parents was to be put to death (Exodus 21:15, 17). This may seem a severe penalty for an oath uttered in hasty anger, but the ancient Hebrews had a profound sense of the power of words. A father's blessing once given could not be retracted, even if it had been bestowed on the wrong son and wrung from the father by deceit at that! (cf. Genesis 27). A blessing had power and so had a curse; the one was as much to be desired as the other was to be feared. Words were not to be used lightly. Once spoken they could not be recalled; one could not act as though he had never said them. It was not only Yahweh's word which should not return unto him void but accomplish that which he purposed (Isaiah 55:11), but man's word as well. Death, then, was the penalty for a child who cursed his parents, as it was also for one willful or disobedient, though in the latter case the elders of the village were to be the witnesses, the judges, and the executioners. A father in debt had the right to sell his children into slavery, in order to save himself from bankruptcy, and a daughter was a commodity to be sold to the highest bidder if the family finances demanded it. Jephthah could even sacrifice his daughter to Yahweh. The power of life and death over the family was unrestrictedly in patriarchal hands. There was little of love here.

It would be a serious error, however, to judge Hebrew life entirely by the Law, which deals after all with infractions and transgressions rather than with the practice of the majority. The Old Testament narrative is a far more accurate portrait, particularly of an essentially historical people. The Israelite never speculated or philosophized; when he wanted to make a point, he told a story. So Jesus was Jewish to the core in his constant use of parables. It is no accident that Abraham Lincoln so often turned to stories to convey his mind; he was steeped in the Bible. The cold and heartless discipline of the Law melts before the warmth and affection of Jacob for his beloved son Joseph. The coat of many colors which so aroused the jealousy of the brothers reveals the tender if unwise favoritism of an aging father for the first child of his beloved wife. And the news of the death of this "son of his old age" broke the old man. "Then Jacob rent his garments, and put sackcloth upon his loins, and mourned for his son many days. All his sons and all his daughters rose up to comfort him; but he refused to be comforted, and said 'No, I shall go down to Sheol to my son, mourning'" (Genesis 37:34–35). This is a gem of tragedy, whose sparkle is not diminished by the reader's knowledge that the boy was not really dead but a slave on his way to Egypt. Jacob's grief was nonetheless real. His suffering is surpassed only by that of David in his agony over Absalom (2 Samuel 18), where again it is clear that a father's love was intense and genuine. Nor was Jacob's fatherly affection unreturned by his sons. When Joseph's ruse of the silver cup hidden in the sack of Benjamin made it appear that the brothers must return to their father without the youngest, they pleaded with Joseph. "When I come," said Judah, "to your servant my father, and the lad is not with us, then, as his life is bound up in the lad's life, when he sees that the lad is not with us, he will die; and your servants will bring down the gray hairs of your servant our father with sorrow to Sheol" (Genesis 44:30–31). Apparently, the elder sons were not jealous of Jacob's affection for Benjamin as they had been over Joseph. Perhaps they felt guilty, but their concern and affection for their father is perfectly plain.

Nor is this one legend an isolated example of love and tenderness between parents and children. One thinks of Hannah's yearly trip to the shrine at Shiloh bringing "the little robe" she had made for her son, Samuel; of Eli's grief over the death of his two sons, Hophni and Phineas, wayward and wicked though they were; of Saul's affection for Jonathan. The most classic example of filial devotion in the Old Testament is curiously that of a daughter-in-law for her mother-in-law; even more curious, the well-known words of Ruth to Naomi are most commonly cited in the context of romantic love between maid and man, "Entreat me not to leave you or to return from following you; for where you go I will go, and where you lodge I will lodge; your people shall be my people, and your God my God" (Ruth 1:16). Solomon's shrewd order to divide the disputed infant between the two women claiming motherhood quickly revealed the true parent, who was willing to forswear her right in order to preserve the life of her baby (1 Kings 3:16–28).

Whatever the Law may have commanded in terms of respect and obedience, it is clear that parents in Israel loved their children and found their love returned after the fashion common to all mankind. This is surely one source of the Bible's power and pertinence through the centuries: the fact that it does not present us with a series of portraits of plaster saints. Rather, its pages teem with men and women of flesh and blood who awaken a sympathetic response in any age, for they are human. They suffer and prosper, they laugh and weep, they love and hate, they hope and despair, they believe and doubt. And they are marked by all the weaknesses that plague the race perennially. Abraham was a liar, Jacob was a cheat, Moses was a stammerer and a murderer, Samson and David were sensualists, unable to resist the lure of a beautiful woman. Solomon was a foolish monarch with eyes bigger than his pocketbook. But if they shared the weaknesses of all eras, the biblical characters also stand forth in strength and heroism, inspiring the heart and moving the mind. They represent man at his worst and at his best. Their significance in the history of salvation lies not in what they were but in the fact that God chose to speak to them and through them to all men, to use them for his own purposes.

The situation between parents and children in the Old Testament is paralleled by that between man and woman, between husband and wife. Under the Law, woman had few rights. The covenant decalogue listed the wife among the man's possessions which were not to be coveted. "You shall not covet your neighbor's house; you shall not covet your neighbor's wife, or his manservant, or his maidservant, or his ox, or his ass, or anything that is your neighbor's" (Exodus 20:17). As we have already seen, the term *baal*, which was used to refer to a god as lord of the land, was used also of a man as owner of his household, domestic animals, wives, children, servants, and slaves. The wife was a chattel which her husband owned. The same legal code speaks of a man as the *baal* of an ox and as the *baal* of a woman.

Divorce was solely in the hands of the husband. All he had to do was to write out a bill of divorcement and give it to his wife with orders to leave his house, and this could be for any reason of which he himself was the sole judge. "If then she finds no favor in his eyes because he has found some indecency in her," is the way the Law expressed it (Deuteronomy 24:1). No provision was made for a wife's release from a cruel husband. There was, however, a high value placed upon wifehood and motherhood, as the laws against adultery, harlotry, and rape clearly show. The Decalogue placed mother on an equal plane with father in the command enjoining filial honor and obedience. But the interest in woman was almost entirely in her role as childbearer and carrier of the family life. She was valued not so much as a person as a sexual being. If her husband died leaving her childless, it was the duty of the nearest male relative to take her to wife and bring forth an offspring who was to be regarded as the seed of the dead man. The laws governing rape and seduction seem far more concerned over the violated rights of father or husband than over the feelings of the woman. The corollary of this patronizing patriarchy was of course polygamy. If woman's chief value was as a childbearer, and if it was desirable to insure one's posterity with numerous children, then the only limitations on the number of wives any man might have were his financial resources and the available supply of women. The law placed no limitation on the number of wives. David married eight women specifically mentioned and added many more to his household in Jerusalem. When he fled from Absalom, he left ten concubines behind. Abraham had both Sarah and Hagar; Jacob's two wives, Leah and Rachel, carried on a contest in motherhood, entering themselves and their maidservants as competitors. Solomon's seven hundred wives and three hundred concubines set something of a record in the marital Olympics. It should be noted, however, that polygamy in patriarchal societies was more a matter of prestige than of sensuality. After all, to maintain a household of several wives and their children and servants was no small item of expense. This is the Old Testament equivalent of what Thorsten Veblen called "the wealth of conspicuous consumption." The larger the harem, the greater the status. The modern suburbanite displays his wealth by driving two cars. The ancient Hebrew married two wives. But the wife was a possession with few rights of her own.

ROMANTIC LOVE

Once again, as in the relations between parents and children, the narrative portions of the Old Testament must be placed beside the books of the law if the full picture is to be obtained. Women in Hebrew society were loved and revered by men as they have been in all ages. It is sometimes suggested that romantic love between the sexes was unknown, at least in the West, until the rise of the so-called courtly love of the Middle Ages. Prior to that time, marriages were arranged by parents partly as a financial or political transaction and partly with an eye to a stable and enduring relationship based on similarities of background and temperament. There is some truth in this contention, but romantic love is by no means a stranger to the pages of the Old Testament. Jacob was obviously smitten by Rachel. Unable to provide a dowry, wandering far from home, he agreed to labor seven years to earn her hand. Then when Laban tricked him, pawning off his elder daughter Leah on the ardent suitor, Jacob undertook yet a second sabbatical of servitude for the sake of his beloved. Who in this modern day would work for fourteen years to buy the approval of a crafty father-in-law? (Genesis 29).

We even encounter the phenomenon of love-at-first-sight in Holy Writ. "It happened, late one afternoon, when David arose from his couch and was walking upon the roof of the king's house, that he saw from the roof a woman bathing; and the woman was very beautiful. And David sent and inquired about the woman. And one said, 'Is not this Bathsheba, the daughter of Eliam, the wife of Uriah the Hittite?' So David sent messengers and took her, and he lay with her" (2 Samuel 11:2–4). This could be dismissed as mere lust, abetted by royal prerogatives, but the subsequent career of the relationship points to something far more enduring. At the end of the king's life when he lay feeble and shivering with the chills of age, Bathsheba still had her way with this man. He named her child as successor to the throne, advancing him over brothers who outranked him in seniority.

Infatuation is the only name possible for the overpowering desire Amnon felt for his half sister Tamar. He was "so tormented that he made himself ill because of his sister" (2 Samuel 13:2). By a clever stratagem he lured her to his bedroom and sought to seduce her. Tamar resisted these illicit advances, seeking an honorable approach. "I pray you, speak to the king; for he will not withhold me from you" (2 Samuel 13:13). But Amnon was either impatient or skeptical and forced her, transforming his infatuation to repugnance. "Then Amnon hated her with very great hatred; so that the hatred with which he hated her was greater than the love with which he had loved her" (2 Samuel 13:15). Love, lust, or infatuation, romance has its place in Hebrew literature.

The place of pre-eminence, however, belongs to a collection of highly erotic love poems which won its way into the Jewish canon by a double fiction. The first was the tradition that none other than King Solomon was its author, and the royal prestige carried half the day. The second was the allegorization of the verses to symbolize the love of God for Israel, a device which finally crumpled the last resistance to the book. The Council of Jamnia in A.D. 100 locked it firmly into the canon, and the early Christians had only to adapt the allegory slightly, regarding the two lovers as Christ and his bride, the Church. Thus the Canticles, or Song of Solomon, has been sanctified as sacred Scripture in both Jewish and Christian Bibles, though it is seldom read in public. The most cursory glance at its eight chapters makes it perfectly clear what its true character is. "O that you would kiss me with the kisses of your mouth!" the song opens, "For your love is better than wine" (1:2). "Behold, you are beautiful, my love; behold, you are beautiful; your eyes are doves. Behold, you are beautiful, my beloved, truly lovely. . . . Your lips are like a scarlet thread, and your mouth is lovely. Your cheeks are like halves of a pomegranate behind your veil. . . . Your two breasts are like two fawns, twins of a gazelle, that feed among the lilies." So speaks the man of his maid.

Nor is she silent and shy. "My beloved," she boasts, "is all radiant and ruddy, distinguished among ten thousand. His head is the finest gold; his locks are wavy, black as a raven. His eyes are like doves beside springs of water, bathed in milk, fitly set. . . . His lips are lilies, distilling liquid myrrh. His arms are rounded gold, set with jewels. His body is ivory work, encrusted with sapphires. His legs are alabaster columns." The poems are explicit not only as to the charms of the two lovers, described in delightful detail, but also as to their relations. "How fair and pleasant you are, O loved one, delectable maiden! You are stately as a palm tree, and your breasts are like its clusters. I say I will climb the palm tree and lay hold of its branches. Oh, may your breasts be like clusters of the vine, and the scent of your breath like apples, and your kisses like the best wine that goes down smoothly, gliding over lips and teeth." Some scholars regard the collection as an ancient marriage cantata, sung by soloists and chorus antiphonally to celebrate a wedding. But no literature of any tongue contains love poetry that is more beautiful or more romantic. The Song of Solomon is a hymn in praise of sensual love with no minor strains of prudery or shame to mar its melody.

We have seen, then, that the Old Testament knows all shades of human love. Man's love for God is not a mystic rapture, a yearning after absorption in the divine life, but rather a reverent obedience which manifests itself in love for one's neighbor. And that love is a steady and sober concern for the welfare of another, a sense of responsibility and respect rather than a precarious and ephemeral sentiment. The two are inextricably related to each other: love for God and love for neighbor. As the popular song has it, "You can't have one without the other." Yet the tenderer feelings of the more intimate relationships of life are not lacking, either. There is devotion between parents and children, between man and woman, between husband and wife. The Old Testament never goes so far as to say that "God *is* love," but it knows the love of God for his creation, especially for his chosen people, and it knows, too, the answering love in the human heart, answering both to the Creator and to those also made in his image.

3

DIVINE LOVE

IN THE

NEW

TESTAMENT

ॐ

IT IS A CANARD and a misunderstanding still far too prevalent that the Old Testament portrays a God of judgment and wrath, while the New Testament speaks of a God of love and mercy. As we have seen, the Hebrews produced out of their encounter with the Lord of the covenant the recorded experiences of Hosea and the Second Isaiah. Here is a God of infinite compassion who cannot turn his back on his beloved, no matter how false and faithless she has proven. Here also is a conception of a love that suffers vicariously, and this represents a summit as lofty as any of the peaks in the New Testament. It is true, as Claude Montefiore, the great Jewish scholar, discovered, that in the Gospels and Epistles of the Christian community, the divine love not only receives those who come in penitence and in supplication but also goes out to seek and to save those who are lost, and that this represents something new, a conviction not found in the old covenant.

But the God of Jesus and Paul is no grandfather in heaven, a sweet and sentimental old gentleman who is so loving that he knows neither anger nor judgment. The prophets of old uttered no fiercer threats and denunciations than came from the mouth of Jesus. "Woe to you, scribes and Pharisees, hypocrites! for you build the tombs of the prophets and adorn the monuments of the righteous, saying, 'If we had lived in the days of our fathers, we would not have taken part with them in shedding the blood of the prophets.' Thus you witness against yourselves, that you are sons of those who murdered the prophets. Fill up, then, the measure of your fathers. You serpents, you brood of vipers, how are you to escape being sentenced to hell?" (Matthew 23:29–33). Jesus was convinced of the imminence of divine judgment which would consume the wicked of the world and burn forever. "Depart from me, you cursed, into the eternal fire prepared for the devil and his angels" (Matthew 25:41). The apostle Paul knew that the wages of sin is death. He proffered to all who would receive it newness of life in Christ, but to those who turned away he promised only the wrath of God. Thus we see that the Bible is a unity, that both Testaments speak of the divine economy as offering love and mercy, but both also know God's judgment on those whose hearts are fat, their ears stopped, and their eyes closed. As C. S. Lewis expressed it in his *Great Divorce,* "In the end, there are only two kinds of people: those who say to God 'Thy will be done,' and those to whom God says, 'Thy will be done.'"

The New Testament is written in Greek, which has a somewhat more diversified vocabulary, containing three words for love: *eros, philia,* and *agape.* Anders Nygren, the Swedish theologian, some years ago produced a study of the first and third of these terms, *Agape and Eros.* He traced the concept of *eros,* love or desire from the human side, through Greek philosophy and culture, and contrasted it with the New Testament *agape,* the uncaused and spontaneous love of God for his creation. The two were synthesized in Augustine's *caritas,* a synthesis which dominated medieval theology and, in Nygren's view, obscured the sharp distinction made by the New Testament. Luther's biblical studies made him aware of the contamination of the pure *agape* of the gospel by the pagan *eros* and he sought to burn away the dross, leaving the unpolluted ore. Various criticisms have been made of Nygren's thesis, but it is not our purpose here to enter that particular debate. The New Testament does not use the term *eros* at all, and we may confine our attention to *philia* and *agape*.

In classical Greek literature, the verb *agapao* was used infrequently as a less colorful synonym for *eros* or *phileo*, but the translators of the Old Testament into Greek showed a decided preference for the neglected word as the equivalent of the Hebrew *aheb*. The early Christian community had an intimate familiarity with the Greek Old Testament (known as the Septuagint from the tradition that seventy scholars did the work of translation), and their writers therefore used *agapao* again and again, giving to the term a wide circulation in the Graeco-Roman world, a circulation it had never enjoyed in the pre-Christian era. But in what sense does the New Testament speak of the divine love?

THE DIVINE INITIATIVE

As in the Old Testament, the love of God is spontaneous and free; it is manifested in historic events, and it is apprehended in the context of a community. Nowhere is there any suggestion that God's love for the world, for the church, or for the individual Christian was earned or deserved in any way. God "makes

his sun rise on the evil and on the good, and sends
rain on the just and on the unjust" (Matthew 5:45).
Jesus insisted that God loves all men, the greatest
sinner in the world together with the greatest saint;
and if there is any inequity, it is in favor of the sinner
because he needs the divine love more than the saint.
The ways of the divine love are strange and paradox-
ical, cutting radically across all human understanding
and calculation. God is like an employer who hires one
group of laborers for a project at nine o'clock in the
morning, another group at noon, and still a third at
four o'clock. When the whistle blows, marking the end
of the working day, all the men are paid exactly the
same wage! When those who had toiled all the day
grumbled at the obvious inequity of this arrangement,
they were told, "Am I not allowed to do what I choose
with what belongs to me? Or do you begrudge my
generosity?" (Matthew 20:1–16). This is also the point
of the famous parable of the Prodigal Son, which, despite all of the attention and allegory lavished by
tradition on the young wastrel and his return, is actually centered on the character of the older brother. It is
a story directed at the Pharisees, who were shocked
by Jesus' association with sinners, with harlots and
publicans, with winebibbers and tax collectors. They,
the Pharisees, had been righteous, God-fearing, and
law-abiding throughout their lives. Why, then, should
God receive these licentious sybarites with such pleasure and joy? Why should there be more rejoicing in

heaven over one sinner who repents than over ninety and nine who never left the fold? It is monstrously unfair. Yet this is precisely the nature of the divine love, which goes out to those who need its healing power. Those who are well do not require the services of a physician. The Beatitudes at the opening of the Sermon on the Mount do not represent so much a classical summation of Christian character as illustrations of the paradox that the kingdom of God is given to those who think they deserve it least. The world rewards and admires the noble, the mighty, the rich, the righteous. These "have their reward" and therefore are unaware of their emptiness, their hunger for the love of God. That can come only to those who ask, who seek, who knock; and those who know themselves to be sinners in desperate need of mercy are the very ones who do search and request. Therefore harlots and publicans go into the kingdom before scribes and Pharisees; it is the poor, the persecuted, the hungry, the meek, the mourners who are truly the "blessed" ones. Not that God does not love the scribes and the Pharisees too. He does, but they dwell under the illusion that they have some sort of claim on his love, that they have earned it; it is their just desert. They have little sense of need. They are self-sufficient and will not ask. God will not force his love; one might even say that he cannot, since love is by its very nature free. Coerced, it ceases to be love, as Svengali, the hypnotist in Du Maurier's novel *Trilby*, discovered to his sorrow.

The apostle Paul, throughout his epistles, underlined and italicized this principle enunciated by Jesus in the Synoptic Gospels.[1] It is not simply that "God shows his love for us in that while we were yet sinners Christ died for us" (Romans 5:8), that "all have sinned and fall short of the glory of God" (Romans 3:23). Paul went still further to condemn the Jews and Judaizing Christians because they failed to recognize their need for God's love and forgiveness. This is what he meant by "walking after the flesh." The Greek term for "flesh" in Paul's letters is *sarx,* which does not imply sensuality. *Sarx,* to Paul, was rather the state of illusion in which the natural, fallen man found himself, believing that he had his life at his own disposal, that he could live out of his own resources, that he was not utterly and wholly dependent upon God. This might take the form of sensuality, of investing the meaning of one's life in material things, but it also was to be found in the quest of religiosity, the belief that one's piety or righteousness provided a guarantee of salvation. Paul referred frequently to the zeal of the Jew in his desire to fulfill the Law as living "according to the flesh." The Jew imagined that he could by his own effort obey the command of God and achieve righteousness.

In the Epistle to the Galatians, Paul was dealing

---

[1] The first three Gospels in the New Testament—Matthew, Mark, and Luke—are called the Synoptic Gospels, not because they present a synopsis of the life and teachings of Jesus, but because they take a common or synoptic view of his career, as opposed to the Fourth Gospel which presents a different interpretation.

with a problem which plagued him perennially. He had
preached a gospel of freedom, of the liberating power
of the divine love which broke the shackles of all law.
No man could, in ten thousand lifetimes, make himself
righteous before God, thereby meriting salvation. Only
the freely given, totally undeserved love and grace of
God could save. But Paul was strenuously opposed in
this view by some in the early church who viewed
Christianity as a sect of Judaism, as making its converts
better Jews. This party pointed to Jesus' sayings about
not having come to destroy the Law but to fulfill it,
about heaven and earth passing away but not one jot
nor tittle of the Law should pass away. These Judaizing
Christians, as they are called, followed the Apostle to
the Gentiles around the Mediterranean world, seeking
to persuade his converts from paganism that they must,
if they would become true Christians, first become Jews
(by submitting to circumcision) and then exercise scrupulous zeal in observing the Law of Israel. To the Galatians, who appeared in danger of being persuaded by
these Judaizing Christians, Paul wrote his indignant
query: "Are you so foolish? Having begun with the
Spirit, are you now ending with the flesh?" Here he
obviously meant ending in observance of the Jewish
Law, not in sensual passions.

Living according to the flesh, which was sinful self-
reliance, expressed itself in what Paul called "boasting."
The Jew boasted of the Law, the Greek of his wisdom;
but, Jew or Greek, man naturally tended to set himself

above his fellows, to think of himself more highly than he ought to think. This was to forget the fact to which Paul pointed in 1 Corinthians 4:7, "What have you that you did not receive? If then you received it, why do you boast as if it were not a gift?" Indeed, all human boasting was impossible to him who knew the nature of God who "chose what is foolish in the world to shame the wise . . . what is weak in the world to shame the strong . . . what is low and despised in the world, even things that are not, to bring to nothing things that are, so that no human being might boast in the presence of God. . . . Therefore, as it is written, 'Let him who boasts, boast of the Lord' " (1 Corinthians 1:27–31). It is clear, then, that Paul and Jesus were one in seeing the love of God as spontaneous, uncaused, and free, open to all who acknowledged the fact that they needed it but did not deserve it. The Pharisees and the Judaizing Christians cut themselves off from the possibility of appropriating the divine love by their illusion that they had earned it.

So overwhelming is the New Testament conviction of the divine initiative, entirely free from earthly or human causation, that it sometimes takes the form of a doctrine of predestination. In the Fourth Gospel, Jesus emphasized to his disciples the fact that he had chosen them, not they him. They were not selected because of any pre-eminence which they themselves possessed. They were weak, fallible, mortal men, who shared all of the foibles of their race. Peter was quixotic

and mercurial; Thomas was a man of little faith who
demanded proof; James and John were ambitious;
Judas was impatient. All of them ran away at the crisis
and trembled behind locked doors. Very unpromising
material on which to build a church! "Many are called,"
warned the Master, "but few are chosen" (Matthew
22:14). The Fourth Gospel on more than one occasion
suggests that the division of those around the Christ
into the children of light and the children of darkness
was less a matter of free human choice than of divine
determination. "No one can come to me unless the
Father who sent me draws him" (John 6:44). "But
there are some of you that do not believe. . . . This is
why I told you that no one can come to me unless it is
granted him by the Father" (6:64–65). The Fourth
Gospel is perfectly clear, as is the whole of the New
Testament, that all men are potentially sons of God,
that the invitation to receive the divine love is in principle open to everyone, and that each man is responsible for his own decision. Salvation is a combination
of divine initiative and human response, but the emphasis falls strongly on the divine initiative. The author
of the Epistle to the Ephesians speaks of God's having
chosen the saved in Christ "before the foundation of
the world" (Ephesians 1:4). "We know," Paul wrote to
the Romans, "that in everything God works for good
with those who love him, who are called according to
his purpose. For those whom he foreknew he also pre-
destined to be conformed to the image of his Son"

(Romans 8:28–29). But there is in the New Testament no doctrine of double predestination, making God directly responsible for those who fail to respond. Paul specifically rejected such an idea in his discussion of Israel's fate in Romans 9 to 11.

LOVE AS ACTION

This is the first thing to be said, then, about the divine love in the New Testament: it flows forth from God because he *is* love—that is his nature—not because the objects of his love are worthy or lovable. "In this is love," says the First Epistle of John, "not that we loved God but that he loved us and sent his Son to be the expiation for our sins" (1 John 4:10). "If we say we have no sin, we deceive ourselves, and the truth is not in us. If we confess our sins, he is faithful and just, and will forgive our sins and cleanse us from all unrighteousness" (1 John 1:8–9). The second feature of God's love, as the New Testament understands it, is that it is manifested in a series of mighty acts in history. In the message of Jesus contained in the Synoptic Gospels, all attention was centered on the near approach of the kingdom, long awaited, expected and hoped for in Israel and among all nations. It was true that the kingdom would mean judgment and damnation for the wicked, for those who were unable to read the signs of the times, who had neither ears to hear nor eyes to see. But it also meant opportunity for those who would heed the warning and take advantage of it. God could, after all, bring about the final judgment with no warning at all. He could simply snap the book of history shut with a bang and destroy all those caught therein. But he sent his messenger ahead, first John the Baptizer and then Jesus himself. It is significant that Jesus began his ministry with exactly the same message as that of his forerunner: "The time is fulfilled, and the kingdom of God is at hand; repent, and believe in the gospel" (Mark 1:15). If Jesus painted the terrors of the judgment to come in vivid colors, it was only to point up more sharply the opportunity of escape which the love of God afforded. No sign was to be given to this wicked and adulterous generation, which meant that the kind of specific timetable of cataclysm found in the apocalyptic writings of the period was rejected. Jesus made use of the prevailing apocalyptic viewpoint, the division of the cosmos into two warring camps, the division of history into two aeons, old and new. He saw the world under the dominion of Satan and his demons, groaning for salvation. But there was in Jesus' message a decided reduction of detail. He refused to predict in elaborate imagery the events preparatory to the end. No sign was to be given save that of the prophet Jonah, that is to say, the preaching of repentance.

Yet Jesus himself, his message, and his mission were signs. When the disciples of John the Baptist came asking if he was the Messiah, Jesus replied, "Go and tell

John what you hear and see: the blind receive their sight and the lame walk, lepers are cleansed and the deaf hear, and the dead are raised up, and the poor have good news preached to them" (Matthew 11:4–5). This was clearly a reference to a messianic passage in Isaiah 35:5–6: "Then the eyes of the blind shall be opened, and the ears of the deaf unstopped; then shall the lame man leap like a hart, and the tongue of the dumb sing for joy." Jesus looked upon his healing activity as the beginning of the overthrow of Satan's reign. "I saw Satan fall like lightning from heaven" (Luke 10:18). The healing miracles were nearly all interpreted in terms of demon exorcism, the routing of the devil's legions. They were signs, not of Jesus' divinity (after all, the disciples also worked miracles, and were they, too, divine?), but of the coming kingdom whose light was already beginning to break up the long night. God was about to inaugurate his final reign upon the earth, and man could do nothing either to hasten or delay it; he could only get ready. The Pharisees were deluded by the belief that the perfect observance of the Law would bring in the kingdom, while the Zealots sought to goad God into action by resorting to arms and hurling the Roman legions into the sea.

But none of this would avail. Man could do nothing except to decide where he stood, for Jesus proclaimed the hour of decision. This was the final hour of history's drama. Any moment the curtain might ring down and the play would be over. Then it would be too late to

choose. Then it would be revealed how men had
chosen. But now, there was still time. The hinges of
heaven creaked ominously as the gate swung shut, but
it was not yet closed. A few desperate seconds remained, and in those seconds Jesus confronted men
with a decisive either/or. Either one said to God with
a single heart, "Thy will be done on earth as it is in
heaven," or he did not, preferring to cling to the world
and its goods.

The demand of Jesus was marked by extreme urgency and drastic decision. There could be no half-way
measures. One man who was invited to follow the
Master asked, " 'Lord, let me first go and bury my
father.' But he said to him, 'Leave the dead to bury
their own dead; but as for you, go and proclaim the
kingdom of God.' Another said, 'I will follow you,
Lord; but let me first say farewell to those at my home.'
Jesus said to him, 'No one who puts his hand to the
plow and looks back is fit for the kingdom of God' "
(Luke 9:59–62). In a cuttingly cruel passage, Jesus
even sundered the closest earthly ties of all: "If anyone comes to me and does not hate his father and
mother and wife and children and brothers and sisters,
yes, and even his own life, he cannot be my disciple"
(Luke 14:26). He himself renounced his family, refusing to recognize their close claims on him. "And his
mother and brothers came; and standing outside
they sent to him and called him. And a crowd was
sitting about him; and they said to him, 'Your mother

and your brothers are outside, asking for you.' And he replied, 'Who are my mother and my brothers?' And looking around on those who sat about him, he said, 'Here are my mother and my brothers! Whoever does the will of God is my brother, and sister, and mother'" (Mark 3:31–35). Jesus did not expect that every man would forsake his home, any more than he required everyone to sell all that he had to give to the poor. But every man must make up his mind what matters most. When a choice is to be made, which comes first: God's kingdom or one's own supposed security? This is why he uprooted his own life and the lives of his disciples from the ordinary cares and concerns of daily existence, to show a singleness of heart and childlike trust in the God who clothes the lilies of the field in a glory transcending that of Solomon.

Any earthly security is, after all, illusory. As James Thurber has observed, "There is no safety in numbers nor in anything else." No man can, by taking thought, alter his height by one inch or change the number or the color of the hairs of his head. He may disguise both with wigs or dyes, but he does not escape either balding and graying or what those conditions symbolize: the inexorable march of time. To the man who rests his soul in his worldly possessions overflowing into ever larger storehouses, God says, "Thou fool! This night your soul is required of you; and the things you have prepared, whose will they be?" (Luke 12:16–21). There seems to be special peril for those who pile up riches.

They become ensnared in a golden trap, unable to escape, so that a camel goes through a needle's eye more easily than a rich man into the kingdom. But not only the rich choose the wrong things whereon to set their hearts. Most men fail, for their preoccupation is with the world and its cares. "A man once gave a great banquet, and invited many; and at the time for the banquet he sent his servant to say to those who had been invited, 'Come; for all is now ready.' But they all alike began to make excuses. The first said to him, 'I have bought a field, and I must go out and see it; I pray you, have me excused.' And another said, 'I have bought five yoke of oxen, and I go to examine them; I pray you, have me excused.' And another said, 'I have married a wife, and therefore I cannot come.'" Then the host threw open the doors and invited all "the poor and maimed and blind and lame" to enjoy the feast spurned by those busy with their own affairs (Luke 14:16-20).

Jesus knew that the way is narrow and the gate is strait and only a few enter into life, while multitudes walk the broad highway to destruction. This is why he urged, "Seek first his kingdom and his righteousness, and all these things shall be yours as well" (Matthew 6:32). Each man must count the cost, must decide what is really important to him and what he will give up for its sake, even as a king planning a war or a builder contemplating the construction of a tower. The kingdom of God, however, is worth any sacrifice. It is like a pearl of great price for which a merchant will sell all that he has in order to purchase it. The kingdom is like a field wherein lies buried a great treasure, and the farmer who discovers it puts all of his house and lands up for sale in order to raise the price of that field. Some will sacrifice tempting hands and offending eyes; some will even make themselves eunuchs for the sake of the kingdom. It is better to enter into life maimed than to remain whole and be lost.

Jesus was not suggesting that the world is in itself corrupt, to be renounced and rejected. He was no dualist, looking with jaundiced eye on the material realm. What he was warning against is the investment of one's heart in the wrong place, finding one's ultimate security and meaning in that which is not ultimate but only proximate and finite. Such an investment is precisely what the prophets of old meant by idolatry, and it is doomed to fail, leading to destruction and death. The attitude demanded for entrance into God's kingdom is genuine inner repentance, what the Greek calls *metanoia*. This does not mean a simple sorrow over past wrongs, a mild regret which passes and forms no firm barrier against repetition of the wrong. *Metanoia* means a radical about-face, a complete transformation of one's whole orientation. Where before, one's back was turned on God and his kingdom, the attention turned to self-seeking, to the world and its cares, now one puts the world behind him and places his entire trust in God. And such a *volte-face* is possible to any man at any time. He can do it now, in this moment. This is the significance of Jesus' saying that "the kingdom of God is within you" (Luke 17:21). To enter the kingdom lies potentially within all. The kingdom in its final state has not yet arrived. It is coming but still not here. But one need not wait for its total consummation; he can belong to it now, by setting his heart where it truly belongs. And he need have no fear; need take no thought for the morrow, what he shall eat or drink or wear. He is not anxious, for God knows his needs, even as he knows the needs of the birds of the air; and God can be trusted. There is no guarantee that one's faith will protect him from the slings and arrows of outrageous fortune, that one is provided with an armor that wards off bacteria or bullets. Jesus told his disciples that the hairs of their heads were numbered, but he did not promise that they would never be bald! On the contrary, he warned that their lot would contain suffering, persecution, perhaps even a cross. But none of these things could cut one off from God who loves and saves, who cares.

It is a merciful God who warns of the impending judgment and offers salvation to all who will reach out their hands and take it. This is a God who loves all of his children and yearns for them, going forth to seek and to save. He is like the woman who lost a coin and dropped everything to sweep the house, concentrating all attention on finding what was hers. He is like the shepherd who searches everywhere for the lost lamb; he is like the prodigal's father running down the road to meet the returning one. Here is once more a God who acts, who finds and is found of men. In post-exilic Judaism, God had become remote, dwelling in the far-off heavens, addressed through the elaborate and ornate prayers of the ritual. His will was made plain once for all in the Law. No longer did he speak as in the days of Moses and the prophets. No more did he intervene dramatically in the events of history. The reign of God over his world had become clouded and unclear. It was a rule of Law, not dissimilar to that conceived by the eighteenth century deists. Now Jesus restored the God of the prophets who is omnipotent, that is to say, the power in and over all things, a dynamic, active will. He hears the prayers of his children; he knows their needs; he broods over them and loves them. Man need no longer come to God only through the intermediary of the Law; he can come directly as to a Father who listens and cares.

There is nonetheless a striking difference in the divine Being as encountered by the prophets of the Old Testament and as portrayed by Jesus. Unlike Amos and Hosea, Isaiah and Jeremiah, who were acutely aware of the destiny and the danger of the nation in its relation to other nations, who saw the hand of God preeminently at work in history, history conceived as the broad sweep of events involving kings and empires, the man from Nazareth appeared indifferent to Israel as Israel, a kingdom in the midst of kingdoms, to the

Roman Empire and its political vicissitudes. He cleverly evaded the dangerous question of tribute put to him by the Pharisees: shall we render tribute to Caesar? An affirmative answer would make him appear weak and lacking in courage, while a negative answer was revolutionary and insurrectionist. "Bring me a coin," he said. "Whose image is inscribed hereon? Caesar's? Then give to Caesar what belongs to him." The question unspoken but clearly implied was, "Whose image is inscribed on you? To whom, then, do you belong?" And the answer was clear. "Give to God that which belongs to him." To Pilate's inquiry whether he claimed to be King of the Jews, he answered, "My kingdom is not of this world." He was simply not attached to the political concerns of men. All the pomp and power of government were offered by Satan in the wilderness temptation and rejected by Jesus. "Those who live by the sword shall die by the sword."

As Bultmann points out in his *Theology of the New Testament,* Jesus radically de-historized God, or rather he reinterpreted the meaning of history, which was seen no longer as the affairs of nations but as the life of the individual. This had happened already to some extent in post-exilic Judaism. Prior to the exile, the religious unit before God had been the nation Israel. Judgment or salvation came to all, and it came as national catastrophe or national deliverance. A sense of community, of social solidarity, pervaded the thinking of all the early prophets, so that responsibility for the sins of the nation fell upon the shoulders of every man, even those of the prophet himself. Amos had no expectation of escaping the divine punishment which must inevitably come upon his people. He, too, shared in a guilt which was necessarily collective. Isaiah, in turning to the future, saw hope in a righteous remnant, but his hope lay not in the personal sanctity of the faithful few as contrasted with the iniquity of the many. The saving power of the remnant was not to be piety but insight, the ability to read aright the signs of the times, to see history as judgment, and to build anew the national life on the sure foundations of the covenant. Jeremiah envisioned a blessed future, when the covenant would be internalized, when it would be written on men's hearts and everyone would experience the intimate relationship to God which had heretofore been confined to prophets and seers. Ezekiel it was, however, who really sundered the knot binding the Hebrews into a national unit and that unit to God. He rejected the old proverb, "The fathers have eaten sour grapes, and the children's teeth are set on edge." Each man was now to be responsible to God for his own sins, his own and no one else's (Ezekiel 18). If he was righteous, he would prosper, rewarded by God himself. If he was wicked, then the divine judgment would surely fall.

From the exile on, the individual became increasingly the religious unit before God as the nation faded into the background. It was in this line of development that Jesus stood, in his recasting of history. But though post-

exilic Judaism de-historized God, it also made him remote. Now Jesus restored the nearness of the divine,
the active, dynamic Presence who spoke through the
prophets of old to the nation. But instead of simply
using individuals as instruments to warn the whole
people, God now confronted each man in his own life
and offered him the decisive choice: the demand and
the promise. The man of old was largely dependent
upon another for his relationship to God: the prophet,
the priest, the Pharisee as interpreter of the Law. Now
all intermediaries were rendered superfluous. The divine love is such that it comes directly to a man in his
own history and offers itself to him who will receive.
The only price tag attached, the only conditions laid
down, the only word written over the portals to life is
"Repent," which is to say, "Admit that you need God's
mercy and love. Turn, and live for him." To any man
who will take that simple step the gates of the kingdom
swing open.

THE COMING KINGDOM

The concept of the divine love as manifested in
mighty acts in history took on new significance in the
faith of the early church. For Jesus, those mighty acts
were centered on the coming kingdom; for the disciples, they revolved around the figure of Jesus himself,
in whom the kingdom had already come. Thus, the
New Testament is described as "realized eschatology,"

which is simply a way of saying that the kingdom is coming, using four-dollar words. Eschatology means literally "a doctrine of the last things," a description of the end of history and the final triumph of righteousness over evil. This triumph, according to the early Christians, had taken place in the life and death and resurrection of Jesus Christ. To be sure, the final consummation lay still in the future, when Christ should return in glory with his angels. But that would only complete what had already been started. C. S. Lewis, in *Mere Christianity,* has used a graphic metaphor to describe the situation. It was, he says, as though the world were enemy-occupied territory. The rightful king had landed in disguise and set up a short-wave broadcasting station. He announced that the work of liberation had begun and called upon all his loyal subjects to rally to him, to join in this great task. The final deliverance was still to come, but it had begun and the outcome was assured. This conviction stands out on every page of the New Testament. Indeed, this is the central content of the message of the early church, called the *kerygma.* In the Greek city-state, the town crier was called a *keryx,* or herald, and he had two major functions. The first was to announce the news, to proclaim the happenings of the day; the second was to call the citizens out of their homes and shops to the assembly in the town square, where they voted as a community on important questions of policy. Christian preachers took the title of *keryx,* heralds of the good news of the gospel, proclaiming the news of what God had done and was doing, and calling upon their hearers to leave their ordinary lives and join the assembly of the church, the assembly of God. The content of the *kerygma,* then, was news and a summons, event and invitation. A rather careful examination of that preaching, that message, is important on two counts: to show its essential unity with the teaching of Jesus and to indicate its function as a bridge between Jesus and Paul.

C. H. Dodd's little book entitled *The Apostolic Preaching* presents under six heads the *kerygma* as it appeared in the pre-Pauline Jerusalem community of the church. First, it was the declaration that the long-expected, earnestly awaited time of fulfillment had come. The prophets of old had foretold it, and now their prophecies were coming to pass. So Peter, in the first sermon in the post-resurrection church, explained the ecstasy of the apostles at Pentecost to those who thought them drunk. "These men are not drunk, as you suppose. After all, it is only nine o'clock in the morning. Rather this is a fulfillment of the ancient prophecy of Joel: 'And in the last days it shall be, God declares, that I will pour out my Spirit upon all flesh, and your sons and your daughters shall prophesy, and your young men shall see visions, and your old men shall dream dreams; yea, and on my menservants and my maidservants in those days I will pour out my Spirit; and they shall prophesy. And I will show wonders in the heaven above and signs on the earth beneath, blood, and fire, and vapor of smoke; the sun shall be turned into darkness and the moon into blood, before the day of the Lord comes, the great and manifest day. And it shall be that whoever calls on the name of the Lord shall be saved' " (Acts 2:15–21). Or, as Peter put it in a later address, "What God foretold by the mouth of all the prophets, that his Christ should suffer, he thus fulfilled. . . . And all the prophets who have spoken, from Samuel and those who came afterwards, also proclaimed these days. You are the sons of the prophets and of the covenant which God gave to your fathers, saying to Abraham, 'And in your posterity shall all the families of the earth be blessed' " (Acts 3:18, 24, 25). This note of prophecy fulfilled, of the dawning of the new aeon, the new age, was sounded again and again.

The second part of the *kerygma* was the assertion that the day of fulfillment had been ushered in by the life and ministry, the death and resurrection, of Jesus the Christ. This usually took the form of a brief summary account of these events, citing the fact of Jesus' membership in the house and lineage of David (from whom the Messiah was to come), his ministry of miracles, his death upon the cross, which was no defeat but a part of the divine plan, and his resurrection and exaltation to glory. "Men of Israel," said Peter at Pentecost, "hear these words: Jesus of Nazareth, a man attested to you by God with mighty works and wonders and signs which God did through him in your midst, as you yourselves know—this Jesus, delivered up according to the definite plan and foreknowledge of God, you crucified and killed by the hands of lawless men. But God raised him up, having loosed the pangs of death, because it was not possible for him to be held by it" (Acts 2:22–24). The Davidic descent of the Christ was linked to a foreshadowing of the resurrection in the words immediately following (Acts 2:25–36): "For David says concerning him [Jesus], 'I saw the Lord always before me, for he is at my right hand that I may not be shaken; therefore my heart was glad, and my tongue rejoiced; moreover my flesh will dwell in hope. For thou wilt not abandon my soul to Hades, nor let thy Holy One see corruption. Thou hast made known to me the ways of life; thou wilt make me full of gladness with thy presence.'" "Brethren" (Peter continued after this quotation from Psalm 16), "I may say to you confidently of the patriarch David that he both died and was buried, and his tomb is with us to this day. Being therefore a prophet, and knowing that God had sworn with an oath to him that he would set one of his descendants upon his throne, he foresaw and spoke of the resurrection of the Christ, that he was not abandoned to Hades, nor did his flesh see corruption. This Jesus God raised up, and of that we are all witnesses. Being therefore exalted at the right hand of God, and having received from the Father the promise of the Holy Spirit, he has poured out this which you see and hear. For David did not ascend into the heavens; but he himself says, 'The Lord said to my Lord, Sit at my right hand, till I make thy enemies a stool for thy feet.' Let all the house of Israel therefore know assuredly that God has made him both Lord and Christ, this Jesus whom you crucified."

The third section of the *kerygma* of the early church proclaimed the exaltation of Jesus to God's right hand where he reigned and whence he should return as the messianic head of the new and true Israel. "The God of our fathers raised Jesus whom you killed by hanging him on a tree. God exalted him as Leader and Savior, to give repentance to Israel and forgiveness of sins (Acts 5:30–31). "This is the stone," said Peter to the leaders of Israel, "which was rejected by you builders, but which has become the head of the corner. And there is salvation in no one else, for there is no other name under heaven given among men by which we must be saved" (Acts 4:11–12).

Fourth in the *kerygma* was the assertion that Christ manifested his position of power and glory at God's right hand by pouring forth the Holy Spirit into the life of the Christian community, not alone at the feast of Pentecost, in the rushing of the mighty wind and the speaking in tongues, but in the power given to the disciples to continue the signs and wonders of the kingdom and to live together in love and fellowship. "We are witnesses to these things, and so is the Holy Spirit whom God has given to those who obey him" (Acts 5:32).

There was a fifth element in the *kerygma:* the con-

viction that the Messianic Age was soon to be finally
consummated in the imminent return of the glorified
Christ. God will "send the Christ [Messiah] appointed
for you, Jesus, whom heaven must receive until the time
for establishing all that God spoke by the mouth of his
holy prophets from of old" (Acts 3:20–21).

This proclamation of the *kerygma,* the news of what
God had done in Jesus, was doing in and through the
church, and was about to do in bringing in the kingdom, was always concluded with a call for repentance,
an offer of the forgiveness of sins, and a promise of salvation and the Holy Spirit. Those who accepted this
call, this offer, and this promise by entering the community of Christians would have a share in the life of
the coming age, the new aeon, the kingdom of God. At
the end of Peter's sermon at Pentecost, he and the other
apostles were asked, "Brethren, what shall we do?" to
which the reply came, "Repent, and be baptized every
one of you in the name of Jesus Christ for the forgiveness of your sins; and you shall receive the gift of the
Holy Spirit. For the promise is to you and to your
children, and to all that are far off, every one whom
the Lord our God calls to him" (Acts 2:37–39).

Peter concluded a later address to Cornelius the
Roman centurion and his family with a general summation of the gospel and an invitation: "You know the word
which he [God] sent to Israel, preaching good news of
peace by Jesus Christ (he is Lord of all), the word which
was proclaimed throughout all Judea, beginning from

Galilee after the baptism which John preached: how God anointed Jesus of Nazareth with the Holy Spirit and with power; how he went about doing good and healing all that were oppressed by the devil, for God was with him. And we are witnesses to all that he did both in the country of the Jews and in Jerusalem. They put him to death by hanging him on a tree; but God raised him on the third day and made him manifest; not to all the people but to us who were chosen by God as witnesses, who ate and drank with him after he rose from the dead. And he commanded us to preach to the people, and to testify that he is the one ordained by God to be judge of the living and the dead. To him all the prophets bear witness that every one who believes in him receives forgiveness of sins through his name" (Acts 10:36–43).

The love of God is made manifest in his mighty acts, acts not in the realm of nations but in the sphere of individual lives. Thus spoke the early church. Three general comments need to be made about this message. First of all, it is obviously organically related to the message of Jesus. If one compares the *kerygma* in Acts with the opening proclamation of Jesus in the Gospel of Mark, the unity becomes readily apparent. "The time is fulfilled," said Jesus, and the early church gave back, "Amen," documenting the statement with prophecies from the Old Testament and showing how they were being realized. "The kingdom of God has drawn near," was the proclamation of Jesus, and the *kerygma* pointed to the life, ministry, death, and resurrection of the Master as the chief evidence of the kingdom's arrival. "Repent and believe the good news," Jesus concluded, and so also did his disciples and followers, promising forgiveness of sins to all who would repent. This is the first thing to notice: the essential identity of Jesus' preaching and that of the pre-Pauline church in Jerusalem.

The second point has to do with Paul himself, who has so frequently and so unjustly been accused of transforming and distorting the simple message of Jesus into a metaphysical mystery cult. Such an accusation is usually made by those who overlook the eschatological element in Jesus' teachings and focus almost solely on his ethics. They welcome and emphasize the Sermon on the Mount, the parables of the Good Samaritan, the Prodigal Son, or the Lost Sheep, but they ignore the plain evidence that Jesus believed in the coming kingdom. "There are those within sound of my voice who shall in no wise taste death till the Son of Man shall come in his glory with his angels." Thus Paul's focus on the activity of God in Christ, an activity which the apostle viewed as eschatological and saving, is distasteful to the admirers of the simply ethical Jesus, and they make of the apostle a villain who created Christianity. The foregoing account of the message of Jesus and the *kerygma* of the early church should make it perfectly clear that the New Testament has a single core, uniting Jesus himself, the early church, the apostle Paul, and the Johannine literature: the saving work of God, reconciling the world to himself in Christ.

The third comment to be made at this point is one which applies to the whole of the Bible as much as to the concept of divine love in the New Testament, and it is simply this: biblical religion deals with events rather than ideas, with the concrete rather than the abstract, with the historical rather than the detached eternal. God is not an idea but Being. He manifests himself in personal encounter in human experience. Supremely does he reveal himself in the events of Jesus the Christ —his life, his death, his resurrection. Only in the experience of personal encounter with the Christ does a man become marked with his sign. Christianity is not an idea or series of ideas to which the mind is asked to give assent, not even the idea that God is love. In fact, one might say that every major heresy in Christian history represents an attempt to transform event into idea. What is central to all the New Testament is the event of the New Being in Christ.

This is not to say that the event does not give rise to interpretations, to theologies. Indeed, man, being a rational creature, must interpret, must seek to relate his experience of this event to every other event. But he must not confuse the one with the other, mistaking his own interpretation or even the interpretation of his church for the event itself. That transcends all particular theories and understandings of it, partly confirming them but also partly contradicting and denying

them. Paul Minear, Professor of New Testament at
Yale Divinity School, has translated the gospel into
a kind of algebraic symbolism. Let the life, death, and
resurrection of Christ equal Event A1. The concrete
encounter and conversion of the individual believer is
Event A2. Event A3 is the creation of the church, the
community of those who have been grasped and called
by Event A1. These three are all inextricably related
to each other. None is complete without the other two.
The divine love in the New Testament is empty and
meaningless as mere theory, as an ideal. It comes
alive only in a concrete event in which the observer
becomes participant, is challenged to decide where he
stands. And his decision becomes his own event.

Before proceeding to a discussion of the final characteristic of the divine love as the New Testament
experiences it, we must deal with one question which
must raise itself in the minds of many readers. If Jesus'
message was so eschatological, if the early church
looked for the early return of the Christ, then what
happened? Isn't there a glaring miscalculation here?
Wasn't Jesus obviously wrong in his expectation of the
kingdom, and weren't the disciples led astray by that
mistaken hope? It is obvious from the epistles of Paul
that he gradually gave up his own belief that he would
live to see the end of history and the establishment of
God's kingdom on earth. The early letters, those to the
Thessalonians, for example, are filled with references to
the imminent coming of Christ in glory. The later

epistles of captivity, Colossians and Philippians, reflect a resignation to an indefinite postponement of the fulfillment. The New Testament itself reflects the alternating ebb and flow of this hope through the first century. The book of Revelation attempted to revive the expectation, seeing in the fiery trials of the persecution of the church under the Emperor Domitian in A.D. 94 the signs of the end. The Fourth Gospel attempted a reinterpretation of the second coming, saying that it had already occurred—in the entrance of the Holy Spirit into the life of the church. Christ had returned and dwelt in the community already, so there was no reason to expect another manifestation.

But what of Jesus and his apparently egregious error? The man from Nazareth was here solidly within the prophetic tradition of Israel. The prophets of old almost without exception expected the judgment of God to take place in a very short time, not so much that they sought vindication of their own threats as that they were overwhelmed by the sovereign majesty of God before whom the world faded away into insignificance and transience. A thousand years in his sight are but as yesterday when it is past, and already the world seemed at its end. Each individual man's destiny was decided by his relation to God, and the hour in which that decision was made was a brief one. Saying no today predisposed one to say no tomorrow and tomorrow and tomorrow, limiting the possibilities of saying yes. This the prophets knew, and that knowledge col-

ored their view of the world's limited status before the
throne of judgment. The word placed in their mouths
became a word of urgency, of immediacy, of a final
choice: either/or, now or never. Your fate is determined once and for all by your decision in this moment.

Jesus shared this view. He was passionately convinced that God demands of man a decision, and the
direction of that decision determines man's fate: salvation or condemnation. So Jesus felt himself at the
razor's edge of time, offering the world its final alter-
natives. He was not, like the Essenes, world-weary
and disillusioned, nor was he one with the apocalyptic
sects, yearning for the dawn of the new age, seeing
signs where none existed. He simply was painfully
aware of the contrast between the awful futility of
men's striving for security in the world and the searing
demand of the Almighty. What is important about
the eschatological message of Jesus is not the temporal
foreshortening, in which he was clearly wrong, but in
his conception of the will of God and its demands and
of human nature and its misdirectedness, in which he
was profoundly right. Most men do lay up treasures in
the wrong places and find, too late, that where their
treasure is, there are their hearts also. But then they
cannot change. They have made their choice and the
judgment is upon them. They have judged themselves,
condemning themselves to futility, emptiness, and
meaninglessness. When the invitation to the great banquet comes, they have other pressing business and

cannot come. To cite C. S. Lewis once more, again from *The Great Divorce,* "All that are in Hell choose it. Without that self-choice there would be no Hell." Not that they know that they are deciding thus. They simply pass up the chance while it is alive and thereby kill it. In these terms Jesus' eschatology is as relevant today as ever. The world may not end next week, but our opportunity to enter the kingdom may very well end. The divine love is long-suffering, willing to wait forever; our destiny is to rush headlong to our fate— life or death. Time, the world's time, stretches out indefinitely. Our time does not. It must, as Thomas Wolfe observed, have a stop.

LOVE IN COMMUNITY

The divine love in the New Testament is, as we have seen, spontaneous and free, uncaused by its objects, and it is manifested in the mighty acts of God, in the events of Jesus Christ. It is also apprehended in the context of a community of forgiveness and grace. If it is true, as Paul declared, that God was in Christ, reconciling the world to himself, then that work of reconciliation goes on, after the ascension of Christ to the right hand of God, nowhere else than within the church itself. The Greek term translated into English as "church" is *ecclesia,* which in classical Greek meant an assembly, the very assembly to which the citizens were called by the *keryx* or herald. But the word had no religious connotations whatever. It was purely a secular or political gathering. In the New Testament the *ecclesia* is solely religious, the company of those who are the "called of God." These are the elect, the new people of God, chosen by him to carry on the mission which the chosen people of the old covenant rejected. From the beginning, God purposed that Israel should be "a light to lighten the Gentiles," that their common life should be so contagious that all nations should be drawn to the covenant relation with their Creator and Lord.

But Israel after the exile grew exclusive and nationalistic, fiercely proud of their privileged position and contemptuous of the Gentiles or *Goyim*. They rejected the Christ whom God sent and therefore God rejected them, turning to the people of the new covenant established by the cross.[2] The church, then, is the new Israel, called of God not out of the world but precisely to go into the world and preach the gospel to every creature. The term *ecclesia* itself is used sparingly in the New Testament. Only one of the Gospels (Matthew) contains the word, and it is absent in eight of the Epistles, but the community of God's people plays a central role throughout, described in other terms.

---

[2] This statement should not be interpreted as anti-Semitism. After all, Jesus himself and all of the earliest Christians were Jews. It was the religious leaders of Israel who rejected Christ, and the continuing Jewish community remains a covenanted people but with a different function. Their task is, as Franz Rosenzweig has observed, to hold the fort, to be what they are, while the church is the reconnaissance arm, sent out to convert the world.

The "little flock" of which Christ is the Shepherd, the vine of which he is the center, the bride of Christ, the body of Christ—all these phrases point to the *koinonia,* the community, the fellowship of which Christ is Lord.

Jesus himself gathered the company of the disciples around him and trained them intensively for the mission which was to be theirs—the preaching of the good news of the kingdom in the interim between his own death and the coming of the Son of Man in glory. He suggested on one occasion that the motive behind his use of parables was not to make plain but to conceal. His meaning would be clear to those whom God had chosen to be the new temple which he would build, to be the heirs of the coming kingdom. Christ had come to establish a new covenant through his death upon the cross. The Son of Man must suffer and die and be raised again on the third day to establish a new covenant in his blood. This is clearly the significance of the institution of the Eucharist, the Lord's Supper, the earliest account of which is to be found in 1 Corinthians 11. Paul said significantly, "I *received* from the Lord what I also delivered to you," indicating that this was no invention of his. He found the practice firmly established already in the church, and his words are clearly a liturgical formula well-fixed in the worship of the new community. The words, "This cup is the new covenant in my blood. Do this, as often as you drink it, in remembrance of me," indicate both a conception of a new Sinai and the expectation that an interim was

to take place between the imminent death and the
final return. These are ideas which permeate the whole
of the New Testament.

Paul never gave up his hope for the ultimate conversion of Israel. The Epistle to the Romans contains
a long agony over the relationship between the two
peoples of the covenant, old and new. But he was
perfectly clear that the old barriers between Jew and
Greek, slave and free, male and female, were broken
down in Christ. The church opened her doors to all,
and her ultimate purpose was the reconciliation of the
whole of mankind to God. But that purpose could be
fulfilled only through the church and her preaching, her
sacraments and her fellowship. The church was literally
the body of Christ, carrying on the great work of salvation which he began. His earthly body was no more,
glorified as it was in the heavens. So the church became the vessel wherein the Spirit dwells, continuing
to carry the message of divine love and grace to the
world. How else could the gospel be carried on? Unlike
the old covenant, men and women were not born into
it, bound by blood to God and one another. They were
born again of the Spirit, entering the community of
faith individually by acts of decision. But they were
not isolated individuals, any more than were the members of the old Israel. They were members one of another, living in the assembly of God, the fellowship
of love. And they were included within the church because God had called them through Christ. The church

is not a human organization instituted by men for their mutual association and benefit. It is a divine organization created by God's act, constituted by his call, and supported by his Spirit which dwells within it. "God so loved the world that he gave his only begotten Son," and he gave the world also the church as the community of reconciliation. "Thanks be to God for his unspeakable gift!"

4

HUMAN LOVE

IN THE

NEW

TESTAMENT

꽃

The essential unity of the two covenants of the Bible is as evident in the conception of human love as it is in the divine. Jesus, asked which is the first and great commandment, responded from the Old Testament, "The first is, 'Hear, O Israel: the Lord our God, the Lord is one; and you shall love the Lord your God with all your heart, and with all your soul, and with all your mind,

and with all your strength.' The second is this, 'You
shall love your neighbor as yourself.' There is no other
commandment greater than these" (Mark 12:29–31).
Or, as Matthew put it, "On these two commandments
depend all the law and the prophets" (Matthew 22:40).
The vertical dimension of life, man's relation to God, is
inextricably related to the horizontal, man's relation to
man. "You can't have one," as Tin Pan Alley insists in
another connection, "without the other." "If any one
says, 'I love God,' and hates his brother, he is a liar; for
he who does not love his brother whom he has seen,
cannot love God whom he has not seen. And this
commandment we have from him, that he who loves
God should love his brother also" (1 John 4:20–21).

As Hosea used one word to describe God's love for
Israel and his own love for his faithless wife, so the
New Testament shows a decided preference for the
term *agape* to indicate the various facets of Christian
love. The Greek *philia* does appear, more usually in the
context of human love, but far less often than *agape*.
This choice of words is not accidental, for the New
Testament sees man's love for God and his neighbor
primarily as a response to the divine love. It is "God's
love shed abroad in our hearts" (Romans 5:5). This, however, is a response awakened in the human heart by the
activity of God in Christ, not a natural love, inherent in
all men. Man in his natural unredeemed state does love,
does set his heart—but on the wrong things. This is
perfectly clear both in the Gospels and in the epistles of

Paul. Natural, sinful, "fleshly" man lives in the illusion that his life is at his own disposal, that he can invest and withdraw his love at will. He believes himself to be his own master. What he does not know, and usually does not discover until it is too late, is that his freedom is sharply delimited. He *can* choose that which he will love, but having made his choice, he has lost his freedom and become a slave. Once he has invested himself in someone or something, he is bound captive, for the ultimate meaning of his life is involved and he can no longer get along without the object of his devotion.

The rich man simply cannot forswear his wealth, even to save his life. He for whom father or mother or family has become an idol loves them unwisely and too well and thus finds entrance to the kingdom barred. The Jew is enamored of the Law, or of his own righteousness, or both. Greeks are ensnared by their wisdom. Whatever the object or the person, once a man loves, he is caught. He no longer is the master; he is the slave, for he finds that he cannot live without his love. Take it from him and life ceases to have meaning. Many a man has cut the thread of his life with his own hand following such a deprivation or loss. The suicide always testifies to his faith in a god that failed. Fortunately for human life on the planet, the gods that fail are few, and men offer less drastic sacrifices upon the altars of their deities. But their love robs them of their liberty; they are faithful devotees of that in which they have invested their ultimate concern. The pantheon of these divinities is crowded, and it is sometimes possible to shift one's allegiance from one faltering idol to another which seems firmer and more glamorous. But no man while he lives has the choice to love or not to love. He can only decide what or whom he will love. That is the character of human existence, at least as the New Testament sees it.

The verb *phileo* is used frequently in the New Testament to indicate a love which is misdirected. The hypocrites "love to stand and pray in the synagogues and at the street corners, that they may be seen by men" (Matthew 6:5). There are those who love mother or father, son or daughter, more than they should so that such a love bars them from the kingdom of God (Matthew 10:37). The Pharisees "love the place of honor at feasts and the best seats in the synagogues, and salutations in the market places, and being called rabbi by men" (Matthew 23:6–7). And "the love of money is the root of all evil" (1 Timothy 6:10). But *phileo* can also be used to mean brotherly love as in 1 Peter 3:8, Hebrews 13:1, or Romans 12:10. The Fourth Gospel contains the word about a dozen times, most notably in the closing chapter when Jesus asks Peter three times, "Simon, son of John, do you love me?" and Peter responds, "Yes, Lord; you know that I love you" (John 21:15–17). "Then," says Jesus, "feed my sheep." If *phileo* is ambiguous in its meaning, varying in the context, the same can be said of *agapao*, for it, too, can connote the wrong kind of love. Luke, for example, uses the latter term to describe the love of the Pharisees for the uppermost seats in the syn-

agogue (Luke 11:43) and the love of sinners for those
who love them (Luke 6:32). The First Epistle of John,
which is a virtual hymn to the divine love (*agape*), also
uses the same word, cautioning its readers not to love
the things of the world, for "if any one loves the world,
love for the Father is not in him" (1 John 2:15).

LOVE AS AGAPE

But the overwhelming preponderance of New Testament usage is in favor of the essential unity of the love
(*agape*) which God manifests to his creation and the love
(*agape*) which Christians are to have for God and for
one another. And this is not an innate possession of the
natural man in his fallen state; it is a gift of grace, bestowed by God on those who have heeded his call
and entered the kingdom. The majority of "the world"
(*kosmos*), as we have seen, loves the wrong things. Only
those who have the ears to hear and the eyes to see know
what it means to love God and neighbor. Only those who
can look at Calvary and see there more than a good man
going to his undeserved death are in a position really
to understand the character of the divine love and to
respond with a grateful and wondering devotion. "In
this is love, not that we loved God but that he loved us
and sent his Son to be the expiation for our sins" (1 John
4:10). The Jew found the love of God in his choosing
Israel as his people and in his revelation in the Law.
The Greek traced the divine love in the orderly processes

of nature. Both were capable of responding after their own fashion with obedience and with wisdom. But they "boasted," as the apostle Paul put it, of their righteousness and their knowledge, regarding their activity as the decisive element in the encounter between themselves and God.

God acts first, to be sure, in ordering the cosmos, in giving the Law, but with the act are set up conditions which must be fulfilled on the human side, and the fulfillment of those conditions is a source of pride, of boasting. The Greek looked down on the ignorant barbarian, and the righteous Pharisee scorned the sinful publican. The love for God displayed in wisdom and goodness was a "work," a human achievement. The New Testament knew better. It acknowledged the divine initiative in every respect. The Christian could not boast before pagans that he loved God, for he knew that this was a possibility opened to him only by the activity of God himself. This is the real significance of such predestinarian notes as are sounded in the New Testament. Whatever one may think of the whole doctrine of election, it does have this one virtue: it renders any boasting on the part of the Christian utterly impossible. He regards himself as having been chosen by God, but not because of any virtue on his part. He is no more pious or righteous than anyone else. The cause of his election remains a mystery of the divine love. He loves God because God first loved him and enabled him to respond in faith and devotion. "Then what becomes of our boasting? It is excluded" (Romans 3:27). No human being, therefore, can "boast in the presence of God" (1 Corinthians 1:29). For all human possessions, including the capacity to love God, are gifts of the divine grace; and since they are gifts, they cannot be regarded as works or achievements.

This, then, is the first characteristic of human love for God as seen in the New Testament. It is *agape*, the same love which God has for man, and is implanted in men's hearts by the Father of the Lord Jesus Christ. The second aspect of man's love for God is its demand for un-reserved dedication to the divine will: "Thy kingdom come, thy will be done, on earth as it is in heaven." Each man must recognize that he cannot serve two masters, God and the world. He must choose between them; loving one, he will "hate" the other. No sacrifice is too great to make for the sake of one's absolute loyalty and love to God. But mere lip service is not enough. "Not everyone who says 'Lord, Lord,' shall enter the king-dom." The love must translate itself into concrete obe-dience. It is precisely at this point that Jesus recast the conception of love and obedience as it was known in rabbinical Judaism.

The Pharisees saw man's duty as loving God and serving him through a scrupulous observance of the Law, or Torah. This was not, for the Jew, as one might assume from some of the apostle Paul's polemical pas-sages about the Law, a burden and a bother, leading to despair. On the contrary, the Jew rejoiced in the Law, regarding it as God's most precious gift to his chosen people. Other nations might grope through mist and darkness, seeking to know the divine purpose and plan, bedeviled by the specters of doubt and uncertainty. Israel knew what the Lord required. He had spoken once for all, revealing his will through his Word. The Torah was the glory of Israel, and the Psalms abound in hymns of gratitude to God for his gracious gift. (See especially Psalm 119.) The Jew was to show his love for the Lord by obeying, by following to the letter the manifest design for living. This required careful study and constant adaptation as the circumstances of life changed. The scribes and Pharisees were the interpreters of the Law, and their goal was to discover the relevance of this revelation of God's will to every aspect of existence. The Pharisees were the "liberals" as over against the conservative Sadducees, the aristocratic party connected with the Temple and its priesthood. The Sadducees were fundamentalists regarding the Torah. It was to be taken literally in every detail. They rejected the so-called oral tradition, the mass of interpretative material which grew up around the Law, representing the efforts of the Pharisees to adapt an unchanging legal code to a changing world. Not that the Pharisees were innovators. Such a suggestion would have scandalized them. They believed in the entire perfection of the Torah no less than the Sadducees, but they felt keenly the necessity of interpretation, of application to a mode of living very different from that known by Israel when the Law was first handed down from on high.

Their motives were beyond reproach, and their influence over the common people was considerable. When
the Temple was destroyed by the Romans under Titus
in A.D. 70, the Sadducees disappeared into the ruins,
never to rise again. The Pharisees, on the other hand,
survived as the real religious leaders of the Jews. They
were the rabbis, the teachers, and they have continued
to instruct and inspire through the subsequent centuries.
The New Testament does them severe injustice, reflecting as it does the conflicts between the new community
of Christians and the enduring Jewish community during
the first century A.D. Doubtless some of them were hypocrites, guilty of casuistry and hairsplitting, but what
religious body has ever been free from such? For the
most part, they were men of deep piety and devoted
scholarship, walking before the world in unblemished
righteousness. Many of Jesus' sayings find parallels in
rabbinical teachings which date from the same period,
including exhortations to obedience out of disinterested
love for God without any other concern, either hope of
reward or fear of punishment. Jesus was clearly not of
their number, for he taught "as one who had authority,
and not as the scribes" (Mark 1:22); that is to say, he
made no reference to the opinion of the distinguished
scholars past and present as to the meaning of the text.
He had not received rabbinical training and thus lacked
his union card, or its academic equivalent, the Ph.D.
Yet Jesus was not opposed to the Law as the medium
through which God's will was clearly revealed. "I have

come," he said, "not to destroy the Law but to fulfill it," i.e., to fill it fuller (Matthew 5:17). Even more emphatic is the ensuing statement: "Till heaven and earth pass away, not an iota, not a dot, will pass away from the Law until all is accomplished. Whoever then relaxes one of these commandments and teaches men so, shall be called least in the kingdom of heaven; but he who does them and teaches them shall be called great in the kingdom of heaven" (Matthew 5:18–19).

What, then, was Jesus' quarrel with the Pharisees, aside perhaps from a kind of professional rivalry? He was not attacking the Law as such any more than the prophets of old had attacked the cult as such. They protested against the assumption on the part of king, priest, and people that the cult represented the heart of man's religious duty to God. So Jesus spoke out against the conception that the Law and its careful observance were the core of the relationship between God and man. The basic problem with any religious relationship conceived in legal terms is that it gives rise to what Bultmann has called "formal obedience." I follow a given course of action because the Law says to me, "Thou shalt," or I eschew another pattern of behavior because the Law enjoins me, "Thou shalt not." If the Law did not forbid me, I would do it; if the Law did not command me, I should not do it; if the Law demanded something else, I would do that. The understanding of man's obligation to God is statutory, and apart from specific commands and prohibitions, man is left free. Such a

view had as a further consequence the conception of
works of supererogation, so that it is possible for one
to go beyond what the Law requires, storing up merit
or atoning for past sins by extra fasts, alms for the poor
greater than those required, deeds of mercy in excess
of duty. That is precisely the rub: man's relation to God
is one of duty, of command and obedience. He does not
affirm the content of the Law with his inner being; he
acts so because he must. This is what Tillich calls
heteronomy—hetero, strange; *nomos,* law—the imposi-
tion of a strange law upon me from outside myself. My
actions are determined but my heart and will remain
free, free to resent and to rebel, to wish that I might do
otherwise than I must. I refrain from adultery since the
Law forbids it, but inwardly I am a mass of lust, men-
tally undressing and seducing every attractive woman
I see. I do not kill my neighbor because I fear the consequences, but I hate him bitterly and passionately wish
him dead (cf. Matthew 5:21–28). Merely formal obedience characterizes the attitude of the servant Jesus spoke
of in John 15:15. The Greek word here usually rendered
into English as "servant" is *doulos,* which means literally
slave. "No longer," said Jesus to the disciples, "do I call
you slaves, for the slave does not know what his master is
doing." He obeys, but he does not know. The obedience
of the scribes and Pharisees, at least as the New Testament portrays them, whatever may be true of them in
fact, came perilously close to this kind of obedience.

Against this Jesus set what Bultmann calls "radical

obedience," which is characteristic of the friend rather than the slave. In radical obedience, what is affirmed is not duty but love, not grudging consent but joyful agreement. I understand not only what it is that God requires of me but also why it is that he requires it, and I respond willingly from the depths of my being. This is Tillich's *theonomy,* or law of God, which confronts me not as master to slave but which I find within myself where dwells the image of God. There is no part of me left free from the divine demand, no area where I can go beyond the claim which God lays upon me and do more. To him I owe everything, a debt which I render joyfully in love rather than grudgingly in duty. God confronts me not as a master, demanding that which I do not wish to give but feel I must. He confronts me as a friend, as One closer to me than my own breath, as him in whom I live and move and have my being. To him I say in love, "Not my will but thine be done." This is the first consequence of radical obedience: the transformation of man's inner attitude. This is what it means to fill the Law fuller, to have a righteousness which exceeds that of the Pharisees.

The second consequence is set forth in the parable of the Last Judgment in Matthew 25. The Son of Man who has come in his glory with the angels divides the sheep from the goats, the righteous who are destined to enter eternal blessedness from the wicked who are doomed to damnation. And the basis for the division is neither the extent of theological orthodoxy nor the de-

gree to which the Torah has been scrupulously observed. The decisive word is the fateful "inasmuch."
"Inasmuch as you have (or have not) done it to one of
the least of these." That is to say, the sensitivity to human need and the response to it make all the difference
between life and death. It should be pointed out, in
this connection, that these are precisely the virtues of
Judaism, which underlines the unfairness of the New
Testament picture of the Pharisees.

If one asks the question "Where do I find God?" the
answer apparently is, "In your neighbor in need." And
what human being is without needs of some kind? This
is the point of the parable of the Good Samaritan, which
follows immediately after the definition of the twofold
commandment of love whose observance leads to the inheritance of eternal life. Count Tolstoi has a short story
about an old Russian cobbler named Martin, who
dreamt one night that Christ would visit his shop next
day. So vivid was the dream that the shoemaker scoured
his shop till it shone with cleanliness and then set feverishly to work so that his Lord might not find him idle.
The day dragged by and no one came. No one except an
old man whom Martin befriended and fed and provided
with a warm overcoat; no one except a poor young
mother and her baby to whom the cobbler gave food
and clothing; no one except an apple woman and a street
urchin between whom Martin made peace and pre-
vented violence and an arrest. But Christ did not come.
That night as the old shoemaker sat down to read his

Bible, disappointment filled his heart as he thought to himself that dreams are after all only dreams. A voice called his name and turning he saw a strange aura of light in the corner behind the stove. Out into the light in turn stepped the old man, the mother and child, the apple woman and the urchin. Each smiled and asked, "Martin, didst thou not know me?" and vanished. Martin turned back to his Bible where his eye fell upon the verse, "Inasmuch as ye have done it unto one of the least of these my brethren, ye have done it unto me." Every man is a brother of Christ. Every man *is* Christ.

Radical obedience, as Jesus stated it, means that there is no obedience to God which does not have to prove itself in the concrete encounter with one's neighbor. This is not a careful and grudging calculation of what the Law requires of me in service to others; it is an outgoing concern, a warm affection, a sincere empathy, and a desire to serve. And there are no boundaries whatever to such a neighborly love. As God cares for all, sending rain and sunshine on good and evil, just and unjust alike, so my love is to go out to all who are in need. "How many times," asked the disciples, "are we to forgive those who wrong us? Seven times, as the tradition has it?" "No," replied Jesus, "Forgive seventy times seven," and he clearly did not mean exactly four hundred and ninety, after which revenge is sweet. As God's forbearance and understanding and acceptance are without limit, so is man's love to be for his neighbor. Even our enemies are to be loved, forgiven, and prayed for. This

demand for love goes far beyond any and every legal
demand. It is not spelled out in detail offering a program
for action, a blueprint for Utopia. Rather, each individual is placed directly before God in such a way that he
has no anxieties about his rights and privileges or about
his future. "Sufficient unto each day is the evil thereof,
so take no thought for the morrow, for the morrow will
take care of itself." Does a man take from you your
coat? Then give him your cloak also. Are you compelled
to walk with a stranger one mile? Then go with him one
more. Are you struck on the face? Offer the other cheek
for another blow. Jesus did not offer this as a prudential
plan of action guaranteeing that such a practice would
shame the aggressor, providing you with the victory. His
own course of nonresistance did not deliver him from his
scourging and crucifixion. But love, as Paul put it, simply
does not seek its own. It is able to surrender its own
rights, to waive all of its claims in its single-minded desire to serve. The psychotherapist who is secure is able
and willing to absorb considerable hostility from his
patients because he is oriented toward their needs.

This is no more, however, a universal prescription
than any of Jesus' teachings. He was not suggesting that
all men should practice nonresistance under all circumstances any more than he was demanding that all should
sell everything they have and give it to the poor, or
that all should forsake their family responsibilities.
There may arise occasions when love for another demands that he be resisted and even hurt. Biblical love

is never mawkishly sentimental. The point is that I resist not to protect my own rights but for the sake of the other, to help him to see the self-destructiveness of his aggression. Such a radical obedience and such a love are utterly incalculable and unpredictable. They cannot be plotted on any scale, reduced to any ethical system, or expressed in any legal code. What is decisive here is the inner attitude. I can sell all that I have and give it to the poor; I can even offer my body to be burned, but if I do it without love, it profits me nothing. Thus, radical obedience transcends the Law and directs me into each encounter with my neighbor. And each encounter confronts me with a question: how shall I respond? Do I serve his need because the Law demands it of me or because I seek the applause of spectators? If so, then I have my reward. Or, do I serve him because I want to do so, because I want to share with him the love which God has given me? If so, then the Law has been filled fuller and the righteousness of the scribes and Pharisees has been exceeded.

Agape, then, is the divine love at work on the horizontal level, operating between human beings. It is radical obedience to God manifested in every encounter between man and man. Precisely the same principle we have seen in the teaching of Jesus in the Synoptic Gospels is to be found enunciated in the Pauline Epistles and in the Fourth Gospel. Paul saw the new life in Christ as a radical break with the old dispensation of formal obedience to the Law, replaced by a radical obedience, which is love. "He who loves his neighbor has fulfilled the Law" (Romans 13:8). According to the Apostle to the Gentiles, the Christian who lives in love has been set free from the Law, so that legal commands and prohibitions have no relevance any longer. "The commandments, 'You shall not commit adultery, You shall not kill, You shall not steal, You shall not covet,' and any other commandment, are summed up in this sentence, 'You shall love your neighbor as yourself.' Love does no wrong to a neighbor; therefore love is the fulfilling of the Law" (Romans 13:9–10). Paul's position was later to be summarized by Augustine and Luther in the famous dictum "Love God and do as you please." *Agape* is the great emancipator, so that Paul could say triumphantly, "All things are lawful for me" (1 Corinthians 6:12). Yet he was not quite a thoroughgoing antinomian, for there are two limiting principles to this dictum. "All things are lawful for me, but not all things are helpful. All things are lawful for me, but I will not be enslaved by anything" (1 Corinthians 6:12).

Here Paul recognized that the man who has been set free by the love of God, set free from bondage to the things of the world (*kosmos*), stands always in danger of falling back into slavery, back into the love of the wrong things. He must thus be on his guard against those idols which heretofore exercised dominion over his will. For the Jew, the Torah itself was dangerous. He might again regard his righteousness, his obedience to the Law as a "work," an accomplishment to boast about, a claim upon God. For the drunkard, alcohol is not "helpful," for he may lose his newly won freedom and sink again into slavery to his habit. Alcoholics Anonymous wisely counsels its members against that first drink. So Paul cautioned his converts against the dearest idols they had known. Not that anything in the world is in itself unclean or unwholesome. All things are created by God and are therefore good. But insofar as anything in the world has been or may become an idol for me, I must approach it with some respect for its power. This is the significance of the declaration, "I will not be enslaved by anything." Man is not, then, set free from obligation in such a way that his capricious and subjective tastes become sovereign. Under such circumstances, those tastes would constantly tend to replace the enslaving shackles stricken off by the love of God. The Christian is free only insofar as he is able to regard the world without care, with indifference; but this is possible only in the context of his being a slave of God, a slave of Christ. "For you are not your own." You have been bought with a price, ransomed from your bondage by the love of God working through the cross. Freedom from the Law is one side of a coin; the other side is bondage to God, which drives one into responsible encounter with the neighbor. So Luther said, "The Christian man is the free lord of all and the servant of all."

This leads to the second principle of limitation on Christian liberty, as Paul interpreted it. "All things are lawful for me, but not all things build up" (1 Corinthians

10:23), that is to say, not all things contribute to fellowship, to community. This statement occurs in the context of the problem in the Corinthian church over the
eating of meat sacrificed to idols. The question was
whether Christians could eat such tainted food. Some
insisted that the fact that the meat had been offered to
pagan gods was a matter of indifference. Such a rite
could not hurt the food in any way. Christians know that
these "gods" are nonexistent, so what harm can possibly
be done? Others in Corinth, however, maintained that
this was to be an accessory to idolatry, that Christians
should give these heathen temples and all their accouterments the widest possible berth. Have nothing whatever
to do with them.

Paul agreed with the former party. There is nothing
harmful about the meat at all. The Christian is free from
such petty and superstitious concerns. But he must recognize that his freedom may serve as a stumbling block
(literally *skandalon,* or scandal) to others weaker in the
faith than himself. Therefore, for the sake of the weaker
brother he renounces his freedom. He is so entirely free
that he can afford to give up his freedom and allow his
actions to be directed by his concern, his love for
others. His conscience is not "other-directed." So far as
his own attitude is concerned, he remains free to regard such matters as ultimately indifferent and unimportant. His conscience is determined only by God. He
seeks by "proving all things," which means literally

"testing" all things, to find what is the good and acceptable will of God for himself in the concrete situation.

But he is under no compulsion to insist rigidly upon
the exercise of his freedom. He knows that not all things
build up and therefore sacrifices his freedom for the
sake of others. "Let no one seek his own good, but the
good of his neighbor" (1 Corinthians 10:24). This is what
it means to be servants one of another, manifesting the
new-found freedom in Christ precisely by renouncing
that freedom to serve one's neighbor. Such a renunciation is the highest liberty of all, akin to that of Christ
himself. Love fulfills the Law by building up fellowship,
by creating community. But such a fulfillment of the
Law through love is not, for Paul, a human accomplishment about which a man may boast. *Agape* is always the
gift of God through Christ, always possible only to those
who have become new creatures in the church.

The Fourth Gospel and the Johannine Epistles manifest this same understanding. The priority of *agape*
as a divine phenomenon is insisted upon again and
again. "See what love the Father has given us" (1 John
3:1). "By this we know love, that he laid down his life
for us" (1 John 3:16). "Beloved, let us love one another;
for love is of God, and he who loves is born of God
and knows God. He who does not love does not know
God; for God is love. In this the love of God was made
manifest among us, that God sent his only Son into the
world, so that we might live through him. In this is love,
not that we loved God but that he loved us and sent

his Son to be the expiation of our sins. Beloved, if God
so loved us, we also ought to love one another" (1 John
4:7–11). The organic and inextricable relationship between the divine *agape* which enters the believer's heart
and the *agape* which he is to show forth to his neighbor
is unmistakably clear in these verses. And the freedom
bestowed by *agape* shines through the marvelous words:
"There is no fear in love, but perfect love casts out fear."

This is not, however, a mystical retreat from the world
into the ephemeral realm of the divine. The love of the
Christian for God *must* translate itself into concrete service to the neighbor. "For this is the love of God, that
we keep his commandments" (1 John 5:3). Reference
has already been made to the closing chapter of the
Fourth Gospel where the risen Christ three times asks
Peter (the three questions strikingly parallel to the three
denials of the big fisherman), "Simon Peter, do you
love me?" And three times the conclusion follows inescapably on Peter's passionate affirmation, "Then feed
my sheep."

The Epistle of James places greater emphasis on the
duty of the Christian to serve his neighbor than on the
source of all Christian love in God's act in Christ, but
the point is underlined that no Christian can claim to
love God while he is indifferent to human need. According to James, the "royal law" of Scripture is, "You
shall love your neighbor as yourself" (James 2:8). The
bodily needs of others must be met (2:14–16); gossip
and slander are to be avoided (chap. 3); no partiality is

to be shown to the noble and rich at the expense of the poor and lowly (2:1–7).

At this point, the New Testament forms a unity, whatever the varieties and diversities of outlook and interpretation. Human love for God must manifest itself in love for neighbor. And love is no mercurial sentiment, coming and going unpredictably. It "never ends" (1 Corinthians 13:8). Prophecy will pass away, tongues will cease, and knowledge will prove ephemeral, for all these things are finite and mortal. But love is of God and therefore is greater than either faith or hope. It does not insist on its own way; it is patient and generous, bearing all things and enduring all things. It is no mere "feeling" but an orientation of the entire personality, a steady inclination of the will. It seeks the good of others; it serves and gives and works. It is not concerned about itself. It take its cue from Christ who, "though he was in the form of God, did not count equality with God a thing to be grasped, but emptied himself, taking the form of a servant, being born in the likeness of men. And being found in human form he humbled himself and became obedient unto death, even death on a cross" (Philippians 2:6–8). On this understanding of love, all the New Testament writers were agreed.

One aspect of human love which has been much discussed in recent years, both in Christian and psychological circles, is self-love. The impression is all too frequently created in church and Sunday school that Christian faith demands a kind of self-hatred, a flagella-

tion of all pride and sentiments of self-worth. Against
this view, the psychotherapists have taken up vigorous
cudgels, insisting that the attitudes toward self and the
attitudes toward others are two sides of one coin, the
one organically related to the other, and that love of
others is possible only on the basis of love of self. Insofar
as a man rejects, mistrusts, and loathes himself, he will
reject, mistrust, and loathe all those around him. The
cultivation of self-abnegating sentiments is from this
point of view a highly dangerous enterprise. To this
contention the theologians have responded with varying
replies. Some have disagreed strongly, pointing to the
long tradition within the church which pillories pride as
the chief of sins and accusing the depth psychology of
being anti-Christian. Others have proved more tractable, underlining the last two words in the command,
"You shall love your neighbor *as yourself,*" maintaining
that this is what Jesus meant from the beginning.

Two comments seem appropriate at this point. The
first is that "discourses on humility," as Pascal observed,
"are a source of pride to the proud." Or, as one poet has
put it,

> *Once in a saintly passion*
> *I cried in deepest grief,*
> *"O Lord, my soul is black with guile,*
> *Of sinners I am chief!"*
> *Then stooped my guardian angel*
> *And whispered from behind,*
> *"That's vanity, my little man,*
> *You're nothing of the kind!"*

An undue concentration on one's sins and shortcomings, as wise confessors have known for centuries, actually represents a subtle form of conceit. One priest, so the story has it, was forced to admonish his penitent that he was bragging rather than confessing. The second comment is that Erich Fromm appears to be profoundly right in his contention that selfishness is the result not of too much self-love but too little. The confusion would seem to be largely a semantic one, arising from the polemical character of the phrase "self-love." Paul Tillich has cleared the atmosphere considerably with his suggestion that various levels of meaning lurk within those two words, and that it is essential to indicate which level is operating in any discussion of the subject:

> The lack of conceptual clarity in the concept of self-love is manifest in the fact that the term is used in three different and partly contradictory senses. It is used in the sense of natural self-affirmation (e.g., loving one's neighbor as oneself). It is used in the sense of selfishness (e.g., the desire to draw all things into oneself). It is used in the sense of self-acceptance (e.g., the affirmation of oneself in the way in which one is affirmed by God). It would be an important step towards semantic clarification if the term 'self-love' were completely removed and replaced by self-affirmation, selfishness, and self-acceptance according to the context.[1]

---

[1] Paul Tillich, *Love, Power, and Justice* (New York: Oxford University Press, 1954), p. 34.

In these terms, self-affirmation and self-acceptance
clearly lie within the sphere of human love as the New
Testament understands it. Selfishness is equally clearly
excluded, though there is still some doubt as to whether
selfishness is simply the quintessence of self-love or due
to the lack of it.

LOVE IN THE FAMILY

Turning from the general area of human love for God
and neighbor to the more specific relationships as they
are understood in the New Testament, let us look at the
understanding of the family. The first thing to note is
the fact that the New Testament appears to call the loyalties and affections of the family into radical question.
Jesus announced that he had come "to set a man against
his father, and a daughter against her mother, and a
daughter-in-law against her mother-in-law; and a man's
foes will be those of his own household" (Matthew
10:35–36). The most extreme statement of the rejection
of family ties appears in Luke 14:26: "If any one comes
to me and does not hate his own father and mother and
wife and children and brothers and sisters, yes, and even
his own life, he cannot be my disciple." These are
strange words in the mouth of a man who laid such
stress upon the law of love. Quite clearly, what Jesus
meant here is better stated in Matthew 10:37–38: "He
who loves father or mother more than me is not worthy
of me; and he who loves son or daughter more than me

is not worthy of me; and he who does not take his cross and follow me is not worthy of me." The decisive phrase here is "*more than me.*" Jesus was simply saying that no price is too great to pay to enter the kingdom, and anything and everything which stands in the way of that compelling goal must be ruthlessly sacrificed. He himself had experienced the surprise, the shock, and the dismay of his own family when he began his ministry. He himself knew what appeals would come from parents and relations to forsake unswerving and single-minded pursuit of the kingdom. He knew the loyalties which would be invoked, the pleas that would be made. He spoke from experience when he said, "A man's foes will be those of his own household"; and again, "A prophet is not without honor except in his own country and in his own house" (Matthew 13:57). When he "went home" after the inauguration of his mission and the calling of the disciples, his friends "went out to seize him, for they said, 'He is beside himself'" (Mark 3:21).

The reaction of Jesus' family and friends is not difficult to understand. Let any reader put himself in the place of a member of the "holy family." A son and brother has grown up a normal, obedient, well-behaving young man, doing his daily work in the carpenter shop, the business which put bread on the table and clothes on the backs of the household. And then suddenly, without warning, he turns his back upon all of this and begins to travel about the countryside preaching, "Repent! The kingdom of God is at hand!" What if your son be-

haved in such a fashion? What parent would not, from
the purest of motives, seek to bring the poor, demented
soul back home and get him as quickly as possible into
the hands of a competent psychiatrist? "Even his
brothers," says the Gospel record, "did not believe in
him" (John 7:5). Even! We might say *especially*. After
all, they had grown up with him, played with him,
doubtless fought with him. Now who did he think he
was, putting on such airs? There was talk going around
that he regarded himself as the Messiah!

Jesus knew foes in his own household, and he knew
that anyone who took the kingdom seriously would encounter similar opposition. If such a man found his
family ties stronger than his longing for the kingdom,
he would miss his opportunity to gain eternal life. In this
sense, he would be no different from the rich man
whose love of his wealth blocked the door to salvation, or the Pharisee whose belief in his own righteousness paralyzed his capacity to repent. What it is essential to understand here is the fact that Jesus was not
condemning the family or wealth or religiosity in and
of themselves. They are aspects of God's creation and
therefore good. They are called into question only when
they become repositories for man's ultimate concern,
when they assume the role of idols. The world and all
its wonders were affirmed by Jesus as the gifts of God.
They are denied only when they are worshiped as deities.
Thus, although it is perfectly clear that the family and
its bonds of affection are questioned in the New Testa-

ment, it is equally clear that the family is not unique in this respect. For all human institutions, all worldly constructions, are likewise questioned. Nothing must be permitted to stand in the way of a man's saying to God, "Thy will be done on earth as it is in heaven." There can be no exceptions, no reservations, no ifs, no conditions. Not every man will be called upon to forsake his family any more than every man is expected to sell all that he has and give it to the poor. Only those whose misdirected devotion to these things makes them build their houses upon sand are warned to move out to safer ground, to the heights where stand the rocks. The family is not ultimate; it is, like everything else in life, including "religion," subordinate to the living God.

Jesus was not, however, a misogynist nor an ascetic. He moved with gaiety and approval among the families of his friends. There may indeed be neither marriage nor giving in marriage when the kingdom has fully arrived and the narrower loyalties of human life are transcended in a realm where all of existence is love, but the beginnings of the kingdom in Jesus' lifetime did not demand the abolition of all natural families. He healed Peter's mother-in-law and counted several of the disciples' mothers as members of his company. He gladly gathered little children to him, rebuking the efforts of the disciples to keep them away, and restored sick youngsters to health and happiness at the request of their worried parents. He "adorned and sanctified" a wedding at Cana with his presence and first miracle. He rebuked the Pharisees for setting aside clear financial obligations to parents by rigid interpretation of oaths vowing gifts to the Temple. He clearly regarded marriage as a part of the divine plan, and intended to last for life. The parables are full of evidences of his keen observation of Palestinian family life and of his affirmative attitude toward it. The ties of human affection are not sundered for those who place the kingdom and its righteousness first in their hierarchy of values. On the contrary, all these things (i.e., love, marriage, family, filial devotion) are added to them.

The Epistles of the New Testament reveal a similar pattern. Paul, in the famous 7th chapter of First Corinthians, joined Jesus in calling marital existence into radical question, a questioning very uncommon in traditional Judaism, expressing the wish that all men were as he (that is, single) and counseling those who had wives to live as though they had none. But, as in the Gospels, the motivation for such a challenge to marriage and family life was eschatological rather than dualistic. In the very same chapter Paul warned married couples not to abstain from sexual relations for too long a period lest their privation prove an occasion for temptation. He ruled that marriage to an unbeliever was no grounds for divorce, that a Christian should continue to live with a pagan spouse willing to maintain the relationship, since the unbeliever was "consecrated" through the faith of the church member. Paul nowhere suggested to the numerous families in the churches he had founded that they should dissolve themselves, that their continuance was in conflict with the gospel. On the contrary, the assumption was that family life should continue within the church and be consecrated and sanctified by the new faith of the family.

The love for husband, wife, parent, children, was not driven out but deepened by the love of God. Marriages were to be made "in the Lord" (1 Corinthians 7:39), which was interpreted specifically to mean that they were to last for life. Children born into Christian homes, even if only one of the parents was in the church, were "holy." As Hosea in the Old Testament saw his own marriage to Gomer as an allegory and a symbol of the relationship between God and Israel, so the New Testament sees the marriage bond as pointing to the relationship between Christ and his Church. "Husbands, love your wives, as Christ loved the church and gave himself up for her" (Ephesians 5:25). "Husbands should love their wives as their own bodies. He who loves his wife loves himself. For no man ever hates his own flesh, but nourishes and cherishes it, as Christ does the church, because we are members of his body. 'For this reason a man shall leave his father and mother and be joined to his wife, and the two shall become one.' This is a great mystery, and I take it to mean Christ and the church; however, let each one of you love his wife as himself, and let the wife see that she respects her husband" (Ephesians 5:28–33). The love that Christians within a family bear for one another belongs not only to the order of creation but has been sanctified and perfected by the new order of salvation.

Fathers are to remember that "every family in heaven and on earth is named" (Ephesians 3:15) from him who is the Father of all, and to act accordingly. A father must be the head of the household, giving to it its essence and substance, acting with firmness and authority, as is fitting for the head. But he must at the same time show love and consideration, loving his wife as himself and refraining from provoking his children to anger, while bringing them up "in the discipline and instruction of the Lord" (Ephesians 6:4). If there are slaves in the household, they are to be treated with kindness. The master of the house must remember "that he who is both their Master and yours is in heaven, and that there is no partiality with him" (Ephesians 6:9). Wives are to be subject to their husbands, as is fitting in the Lord (Colossians 3:18 and 1 Peter 3:1–6), and to join with them in planning for the future of their children (2 Corinthians 12:14). The mothers are to "bear children, rule their households, and give the enemy no occasion to revile us" (1 Timothy 5:14). Their good deeds are to include bringing up children, showing hospitality, washing the feet of saints, relieving the afflicted, and a devotion to doing good in every way (1 Timothy 5:10).

But the chief role of the woman in the household is to show forth the glory of the new life in Christ in her relationship to her husband. She recognizes that "man was not made from woman, but woman from man.

Neither was man created for woman, but woman for man" (1 Corinthians 11:8–9). She willingly accepts the fact that man is the head of the woman and submits to her husband's authority not grudgingly and in fear but willingly, freely, and in joy. This, after all, is precisely what the Christian life is. Christians are to be servants not only of one another but of all men. The children of the world, the Gentiles, seek power and authority; they love to lord it over others, to seek the chief seats at a feast, and to receive the bows and respectful salutes of men. So does many a husband act with his wife. Such behavior makes it clear that these poor unfortunates have not learned the lesson that Christ taught in his person no less than in his words: "Let him who would be greatest among you be the *servant* of all." He himself washed the disciples' feet. He himself gave up his glory in the heavens to take upon himself the form of a slave, to suffer and die for the sins of men. So all Christians who understand the full implications of their new faith are set free from being "men-pleasers," striving after the things of the world, including power and authority over others. They are no longer worried about what the world will think of them or do to them. Everything they do is "to the Lord," and their primary concern is to love and to serve. Not that they are compelled to act so. They do so willingly, freely, gladly. They show how free they are by being able to renounce their freedom, to throw it away. They gain their lives by losing them. This is the real significance of the feeding of the five thousand

—not a miraculous wonder in which Jesus amazed the
people by his strange powers. What is really being said
here is that if you begin to give away what you have, no
matter how small and insignificant, to share it with
others, you will find that the supply is inexhaustible and
you will gather up at the end more than you had in the
beginning. This principle of loving service is pre-eminently manifested in the home in the person of the wife
and mother who freely surrenders her freedom out of
love. "So it belongs to woman, in her capacity as a
woman, to bear witness more particularly to what is
the stuff of the whole Christian ethic."[2]

2 H. Mehl-Koehnlein, in *A Companion to the Bible*, J. J. von Allmen,
ed. (New York: Oxford University Press, 1958), p. 459.

5

SEX ATTITUDES
AND PRACTICES:
ISRAEL
AGAINST HER
NEIGHBORS

ॐ

ONE OF THE CHIEF OBJECTIONS to the so-called higher criticism of the Bible has been the tendency of some scholars to lay such emphasis upon the indebtedness of Israel to her neighbors in the Fertile Crescent that they have obscured the uniqueness of the Old Testament. There can be no doubt that the horizontal lines of influence are present. A comparison of the Gilgamesh Epic,

161

an early Babylonian flood story, with the narrative of
Noah in Genesis reveals striking similarities. There are
also parallels of the creation account, of the legend of
the Tower of Babel, and of numerous strands of biblical
legislation in the religious literature of Mesopotamia and
Canaan. Evidence also exists to suggest that Yahweh was
worshiped by the Kenites before he was known to Israel, that Moses found this deity in the cult of his wife's
family. Indeed, his father-in-law, Jethro, seems to have
been a priest of Yahweh. Results such as these of the research of the higher critics have proved illuminating and
useful, but they have been so emphasized that the vertical lines have faded into obscurity. Old Testament
scholarship of the last three decades, while gratefully
acknowledging the contributions of the earlier compara-
tive studies, has increasingly stressed the differences between Israel and her neighbors rather than the similarities. It is doubtless true that the Hebrews made use of
materials that came to their hands from the surrounding
peoples, but these materials were all transformed and
made into vehicles for passionate Yahwism. That there
should be similarities, we might expect. This is no occasion for surprise. All cultures borrow and adapt from
their predecessors and contemporaries. What is significant is the difference, the radical changes which were
made in the appropriated legends, laws, and lore.

Nowhere is this contrast more dramatically illustrated
than in the realm of sex attitudes and practices. Israel
was surrounded by peoples whose religions were es-

sentially nature cults, bound to and celebrating the cyclical rhythms of the seasons. They were overwhelmed by the consciousness of man's dependence upon nature and of the curious paradox of nature manifesting both order and chaos, both dependability and capriciousness. On the one hand, one could predict the regular appearance of summer and winter, autumn and spring, the movements of the various planets and the stars. The Egyptians and Babylonians both had an elaborate and accurate astronomy. On the other hand, the rivers could rise in flood, plagues and droughts could appear, disease could strike. All of these wrought havoc with "the best laid plans of mice and men," bringing suffering and death in their wake. In the primitive stages of mankind, religions tend to stress the disorder, the unpredictability, the capriciousness of natural forces. Man as a hunter or as a keeper of flocks had little occasion or opportunity to study the seasons, to learn of the recurring cycles of the world. The forces to which he had to adapt seemed infinite in number and incalculable in action. He followed where game was to be found, where fodder for his flocks was plentiful, and both lay to a large extent beyond his control. He was utterly dependent upon forces outside himself, however skillful a hunter or careful a shepherd he might have been.

But as man became a farmer, as he began to till the soil and plant the seed, he became aware of a certain order, a degree of dependability, to his environment. The strange, impersonal spirits of forest and desert became

anthropomorphized. They took on a personal quality,
became like man, and proved tractable to propitiation
and influence. The polytheistic religions which grew up
in the Fertile Crescent represented a considerable advance over the primitive animism of earlier times. For
they recognized still that the forces in nature to which
man must adapt are many, but they were possessed of
a certain order, a coherence and an intelligibility which
they lacked before. As man moved into a pluralistic society, with a division of labor—some to rule, some to sacrifice, some to fight, some to plant and harvest, some
to buy and sell—so the pantheon of the gods was organized and regulated. The cosmos was a state and the
various deities were responsible for its numerous functions. Each god had his sphere of influence and power,
and he had also his goddess with a complementary task.
Together they begot children who assumed their proper
roles in the overarching scheme of things. The opposing
forces of nature—light and darkness, summer and winter, life and death—were engaged in constant conflict
with one another. Yet the struggle was so arranged that
each day, each season, each year, life could go on. A
great dragon sought daily or annually to swallow the
sun, plunging the world into darkness, but always the
sun emerged victorious from the battle, so that light
once more radiated from the heavens. The goddess of
fertility was carried off to dwell captive in the underworld, and winter held the earth in its deathlike grasp.
But the goddess escaped her abductor and spring came

again. The metaphors of these polytheistic cults were for the most part drawn from nature, for their awareness of deity was drawn from a numinous awe of the powers on which they depended. Their gods were symbolized as idols who combined in weird and grotesque ways the forces to be found in the natural order. Heads of beasts, actual or mythological, wings of birds, hair composed of serpents, claws, talons, teeth, abounded together with stars, moon, sun, wind, rain, trees, and flowers.

The gods, then, were rooted in nature and in some sense identical with it. Man's basic problem was to adjust himself to this cosmic rhythm, to integrate his own existence into the larger whole of which he was a part. His life was simply a reflection of the life of the gods. Babylonian religion saw man as created by these deities, who sought to escape the weary necessities of agriculture and made for themselves slaves to take such responsibilities off their shoulders. Man must obey the gods as a slave obeys his master. And he showed his obedience by fitting into the divinely established hierarchy upon earth. As there was a chief among the gods, so there was a king among men, and the latter had been established and appointed to his task by the former. The hierarchy of human political life, beginning with the elders in the local village and ascending to the king himself, was a symbol of the divine order, and he who rebelled against human political authority rebelled also against the will of the gods. Sin was therefore disobedi-

ence, willfulness, and it risked disruption of the cosmos.
Its punishment was not purely social but might be cosmic as well, bringing flood or famine, disease or disaster.
The king as the descendant of the gods (as in Egypt) or
as their vice-regent (as in Mesopotamia) was always
right, and failure to respect and obey him was to court
the displeasure of heaven. Polytheism of this sort was
always a religion of the *status quo,* and it never sired a
revolution in the social order on behalf of justice for
the downtrodden or oppressed elements in the population. When a nation or empire with such a cult perished,
the religion always perished with it, so inseparably were
the two related.[1]

EGYPT

Now all of this had profound implications for the religious life of these peoples and for the relationship between sex and religion. These were nature cults celebrating fertility, and the sexual element loomed large,
not only in the life of the gods, but in the sacred rituals
as well. In Egypt, the sky and the Nile were the greatest
of the gods. All things that are were born as the result
of the copulation of the sky god Sibu and the earth
goddess Nuit. The moon and stars were deities. Sahu
(Orion) ate gods regularly, and occasionally a monster

---

[1] I am indebted for the foregoing discussion to George Ernest
Wright's article, "The Faith of Israel," in Volume I of *The Interpreter's
Bible.*

deity would swallow the moon, but the insistent prayers of men and the wrath of the other gods forced a quick regurgitation. Thus the eclipse was ended. The greatest of the sky gods was the sun, Ra, or Re, and his function was the fertilization of the earth, the Great Mother. And not alone the source of life was an object of worship, but the various forms of life as well. Plants, animals, birds, reptiles, were all revered at one time or another in Egyptian history, most especially the goat and the bull as symbols of sexual power. Even after the gods became humanized, they retained their animal forms and counterparts, sometimes as companions, sometimes as symbols, and occasionally even as incarnations. Osiris, the great god of popular religion, was thought to dwell in the bull and the ram, and he was depicted with large sexual organs as signs of his tremendous power. Images of Osiris as a bull or with a triple phallus were carried in religious processions, and phallic symbols manipulated with strings were often borne by women. Many temple reliefs show gods portrayed with impressively large sex organs, erect, and the Egyptian *crux ansata,* the cross with a handle, was a symbol of sexual union and vigor.

Equally popular with the masses was the goddess Isis, the Great Mother, the loyal wife and sister of Osiris. As her husband symbolized the fertilizing Nile, she was the rich black earth, bringing forth from her womb the grain and vegetation which brought life to Egypt. In her lay the secret of the mysterious power of creativity from which sprang the earth and all living things. She was to Egypt what Kali was to India, Ishtar to Assyria, and Demeter to Greece—the feminine principle in fecundity, prior to and in some sense independent of masculinity. Isis, so the myth had it, discovered the arts of agriculture and revealed the secrets to Osiris. Woman enjoyed a special place in all fertility cults, and Egypt was no exception. Isis was symbolized as a jeweled Mother of God and worshiped with piety and affection. An especial festival of hers was celebrated in late December, at the time of the annual rebirth of the sun. Her divine child, Horus, was displayed being nursed by his holy mother in a stable. Woman thus became the Mother of God, as she was mother of everything else, the creative principle behind all things.

This belief had several consequences. In the first place, it gave rise to temple prostitution, though this seems to have been practiced on a small scale. At the time of the Roman occupation, the most beautiful daughter of the noble families of Thebes was consecrated to the god Amon, another name for the sun deity. When she grew too old to satisfy the god, she was released with a suitable dowry, usually married, and was held in highest esteem. In the second place, Egypt seems to have been something of a matriarchy. Woman had as high a place there as she has ever known before or since. Egyptian husbands were regarded by the Greeks as henpecked, and one satirist reported that the wedding ceremony required the husband to promise obedience to his wife. Women owned their property and bequeathed it as they chose. All estates were handed down through the female line. One historian reports that "even in late times, the husband made over all his property and future earnings to his wife in his marriage settlement."[2] This gave rise to a third consequence, the practice of incest. The Pharaoh regularly married his own sister, and the nobility frequently followed suit. In the royal family this practice was apparently motivated by the desire to preserve the purity of the royal blood, which was divine. In the wealthier classes, the motive was more mercenary. Sisters married brothers because the family inheritance passed from mother to daughter, and the desire was strong to keep the family's wealth in the family.

In later times, the society became more patriarchal, probably through contact with the Hyksos tribes, who dominated Egypt from around 1800 to 1600 B.C. During the reign of the Ptolemies, after the breakup of the Alexandrian Empire, divorce customs shifted markedly. Under the old dispensation, a man could divorce his wife on grounds of adultery. Any other cause required him to give her the largest part of the family property. Divorce was therefore rare, and marital fidelity the general rule. Further, the privilege of divorce was equally extended to both sexes. In the time of the Ptolemies, this became the exclusive possession of the husband. Even so, these new ways were limited to the nobility. The peasants

---

[2] Sir W. Flinders Petrie, *Egypt and Israel* (London: S.P.C.K., 1925), p. 23.

continued in the ancient customs of the land. Infanticide was rare at all times. The Greek historian Diodorus commented on the strange fact that every child born in Egypt was raised, and punishment for killing offspring was severe. The population steadily grew and many families found it difficult to keep track of their numerous children.

The Pharaoh was the chief priest of the national religion, regarded as descended from Amon-Ra, a god come to earth to rule over his people. He wore the headdress carrying the falcon, a symbol of Horus, and the serpent with its magical powers curling upward from his forehead. He led the great rituals and processions which united the nation in worship of the gods of Egypt. Rebellion was rare and dangerous, since it was not only unpatriotic but also sacrilegious. There was little connection, however, between religion and morality. The chief concern was the guarantee of immortality, at first reserved solely for the divine Pharaohs, but gradually extended to all the people. In some liturgical writings, passage to the other world required a declaration of innocence of major sins, such as murder, theft, injustice, oppression, blasphemy. But on the whole this inheritance of eternal life was secured not by morality but by charms and magical incantations. The greatest libertine in the kingdom could purchase amulets and spells which would cancel out all his sins and open the gates of the hereafter. The gods grew indifferent to the daily conduct of life and concentrated their concern upon the proper performance of the ceremonial rites.

In 1380 B.C. there came to the throne of Egypt a Pharaoh who sought to reform the religious life of the nation—Amenhotep IV, who took for himself the name of his god, Ikhnaton. The great temple of Amon at Karnak was crowded with concubines, supposedly for the exclusive use of the god himself but in reality at the disposal of the temple priests. The bloody sacrifices of rams and bulls, the sacred prostitution, the superstitious traffic in magical spells and amulets, revolted the sensitive young monarch. He proclaimed that all the many gods and their indecent rituals were gross idolatry and that in fact there was only one true god—Aton, the sun. He changed his name to read "Aton is satisfied" and sought to reform the religious beliefs and practices of his people. He forbade the worship of the old gods, defaced temples and tombs, and moved his capital to a new city which should stand as a monument to the one true God, who is the power in all nature, in sea and earth and sky, and in all forms of life. This god was not to be represented by images and he was a god of compassion and love, demanding like behavior from his worshipers. Ikhnaton thus set himself against the ancient folkways of his people and against a powerful and entrenched priesthood. His vacillation in foreign policy due to his lofty moral code resulted in the loss of much of the Egyptian Empire, whose provinces successfully declared their independence. This aroused the ire of the military and the court nobility, and Ikhnaton died a failure, with strong hostility felt toward his royal person throughout the land. His successor, Tutankhamen, restored conditions to the state they had been in before the reign of Ikhnaton and banned the mere mention of the name Aton. Various speculators have seen some influence of Ikhnaton upon Moses and it may be that they possess a measure of truth. But, as we shall see, the one God of Moses was vastly different from Aton, who was essentially a deity of nature, not of history.

BABYLON

In Babylon, the king was not a god or descended from a god, but rather simply the agent of the deity who commissioned him to rule. He could not assume the power of the throne until he had been duly crowned by the priests, who were the representatives of the divine pantheon. He "took the hands of Bel" and carried an image of Marduk in solemn procession, wearing the vestments of a priest. The power of the clergy was far greater than that of the monarch, and Babylon was consistently a theocracy. The gods of Babylon were considerable in number; sixty-five thousand of them were counted in a census taken in the ninth century B.C. Each local village and township had its own deity, its patron god or goddess, who were rather like the gods of Greece and Rome—human, warm, subject to foibles and failures. Their appetites were large—for food, for drink, and for sex. There were gods of the sky, of the earth, of the family, of the fields, of each individual. Gradually, these were organized into a pantheon with Marduk, initially a god of the sun, as the supreme deity, Bel-Marduk or Marduk *the* God. Side by side with this reigning male divinity sat Ishtar, the goddess of fertility and creativity. Under her jurisdiction were both love and war, both motherhood and prostitution, both masculinity and femininity. She was portrayed on occasion as bisexual, wearing a beard, and sometimes as a nude female with breasts invitingly offered for suck to her devotees. Known as the Holy Virgin or the Virgin Mother, she was careful to keep herself unwed but by no means unbedded! Her love affairs were numerous and colorful. The Gilgamesh Epic reports that she once wooed, seduced, and slew a lion.

One of the most popular of the Babylonian myths had Ishtar as the central character. Her lover-brother-son, Tammuz, was killed by a wild boar and his shade went the way of all the dead to the underworld ruled over by Ishtar's sister, Ereshkigal. Ishtar wept for her lost lover and journeyed to Aralu (the Babylonian name for the realm of the dead) to restore him to life. The myth recounts the meanderings of the goddess through the labyrinthine underworld, compelled to surrender her clothing as she went, since only the nude might enter Aralu. While Ishtar was below, the world forgot the ways of fertility and all life languished. "The bull did not mount the cow, the ass approached not the she-ass; to the maid in the street no man drew near; the man slept in his apartment, the maid slept by herself." Vegetation died, population shrank, and the world began to neglect the sacrifices to the gods. The deities grew alarmed and ordered Ereshkigal to release Ishtar, who demanded that Tammuz be allowed to accompany her. Her terms were met and she triumphantly returned to earth in a surrounding glory of reviving vegetation and fertility. Love had once more triumphed over death, as in Venus and Adonis, Demeter and Persephone, and many such legends of a dying and rising god. This event was annually celebrated in Babylon with a sacred festival, mourning first for the dead Tammuz and then rejoicing with wild orgies at his restoration to life.

The nature-cult character of Babylonian religion is still further evident in the elaborate mechanics of divination and demon exorcism. The observation of the movements of heavenly bodies gave rise to a highly developed astrology, and omens of various sorts were listed and their interpretations given on the tablets uncovered by archaeological excavations. The entrails of animals were carefully examined, with the liver playing an especially important role. All crucial decisions required a consultation of the signs of nature, which could be read only by the trained priest. The behavior of the rivers, the position of the stars, even the movements of a dog, were all portents of the future.

As in Egypt, the religion of Babylon had little connection with morality, at least among the upper classes. The great city became a byword in the ancient world for immorality and unbridled license. Herodotus reports one interesting custom in a passage worth quoting:

> Every native woman is required, once in her life, to sit in the temple of Venus, and have intercourse with some stranger. And many disdaining to mix with the rest, being proud on account of their wealth, come in covered carriages, and take up their station at the temple with a numerous train of servants attending them. But the far greater part do thus: many sit down in the temple of Venus, coming in, and others are going out. Passages marked out in a straight line lead in every direction through the women, along which strangers pass and make their choice. When a woman has once seated herself, she must not return home until some stranger has thrown a piece of silver into her lap, and lain with her outside the temple. He who throws the silver must say this: "I beseech the goddess Mylitta to favor thee"; for the Babylonians call Venus Mylitta. The silver may be ever so small, for she will not reject it, inasmuch as it is not lawful for her to do so, for such silver is accounted sacred. The woman follows the first man that throws, and refuses no one. But when she has had intercourse and has absolved herself from the obligation to the goddess, she returns home, and after that time however great a sum you may give her you will not gain possession of her. Those that are endowed with beauty and symmetry of shape are soon set free, but the deformed

are detained a long time, from inability to satisfy the law, for some work for a space of three or four years.[3]

Various theories have been advanced to explain this custom—suggestions that it represented a sacrifice of virginity to the goddess of fertility; that it was a preparation for marriage, sparing the bridegroom the necessity of breaking the hymen; that it was the vestigial remnant of an earlier sexual communism. No one really knows the true answer, though one thing is clear. These women were not prostitutes proper. There were, however, numbers of temple prostitutes dwelling within the sacred precincts, and many of them became very wealthy. This was a custom widespread in the Fertile Crescent among the nature cults. The worship of the principle of fertility logically included the sexual act, and sacred concubines, both male and female, were common. This practice by no means excluded secular prostitution, which also flourished in Babylon and in other similar cultures.

The sexual customs of Babylon were curiously wrought. A large amount of freedom in premarital relations was combined with a rather rigorously monogamous marriage with strictly enforced fidelity. Trial marriages between a couple were perfectly permissible, but the woman in such a casual union was required to wear a symbol of the fact that she was a kept concubine. Regular marriages were arranged by parents and characterized by the usual exchange of gifts. The dowry varied

---

[3] Herodotus, I, 199.

in size in accordance with the financial circumstances of the family, and the father of the bride was expected to reward the groom with a gift even larger than the bride's price. Sometimes there was an outright sale of daughters, with an auctioneer employed to cry their worth. The code of Hammurabi, the great Babylonian king and lawgiver, took especial notice of adultery, enjoining drowning for a guilty wife. A man could divorce his wife for other cause simply by returning her dowry to her, but the wife had no rights to divorce, under the code. Actual practice, however, permitted a woman wedded to a cruel husband to return to her parents, taking her portion with her. A woman left by her spouse for a prolonged period had the privilege of establishing a liaison with another man without terminating her first marriage.

In the last days of Babylon's glory, prior to her overthrow by the Persians in the sixth century B.C., her morals seem to have degenerated substantially, a degeneration that continued on into Roman times. Effeminacy among the men and looseness among the women were apparent on every side, and the city was filled with sybarites, pursuing sensual pleasure in a great variety of ways. Herodotus records the rouging and bejeweling practiced by men, and the prostituting of their daughters for money by the poor. The city became a byword for voluptuous delights, and no barrier seems to have been set up by their religion. Ishtar could scarcely disapprove. Imitation is the sincerest form of flattery!

ASSYRIA

Assyria presents a different picture, yet with the same underlying features of the nature cult. Located as it was in Mesopotamia, side by side with Babylon, it was influenced by the latter, sharing the worship of Ishtar under the name Astarte, and manifesting the same superstitious consultation of natural phenomena for signs and portents. Assyrian religious texts uncovered by archaeological excavations contain long lists of these signs and their meanings in terms of predictions, together with the proper formulae for warding off evil and protection against demons. Ashur, the supreme deity, was like Marduk and Amon-Ra, a sun god, who was extremely warlike and utterly without mercy to his enemies. The chief function of the religion was to encourage obedience to authority, more particularly to the authority of the king, who was less dependent upon the priests than his counterpart in Babylon, although he was not like the Egyptian Pharaoh, himself a god.

The Assyrians were pre-eminently a military people and as such had a strongly patriarchal viewpoint. The virtue of women was zealously guarded, and their freedom was strictly limited. State-supported prostitution flourished, under both sacred and secular auspices, and men were permitted as many concubines as they could afford. Wives could not go out in public without a veil, a forerunner of the later purdah found in the Middle

East, and the occupants of the king's harem were forbidden to go out at all. The state policy of encouraging a rising birth rate in order to produce soldiers for the fighting force made abortion or its attempt a crime punishable by impalement on a stake. The entire culture was characterized by a severe brutality and primitive cruelty which made them a terror to their foes. The monuments erected by the kings of Assyria celebrating their victories boasted of the terrible atrocities visited by them upon their defeated enemies. All of this Ashur not only countenanced but commanded.

THE CANAANITES

The closer neighbors of the Israelites, the Canaanites, worshiped a variety of deities, called in the Old Testament by the generic term *baal*, a basket into which all the pagan gods were dumped. The Baal against whom Elijah contended on Mount Carmel was in all likelihood Melkart, the god of Tyre, whence came Queen Jezebel, wife of Ahab. The deity worshiped by the Moabites was Chemosh, while the Ammorites bowed before Milkom, a proper name which came from the common noun *melek*, meaning king. This was probably the god worshiped in the form of a metal idol, heated to a blazing white, into whose lethal arms worshipers placed their first-born infants in order to secure further children. Dagon, god of the Philistines, bears a name derived from the Hebrew word *dagan*, meaning corn, pointing clearly to his close connection with vegetation and fertility. Tammuz, the Babylonian consort of Ishtar, seems to have penetrated to the Temple in Jerusalem, according to a reference in Ezekiel 8:14: "Then he brought me [in a vision] to the entrance of the north gate of the house of Yahweh; and behold, there sat women weeping for Tammuz. Then he said to me, 'Have you seen this, O son of man? You will see still greater abominations than these.'"

The local Baals included the god of Shechem, Baal Berith (Judges 8:33) and the god of Ekron, Baal Zebub, god of flies possessed of curative power. This latter may be related to the Beelzebub of the New Testament. The Canaanite pantheon also included goddesses, such as Asherah, consort of El and of Baal. She, too, was a nature deity, symbolizing sexuality and fertility. In some passages in the Old Testament there are references to an *asherah* as a wooden pillar, an object of cultic devotion. This is clearly a phallic symbol, occupying a place similar to that of the Hindu *lingam* in the temple of Shiva. Astarte or Ashtoreth in the Old Testament is plainly the Babylonian Ishtar, the goddess of war and of love, symbolized by the morning star, Venus. Many other female deities were merged with her, so that the Bible speaks of Astartes in the plural, referring to all goddesses. As the queen of heaven, she apparently developed a sizable following in Jerusalem during the career of Jeremiah (cf. Jeremiah 7:16–20 and 44:15–30). All of these gods and goddesses worshiped by Israel's neigh-

bors near and far were intimately and organically related to nature and the various forces and powers encountered there. For the most part, they appeared in
male/female pairs and were pictured in the myths and
legends as creating the world by copulation. They had
special responsibility for fecundity and fertility of all
sorts and conditions. Their worship apparently required
a kind of imitative magic in which male and female devotees yoked their bodies sexually and spilled their
seed upon the fields they desired to yield bounteous
crops. Orgies involving the use of intoxicants and in-
discriminate sexual activity played an important part
in these cults, and many Israelites gladly became apos-
tates to these weird and wondrous deities. Part of the
explanation for their seduction we have already mentioned. The inexperience of the nomadic Hebrews in the
tasks of agriculture in their new homeland made them
easy converts to the local Baals who promised good
harvests. The exotic character of the cult with its mystic
roots extending far back into antiquity, together with
the highly sensual pleasures afforded in the worship,
combined to make it an attractive type of religious experience. Any such temple in modern society would
encounter no difficulty in attracting large numbers of
devotees, though it is doubtful if it could qualify under
the rubric guaranteeing freedom of religion!

The Old Testament itself contains numerous passages
pointing to the participation of Israelites in these beliefs
and customs. In Judges 7:1 Gideon is called Jerubbaal,

explained in the text as meaning "contender with Baal"
but this is probably a pious explanation of later date.
The more likely meaning is "contender for Baal," a name
given him by his father at his birth, as Saul called one
of his sons Ishbaal, or "man of Baal." The festival of
Jephthah's daughter described in Judges 11:39–40 is
unquestionably an ancient pagan ritual given by this
tale a Hebrew cast. In Judges 21:19–23 we read of a
vintage festival at Shiloh with maidens dancing, doubtless inspired by the fermented juices of the grape. Jotham's fable of the trees in Judges 9:8–15 clearly has
roots in Canaanite nature cults and their mythologies.
Hosea refers to the gold and silver lavished upon the
Baals by those who believed that the grain, the wine,
and the oil of their new homeland came from the local
deities, instead of from Yahweh. *Hebrew Religion,* by
Oesterley and Robinson, devotes several chapters to a
description of the elements of paganism imbedded in the
Old Testament. These are the horizontal lines of influence from Israel's environment, and this is exactly the
sort of cultural osmosis that one would expect to find.

The defection to these pagan fertility cults on the
part of many of the Israelites immigrating into Canaan
aroused passionate protest from the religious leaders of
the nation. The judges, as we have already noted, interpreted the invasions of powerful desert tribes and their
oppression of the land as the punishment of Yahweh
upon his faithless people. But the protest of these charis-
matic leaders was sporadic and short-lived, silenced and

slumbering as soon as the emergency was at an end. Somewhat more enduring but apparently little more successful was the dramatic witness of two groups, the Nazirites and the Rechabites. Both Samson and Samuel were Nazirites, consecrated from birth to the service of Yahweh. This involved a double vow, the renunciation of wine and the rejection of the razor. The significance of this is in itself difficult to fathom without an understanding of the background. What this dual denial represented was a protest against the effete and sybaritic ways of the new life in Canaan in the name of the simple hardihood of Israel's former nomadic existence. The drunken revels at the shrines of the Baals were accompanied by purely secular imbibing for social purposes, leading to a blurring of the moral standards and the virtues of the desert shepherd. Hence, the Nazirite would not touch fermented beverages. He would remain sturdily loyal to the older ways of his people. Nor would he cut his hair or shave his beard as was the wont of the Canaanites in their concern for personal attractiveness and physical cultivation. The Nazirites and Rechabites sought to remind Israel of her heritage as a people of the desert, even as certain Roman moralists and historians of the early empire recalled to their readers the glories of the republic and the virtues of its citizen-farmer soldiers.

But the protest of these semi-ascetics (their self-denial did not, significantly, include sex) went for the most part unheeded. Amos records the fact that the Nazirites

aroused hostility in some circles, so much so that they
were forced to drink wine (Amos 2:12); but if they
represented an ineffective minority on one extreme,
the enthusiastic converts to the Baals and the rites
of their shrines were likewise a minority without a
sizable following in Israel. The majority of the Hebrews
apparently vacillated between these two powerful poles
of attraction, moving now in the direction of the native
cults, without altogether forsaking Yahweh, and then
toward the call to exclusive Yahwism, but without entirely forsaking the customs of the country. The strongest note of condemnation of these pagan fertility deities
was of course sounded by the prophets, and it is in
their messages that the contrast is most sharply drawn.
For Yahwism was not a cult of nature. It was a religion
of history. At the very beginning of Israel's self-consciousness as a people with a unique destiny and direction, Yahweh appeared to Abraham not as a god of
nature, manifesting himself either in the cyclical order
of the skies or the seasons or in wonders and signs apparent in a disruption of natural processes. He intervened and acted not in plants or planets, not in storms
or siroccos, not in beasts or birds, but in the sphere of
human experience, in history. He said to Abraham
simply, "Go from your country and your kindred and
your father's house to the land that I will show you. And
I will make of you a great nation, and I will bless you
and make your name great" (Genesis 12:1–2). Already
at the outset Yahweh announced where he would act—

among the nations, among "all the families of the earth." This is where his will and his work were to be seen—not in the heavens, not in the entrails of animals or the flight of birds, not in the cycle of seedtime and harvest, but in the affairs of men.

His most decisive and dramatic activity occurred, of course, at the Exodus. Here he entered the lists against the most powerful monarch of the ancient world and defeated him. One of the oldest verses in Scripture celebrates that triumph. "Sing to Yahweh gloriously. The horse and rider he has thrown into the sea!" (Exodus 15:1). Whenever the prophets used a phrase to describe their God, it was not, characteristically, "Lord of heaven and earth," but rather, "who brought thee up out of the land of Egypt." It is true that the life in Canaan tended to extend the sway of Yahweh over nature so that he became the creator and ruler of the world, and some of the Psalms celebrated his sovereignty over the processes of the cosmos, but this was always a minor note in the religion of Israel. The dominant theme was always his activity in the destinies of the nations. And his relationship to nature was entirely different from that of the neighboring deities. Even Ikhnaton's Aton was a god who was immanent in the world, the indwelling soul of nature, the life-process quietly and pervasively at work in all things. Yahweh, in contrast, was transcendent over the world, somehow "totally other" than any thing or principle observable in heaven or earth or sea. He was one, while the gods of nature were many. He had no

goddess or consort of any kind at his side, nor did he
beget offspring. There was no divine family, no sexuality within the Godhead. Yahweh embraced both masculinity and femininity within himself, transcending them
both as he embraced and transcended the divine and
the demonic. Thus, the natural metaphors with which
paganism abounded were cast aside by Israel in favor
of those drawn from the realm of human experience.
Where the nature gods were represented by elaborate
images combining weird and wondrous elements of
animals, birds, and reptiles, actual or mythological,
Yahweh was not to be portrayed at all. In fact, no
graven images of any kind were to be fashioned. Yahweh
was to be glorified not in the graphic arts which characteristically imitate nature but in the spoken word,
the unique and distinctive mark of man. He was "Lord,"
"King," "Judge." "The basic language of the ьible . . .
is an anthropomorphic language, draw from the categories of personality and community. Confusion with
metaphors drawn from other realms should be avoided
because there is a basic relatedness and kinship with
God and human life which does not exist in the same
sense between God and 'nature.' "[4]

This historical character of Israel's religion had profound implications both for the life of the people as a
whole and for their sex attitudes and practices. As
against the static quality of the nature cults of the
Fertile Crescent, which saw man's basic problem as

---

[4] George Ernest Wright, "The Faith of Israel," *op. cit.*, p. 359.

adaptation to the cyclical rhythms of the cosmos, Israel's faith proved dynamic, interpreting the human situation as a state of tension between man and God, a God who acted mightily in history to bring to pass his holy will. Revolution, change, progress, were to be expected in Israel, for Yahweh was at work. He was, as Jeremiah says, "awake," "watching" over his word to perform it (Jeremiah 1:12). And his word and his will were passionately ethical, deeply involved in the concerns of personality. His followers were to live together in righteousness and justice and community. This is why the Old Testament was so violently opposed to the sexual practices of the fertility cults. It is not that the Hebrews were prudes. Far from it! It was not sexuality in itself to which they objected, but rather the uses to which it was put, the quality of the relationships involved and their consequences. The sacred prostitution in the temples of the Baals confused the worshipers as to the character both of God and of human life. It further misunderstood and degraded sexuality itself.

It was not the Baals who were the lords of nature. They did not produce the fertility of the soil and the growth of crops. Yahweh was creator and ruler of the world he had made. That is the significance of the creation stories in Genesis 1 and 2, both of which are comparatively late in Israel's literary history. The Hebrew did not, like his pagan neighbors, become aware of the divine in nature and respond with numinous awe to that mysterious aspect of his experience. He began his encounter with God in history, and there came to see that Yahweh was also Lord of nature as well. There was, to be sure, religious syncretism in Canaan, a blending of ideas and concepts. But it was Yahweh who absorbed the functions of the Baals and not the reverse. And in absorbing these functions he transformed them as well. There are parallels between the Genesis creation story and similar legends among Israel's neighbors. What is striking in any comparison of these accounts, however, is not their similarities but their radical differences. Man was not created to serve as a slave for the gods, relieving them of the onerous tasks of cultivation of crops, as in Mesopotamia. Man was created in the image of God! And he was created for community. It was not good that he should be alone, and the woman was brought forth from his own body. She was the doorway into community. She and her husband were absolutely open to one another and to God. They were naked, they had nothing to hide, and they were unashamed. From them no secrets were hid. Their task was simply to obey, to hear the divine word and answer. Their lives were oriented toward him who is the rightful Lord of creation. They "knew" one another, which is to say that in their sexual life they discovered the deepest possibilities of human companionship and mutuality. Adam found what it meant to be a man only through Eve, and she became aware of her femininity only through him.

But then they fell into sin. Was their sin sexual? An

incredibly large number of people still believe that it
was, which is testimony to the extent of biblical illiter-
acy. Anyone who will take the trouble to read the first
three chapters of Genesis will discover that God *commanded* the man and the woman to "be fruitful and
multiply." How, then, could they be sinning if they
simply obeyed? The clue to the nature of their sin lies
in the tempting words of the serpent to Eve. "When
you eat of the fruit of the tree, your eyes will be opened,
and *you will be like God.*" This is where Adam and
Eve went astray and it is where everyone goes astray,
in placing himself in the center of his universe, in making himself God. This disrupts all dimensions of existence, including the sexual dimension. The innocent
"knowing" of man and woman, a symbol of their
mutual and unashamed revelation of their deepest selves
to each other, now was corrupted into a desire and a
need to use one another, to exploit and to abuse. Their
nakedness, then, became a source of embarrassment
and they covered up. They made for themselves aprons
which hid what they were, not only from each other
but from themselves. One's nudity, then, is a symbol
of what he is, and it is to be revealed in the act of
"knowing" only to another with whom one shares the
depths of his being.

This is why the Old Testament is so concerned about
the prevention of what it calls "the uncovering of
nakedness." This is why the hatred was so strong against
the lewd and obscene fertility goddesses and their

naked images, against the phallic symbols of the nature
cults, against temple prostitution. Sexuality and personality belonged together, subject to the reign of a God
who cherished and sanctified personal existence. To
use sexuality as a manipulative device, either in imitative magic or as the purely sensual use of another human
being, was to divorce it from its roots in the personal
life. This was the real sin of Amnon—not so much his
incestuous desire for his half sister, for she herself
suggested that the king would give her to him. Nor
was rape the real villain, though this is clearly to violate
and to wound the personal relationship. The real sin
was, as Tamar herself said, "This wrong in sending me
away is greater than the other which you did to me"
(2 Samuel 13:16). He used her and then flung her away
in disgust, a reaction not unfamiliar in sexual relations
which are not rooted in something stronger than mere
physical attraction. David's sin with Bathsheba was not
so much his possession of her body as his ruthless
elimination of her husband. Seeking to become "like
God" means making one's self the center of existence
and using other human beings as one chooses. The
whole of the Old Testament is permeated with a demand for recognition of God as the true center, as One
who demanded that human life be regarded with
respect and even reverence. Persons were not to be
treated as things in the sexual realm or anywhere else.

   In our own society, the feeling is strong that sex
should be linked to love. Hebrew society knew little

of the kind of love so celebrated in our culture. It was more concerned with responsibility and respect, as one might expect in an age when marriages were arranged by parents and families. Today, the ties binding individual young people in responsible relations to their families and to the wider family of the community and the nation are tenuous indeed. They are inclined to think only of their love for each other and of their needs, oblivious to the concern of others for them. Hebrew mores always saw the individual embedded in society, in the family, the clan, the tribe. And the individual had to be prepared to take the consequences of such sexual freedom as he sought. He was responsible. This is the significance of all the legislation about sexual relations which is always concerned for the personal *and* the social, the individual *and* the society.

This concern for personal responsibility, for respect and reverence, was altogether lacking in the sex attitudes and practices of Israel's neighbors. The temple prostitutes were used and left. The orgies of the fertility cults tore sexuality away from personality and reduced it to a mere symbol of nature. Further, these pagan religions buttressed societies that were agricultural and commercial, producing competition and growing inequality. Against this the religious leaders of Israel set the demands of the covenant God for justice, for community, for brotherhood. Because Yahweh was one, all of life was to be a unity, as against the plurality of polytheistic life; and that unity was between man and

God in history, between man and woman in the family, between man and man in society. Nature was not divine. It was God's handwork, and God gave to man dominion over nature, so that he was not enslaved by its cosmic rhythms. He was free to live in history which he made in co-operation with and in response to him who was the Lord of history.

6

SEX ATTITUDES

AND PRACTICES:

THE EARLY CHURCH

AGAINST

THE GRAECO-ROMAN

WORLD

❧

IN THE OPENING PARAGRAPHS of Paul's Epistle to the Romans there is a passage which scathes and scalds the Gentile world of his day. "What can be known about God," said the apostle, "is plain to them, because God has shown it to them. . . . his eternal power and deity has been clearly perceived in the things that

have been made. So they are without excuse; for although they knew God they did not honor him as God
or give thanks to him. . . . Claiming to be wise, they
became fools, and exchanged the glory of the immortal
God for images resembling mortal man or birds or
animals or reptiles. Therefore God gave them up in
the lusts of their hearts to impurity, to the dishonoring
of their bodies among themselves, because they exchanged the truth about God for a lie and worshiped
and served the creature rather than the Creator. . . .
For this reason God gave them up to dishonorable passions. Their women exchanged natural relations for unnatural, and the men likewise gave up natural relations
with women and were consumed with passion for one
another, men committing shameless acts with men and
receiving in their own persons the due penalty for their
error" (Romans 1:19–27). Thus the pagan world was
described as filled with sexual impurity, including
homosexuality; and its corruption was traced to idolatry, to "serving the creature rather than the Creator."
How accurate a portrait did Paul paint? Was the
Graeco-Roman world as deserving of condemnation as
he suggested? In order to answer that question, it is
necessary to look rather closely at the contents of the
various cultural channels that flowed into the Mediterranean basin in the centuries before and after the birth
of Christianity. Three streams in particular are of importance: the Greek, the Roman, and the Oriental.
Each of these requires separate examination, and then

we shall be in a position to see what resulted from their blending in the days of the Roman Empire.

GREECE

To look first at the Greeks, there is evidence that the regions surrounding the Aegean Sea were in pre-Homeric times involved in the worship of a great mother goddess, adored in her triple role of feminine function, as mother, as wife, as daughter. This seems to have produced a kind of matriarchy, in which women served not simply as priestesses in the prevailing cult but also as rulers of state and household. A recent novel by Mary Renault entitled *The King Must Die* describes the curious customs of these peoples, whose queen annually took to herself a new male consort, whose only function was to share the royal bed, as a sort of sacred stud. At the end of the year, the "king" had to die, either in mortal combat with his chosen successor or as the sacrifice in a bloody orgiastic ritual. His role reflected the status of all males in the society as subservient to the women—in sex, in statecraft, and in religion, no less than in the household. This dominance of the female sex was described in Greek legend in the stories of the Amazons, regarded by the Greeks as portraying their own early history. Since women were also warriors, it seemed necessary that they should render themselves physically capable of bearing arms, of wielding sword and spear, bow and arrow. Hence, the belief arose that the Amazons burned off their breasts, whence they derived their name—*a-mazone,* without breasts. This is a late legend, however, as the Greek statues of the Amazons reveal. As warriors, they refrained from sexual relations with men, but they obviously could not follow the example of their patron virgin goddess absolutely or their race would soon have become extinct. They therefore did copulate with men, but of their choosing and in their own manner. Stories suggest that the male was expected to lie passively on his back while the female mounted his member and rode it to satisfaction and impregnation. Nature had dictated that women must bear children, but their nurture could be the responsibility of either sex, and in the pre-Olympian civilization of the Aegean Sea, this was apparently a function of the male. The household chores were also in his hands, freeing the superior women to devote themselves to the cares of state.

Robert Graves in his *Hercules, My Shipmate,* has described the early conflicts between the ancient triple mother goddess and the new Olympian deities, who were masculine and rebellious. The two heroes of the triumph of the new male cult were Jason and Theseus. Jason was able to win the Golden Fleece for Zeus only with the aid of the priestess Medea, but he ultimately put her in her proper place and made himself master. Theseus conquered the Amazons and made their queen his docile and obedient wife. The Greeks never ceased to worship the feminine principle embodied in their goddesses, and even Zeus, king of the gods, was perennially plagued by a nagging wife, Hera. But on Olympus, the male deities ruled, and Hellenic society followed suit. The matriarchy was at an end. "Yet the Amazonian concept of the interchangeability of the sexes," as Dr. Richard Lewinsohn has observed, "lies at the root of Greek aesthetics."[1] The Middle East and the Orient, in their sacred art-forms, emphasized and exaggerated the specifically feminine. Their fertility goddesses always had wide hips, bulging buttocks, large, pendulant breasts, and full bellies. The face was entirely unimportant, and no one could possibly mistake these figurines for anything but symbols of feminine sexuality. The Greeks seem to have derived their ideal from the Cretan culture which centered at Knossos about 1500 B.C. This was the home of the famous bull-dancers who have recently aroused considerable attention. Archaeological excavations of the temples and palaces have revealed elaborate frescoes of this curious and highly interesting dance, and it is difficult to know whether the figures portrayed are male or female. Both sexes seem to have prized a lithe, lean figure, characterized by a boyish grace. Homosexuality or bisexuality apparently flourished in Crete, and this gave rise to a blurring of anatomical differences, which had clear influence on Greek art and sculpture. The

---

[1] Richard Lewinsohn, *A History of Sexual Customs* (New York: Harper & Brothers, 1958), p. 41.

acrobatic occupation of the bull-dancers, with its at-
tendant necessity for litheness, apparently created a
special conception of beauty.

In neither sex were protuberances of any kind prized
or glorified. Whether one looks at the statues of the
archaic period of Greek culture in the eighth and seventh centuries B.C. or at the products of the classical
Periclean Age, it is difficult to distinguish the sex,
where any drapery conceals the primary genital organs.
The hair and the clothing are sometimes helpful, but
the face and figure are strikingly similar. This dulling
of sexual differentiation does not spring from prudery
or any desire to hide the facts of sexuality. The Greeks
suffered from no such malady! Sex and aesthetics went
together and there was no hesitation in portraying the
nude bodies of gods or goddesses, as there was no
hesitation in the naked participation of both male and
female athletes in the Olympic games. It is not that
sex was concealed. Rather, it was subordinated to the
higher values of aesthetics, which had laws of its own.
Proportion, balance, rhythm, harmony—these things
applied equally to both sexes, and the ideal of beauty
was such that the spectator was attracted or repelled
to the extent that the object or person fulfilled the
canons of aesthetics, without regard to sexual differentiation. That a beautiful boy should be attractive only
to women was a thought utterly foreign to the Greek
mind, as was any suggestion that a lovely lady's desir-
ability was limited to male admirers. Beauty was

beauty, and one always desired to draw near and if possible to possess it.

Thus, Greek society produced a bisexual orientation, a fact that modern homosexual cultists sometimes forget. These latter point with pride to the creativity of Periclean Athens and ascribe it to the sexual inversion of poets and philosophers, artists and architects. But these creators, including Socrates, were for the most part married men with families! They loved boys, it is true, but they were by no means repelled by heterosexual relations, nor did they regard women with disgust. The Greek found beauty magnetic without respect to sex. The perfect symbol of this genteel neutrality is embodied in the myth of Hermaphroditus, who was the divinely fused body of a beautiful boy and an adoring nymph, possessed of the organs of both sexes, able to love and be loved at will. Aristophanes, in his speech in Plato's *Symposium*, declared that man was originally created androgynous—the two sexes united in one body—and was rent in twain as punishment for sin. Ever since, each half has sought its mate nostalgically, and when the quest was won, has striven with all its energy to reunite its body with its mate.

So far, it would appear that the apostle Paul was right. In Greece, at any rate, we have found "men committing shameless acts with men," though there they were certainly not regarded as shameless. It must not be thought from the foregoing, however, that all Hellas whiled away its hours in *paedophilia*. There were marriages between the sexes, and female prostitution flourished. The *hetairae,* as the courtesans were called, frequently rose to positions of very great wealth, influence, and power as they became the objects of the affections of men like Pericles or Alexander the Great. Pericles, the most powerful man in Athens, passed a law in 451 B.C. forbidding the rights of inheritance to marriages between citizens and slaves. A man might establish a liaison with a slave or daughter of a slave, using her as his concubine, but neither she nor any children born of the union could inherit the property of her citizen-lover. This was a desperate attempt to protect concentration of wealth from dispersion among the lower classes. This attempt was further strengthened by laws permitting the marriage of near relations, including even the children of one father, provided that the mothers were different. Pericles himself, however, became enamored of a *hetaira,* Aphasia by name, and he separated from his wife, the mother of his two sons, taking Aphasia into his home and living openly with her as though she were his wife.

But the majority of the Greek *hetairae* were not exceptionally gifted and witty companions of the great. They were rather like their sisters in every age and clime, simple prostitutes plying their trade for their own profit and the pleasure of their customers. It was the rare man who was interested in conversation with his companion of the hour. A modicum of physical attractiveness and skills in the arts of Eros were far more important. Most of these women worked in large brothels maintained by owners and investors. These houses of joy varied widely according to the class they were intended to serve. Some of them were luxurious and elaborately decorated, with accouterments of all sorts designed to please their patrons of wealth and position, and the price was high. Others were simple and cheap, aimed at a proletarian clientele. The girls were for hire either for brief periods or for longer times, according to the desire and pocketbook of the customer. For approximately thirty pieces of silver a girl could be bought outright, transforming her from a *hetaira* to a *pallakis,* or concubine. Some temple prostitution made its way from the East into Greece, but few Greek cities regarded it as proper to sanctify whoremongering with the worship of Aphrodite. Corinth, a seaport town strategically located at a much-visited isthmus, adopted the practice and did a highly successful business with tourists. Strabo commented at the beginning of the Christian era that over ten thousand *hetairae* were employed at the temple of Aphrodite at Corinth, though this seems undoubtedly exaggerated.

Prostitution was not confined to the female sex. Adult males in Athens were perfectly within the law in selling their affections to men who desired them, and they seem to have done so in considerable numbers. Young men or boys were protected by law from being sold into prostitution by their fathers or uncles,

but no barriers were placed in the way of their volun-
tarily assuming the trade. Free love, in the literal sense
of that term, was virtually unknown in Greece between
a man and a maid. Payment in such a relationship was
taken for granted. But love affairs with *ephebi,* or
young men, were commonplace. Solon's code of laws
made it a crime to bribe boys into paederasty, insisting
that such relations should be confined to freeborn citizens. Homosexuality practiced with slaves was thought
to endanger class dignity, and citizen youths not naturally inclined to such activities required protection
from their own greed. Money did in fact exchange
hands, however, as did presents of various value. It was
not uncommon for a man smitten by a fair youth to
take the boy into his house and provide for his room,
board, clothing, and education—a state of affairs often
helpful to a family financially pressed.

Homosexuality was common, as it still is today, all
over the region of the eastern Mediterranean far more
than in the West. But the Greeks had a special taste
for it. No physiological differences are apparent as
explanatory of this phenomenon, and the cause must
be sought in the environment. The ideal of beauty as
the slim, boyish figure probably had much to do with
it, as Lewinsohn suggests. But this does not account
for the willingness of handsome youths to submit to
the caresses of older men as ugly as Socrates, and even
to return those caresses. That appears to stem from a
combination of vanity and avarice. The extravagant

admiration of men of wealth and position and the offers
of impressive gifts were difficult for growing boys to
resist, the more especially as so many of their contemporaries profited by the practice. The existence of such
accepted relationships in the society made in itself for
a certain predisposition. Kinsey's studies indicate that
Freud's contention that children are "polymorphous
perverse" is probably correct. The first sexual experiences are strongly determinative of future attitudes and
practices. Boys early seduced by older men, appealing
alike to curiosity and prurience, to vanity and greed,
were not averse to continuing such relationships, especially where no social censure accompanied these
pleasures.

Homosexuality in Greece, however, was primarily a
male phenomenon. The famous Sappho, with her school
for girls on the isle of Lesbos, loved one of her students
and wrote lyric poems celebrating her beloved. Her
passion was unreturned and unrequited, and she
drowned her grief and herself in the sea. Her island has
given its name to sexual love between women; it is
called Lesbianism. The Greeks had another word for
it. They called such women *tribades,* derived from
tribein, meaning to rub two bodies together. Doubtless
the Greek code of aesthetics produced love between
women as it did between men, but the female lovers
were either far less numerous or far less vocal than
their male counterparts, for the cult of Lesbos had
fewer devotees whose names or verses have survived.

Imperial Rome was more versed in these arts than was Greece. The woman in Greece paid for her earlier position of dominance. Man declared his independence by worshiping his own form, his masculine beauty, and he demanded that the woman conform to his ideal. Her breasts must be small, her shoulders broad, her hips narrow. She lacked a penis, which was a liability, but in all other respects she was forced to imitate male physiology. The old proverb had it, "Women for breeding, but boys for pleasure." So successful was this as a cultural ideal that the Greeks evidently even repressed love of women for each other. They, too, adored the boy. They too were *paedophiles*. This decided preference for the male figure in classical Greece is obvious from the sculpture. The voluptuous female statues are all later productions, dating from the Hellenistic Age. Goddesses dwelling on Mount Olympus could be portrayed as feminine and full-busted, but merely mortal females were subjected to masculinization.

Aristotle spoke for Greece when he discoursed on the natural inferiority of women to men. An examination of the animal kingdom showed clearly that the male was stronger, larger, and faster than the female. Equality of the sexes was therefore unnatural. Further, in Aristotle's philosophy, all things were divided into matter and form. The matter, or *hule*, was the inferior, formless stuff, which was ineluctable and resistant to purposeful shaping. The forms worked upon the matter and impressed upon it useful and beautiful shapes.

Needless to say, the form was masculine, the matter feminine, and it was clear which was superior. Man was energy, heat, life. Woman was matter, cold, listless. Thus, despite several attempts in Greece to emancipate women, to raise them to equal status, the male remained supreme. Women could neither vote nor own property. Divorce was the sole prerogative of the husband, and a father could sell his daughter into slavery if she lost her virginity. Aristophanes put forward his suggested program for women in their struggle for power in his *Lysistrata*. If they would deny their bodies to the men, they could soon name their own terms of capitulation, but no one took this very seriously. Aristophanes was a writer of comedy!

ROME

Turning to Rome, we find a somewhat sterner stuff, as we might expect. The Romans appear to have invented sex—the word, that is! *Sexus* in Latin literature means the difference between male and female, deriving from the verb *secare*, meaning to cut or sever. The Romans made much of this biological difference. Unlike the Greeks, who blurred the distinction between masculinity and femininity, they glorified heterosexual love and were repelled by all sexual abnormalities. Homosexuality, called "the Greek practice," was not a crime, but it was weak and feminine, uncharacteristic of the manly Roman citizen-soldier. A full sex life was indispensable to both men and women, and was to be savored and enjoyed. Neither virginity nor monogamous fidelity were Roman ideals. The separation and remarriage of a couple who proved sexually incompatible was taken for granted. Marriage as a monogamous relationship apparently arrived late on the Roman scene. Early life among the seven hills was primitive. Initiation ceremonies carried on in connection with the cult of the god Tutunus Mutuus were wild and obscene, ushering twelve-year-old girls and fourteen-year-old boys into the mysteries of sexuality. After their initiation both were expected to carry on for themselves with little interference. This contributed substantially to a growing and vigorous population which was gradually able to subdue its neighbors. As marriage relations began to take shape, they assumed the form of purchase. A man bought his wife from her father. If he could persuade a maid to live with him for a year, without absenting herself from his side more than two nights, he was entitled to claim her without price. The marriage was accepted as common-law.

The earliest written law in Rome, the so-called Twelve Tables, dating from the middle of the fifth century B.C., reveals a concern to prevent mixed marriages—between patricians and plebeians. The law was soon repealed, however, and romance crossed the picket lines of class snobbery. In early Rome, the power of the *pater familias* over his family was absolute. He could kill or sell his wife or children for cause.

Changing economic conditions gradually modified marital customs, limiting the husband's rights. His power of life and death gave way first to circumstances of clear and proven adultery, and then in the Empire even this disappeared. As agriculture was replaced by manufacturing and commerce as the principal sources of income in the city, the wife became less an economic asset than a liability and the bride-price was supplanted by the dowry, a financial remuneration to the husband for his increased responsibilities of support. But since some husbands proved improvident, the custom grew of granting the dowry directly to the wife, and she had the right to take it with her if she left her husband's household and returned to her father. The wife thus became relatively independent; so long as she cared for her husband properly, he had no grounds for divorce. But if the match proved incompatible, a dissolution was simple and quick. After the second war against Carthage, women won the right to divorce on sufficient grounds, which included prolonged absence on military service. Under the Empire, a divorce was attainable by the declaration and desire of either husband or wife, thanks to legal reforms which took place over a period of more than a century.

If marital ties in Rome were always somewhat loose and easy to slip, this does not mean that women were lightly regarded. Rape was a serious crime, and anyone tempted to violence had always before him the grim reminder of the fate of the Tarquin monarchy, brought to a bloody end by the indignation stirred up over the rape of Lucretia. Not even a king could ravish a woman of Rome with impunity. The early legends of the city included also the "rape" of the Sabine women, a highly shady episode from start to finish; but the results were a treaty of unification between Romans and Sabines, testifying to the power of woman as a cohesive force.[2] But by the beginnings of the Empire, the female sex was, among the effete aristocracy, chiefly prized as a source of pleasure rather than as a breeding ground. Childlessness began to be much desired by the upper classes and was secured through contraception and *coitus interruptus,* or failing these, through abortion or even infanticide. It became highly fashionable to seek out wealthy persons who were without heirs, and to cultivate and flatter them assiduously in the hope of being remembered in the last will and testament. This made heirlessness attractive and depressed the rate of childbirth. One might not have offspring to brighten one's declining years, but if he possessed any property at all, he could be assured of a sizable coterie of sycophants. This tended to increase the number of wealthy Roman men who avoided marriage altogether, finding their sexual pleasure with prostitutes and concubines. Divorce was easy, but marriage did carry with it responsibilities and these were burdensome to many.

The emperor Augustus grew alarmed at the break-

---

[2] Of course, this was not really "rape" but the seizure of women as wives.

down of marriage and family life and sought to restore some of the old, hardy virtues of the earlier days of the Republic. First of all, he passed a law requiring marriage of all men under sixty and all women under fifty. Anyone who remained single was unable to inherit the estate of a nonrelative unless he married within three months of the testator's decease. No bachelor or spinster was permitted to attend public games, and sharp limitations were placed on the amount of money that could be left to a childless wife. Barriers were erected against mixed marriages between upper and lower classes. Large families were encouraged by a variety of measures. Marriage was brought under the protection of the state, and laws were established regulating and punishing adultery. Heretofore, this had been entirely an individual matter, and crimes of passion were rare in Roman history. It was far more common for a cuckolded husband simply to turn over his faithless wife to her lover than to murder the guilty person. If they wanted each other, why not? After all, now he was free to find someone else. Augustus sought, vainly, to tighten up the marriage vows, to recall Rome to the old virtues, the old morality, the old faith. Youngsters were barred from public spectacles unless accompanied by an adult; women were not permitted at athletic events and were relegated to the remote galleries at the gladiatorial exhibitions. Tacitus, writing a century later, declared the efforts of Augustus to be failures. "Marriages," he said, "did not become frequent, so powerful are the attractions of a childless state."

One of the reasons why the estate of matrimony waned under the Empire was the rise of prostitution. No less august a person than Cicero, however, regarded prostitution as an institution *protecting* the sanctity of marriage, and Cato the Censor and Seneca concurred. If a man were unmarried or unsatisfied with a frigid wife, he had two possible sources of sexual satisfaction: a prostitute or another man's wife. The first protected the second. But in Rome, as in most of Greece, prostitution was secular rather than sacred. Oriental temples built in the imperial city sometimes included priestesses who specialized in erotic ritual, like the temple of Isis, but these were foreign imports not indigenous to Roman society. With the Romans, this was a business, not a rite. They called their harlots *meretrices,* or earners. They were not, for the most part, self-employed, and they did not accumulate large fortunes. Collected in communities by brothel-keepers, they were to be found in every provincial city. The larger metropolitan centers had whole quarters devoted to the trade. In Rome itself the most famous of these "red-light districts" was the *Subura.* The practice of exposing unwanted children provided an ever fresh supply for these brothel-keepers who raised them to carry on the trade. Both boys and girls were trained to earn their keep in brothels. As in Athens, the quality and price of these establishments varied with the financial status of the client. Some were cheap and tawdry, called *lupanar,* or the den of the female wolf. Others, however, were elegant and luxurious, with desirable and delectable girls whose cost was high.

One of the more elaborate of the latter type has been uncovered in the ruins of Pompeii, preserved for centuries beneath the volcanic ash of Vesuvius. Its walls are decorated with frescoes of sensual delight, with pictures of the limitless possibilities of sexual positions and postures. Such surroundings swiftly titillated the customer and put him in the mood to take full advantage of his opportunities. This genre of pornography also found its way into private villas in Pompeii, where wealthy Romans passed the hot summer months. Some viewers of these frescoes have seen in them evidences of flagellation as a popular theme, together with orgies of the Dionysian cult. Poetry as well as the depictive arts was called into the service of the sensuality of the wealthy. Propertius and Horace wrote many an ode to the joys of love and were much in demand at fashionable parties. Of the large number of writers competing in this lucrative market, none was more skilled than the young Ovid. Married twice and twice divorced, he found ample room for his appetites in the lax atmosphere of the Eternal City. Livy and Virgil might glorify the older times of the Republic, wagging their heads at present degeneracy. Not so Ovid. "Let the past please others," he wrote; "I congratulate myself on being born into this age, whose morals are so congenial

to my own." His first series of verses, called *Amores,*
sang of the beauty of his beloved, Corinna, the wife
of another man. He instructed her in the art of deceiv-
ing her husband so that she might be with him. "When
he lies down on the cushion, go to him with modest
demeanor. Lay yourself down by his side, but see that
your foot presses mine." His most famous work was
the *Ars Amatoria,* which served as a manual of seduction as well as a detailed description of the sexual act
from preliminaries to climax, carried on in such a way
as to produce maximum delight. Unhappily for him, he
ran afoul of the puritanical Augustus and was later
banished from Rome. He never lost his popularity with
the reading public, however, and his verses have survived for centuries. These Roman poems all strikingly
anticipate the cult of medieval courtly love, where the
beloved is almost always another man's wife, remote
and difficult to attain. But stolen fruits are ever the
sweetest.

With ladies of easy virtue and good family "as numerous as the stars in the sky," as Ovid observed, it
seems odd that prostitution should have flourished as it
did; but seduction was a wearying occupation confined
to the upper classes, and the patrician men sought
easier prey on occasion, as the plebs desired cheaper
company regularly. Brothels were by law confined to
quarters outside the city walls and permitted to open
only at night. Prostitutes were required to wear distinctive dress identifying their profession. Male prosti-

tution also was widespread as the city became the center of Empire, and Greeks and Orientals came to Rome in growing numbers. Even Roman citizens in this decadent age fell victims to this malady. "I am stricken with the heavy dart of love, for Lyciscus, who claims in tenderness to outdo any woman"; so Horace sang of his passion for a slender youth. A collection of pornographic poems celebrating the raptures of sex between men circulated under the title of *Priapeia*, and both Martial and Juvenal contributed to the literature of the cult.

Marriages continued to take place and children to be born, else Rome's decline and fall would have come some centuries earlier than it did. A girl who reached her nineteenth birthday unmarried was considered an old maid—in itself a testimony to the rarity of the phenomenon. Nearly every young lady was married at least once, if only temporarily. These unions were for the most part arranged by marriage brokers with the parents concerned. The betrothed couple seldom had an opportunity to make each other's acquaintance before the ceremony. Seneca remarked cynically that no one bought anything without testing it, but that such a privilege was denied a prospective husband with his intended bride. Love and romance came, if at all, after marriage, and more commonly in extramarital affairs. Ovid declared that a pure woman was merely one who had never been approached and that any husband objecting to his wife's amours was a country bumpkin.

Seneca believed that any married woman who confined herself to two illicit affairs was a rare and virtuous creature indeed.

Nonetheless, beneath this veneer of the aristocrats and *nouveaux riches,* the old virtues of marriage, fidelity, and parenthood survived among the common people who could not afford such luxuries, nor were they by and large interested in them. Pliny's *Epistles* described the wholesome and healthy home life of numerous families who kept to the old ways, nourishing the flame on the traditional altars of Rome with the fuel of piety, gravity, and simplicity. There were writers who refused to season their works to the lowest public taste, who sang of virtue and morality and bemoaned the decadence of the times. These sturdy souls, though doubtless more numerous by far in the Roman Empire than their lascivious contemporaries, were also less spectacular and therefore did not stand out. As moderns lament the attention lavished by the newspapers on crime, violence, and sin, so history preserves the colorful, the strident, the obscene, leaving the "normal" folk to quiet oblivion. Yet there is comfort in this all the same. The day when newspapers begin to headline stories of virtue, kindliness, and courage will be the day when such things are the exception rather than the rule. As it is, we take marital fidelity, responsible parenthood, filial piety, for granted and raise our eyebrows at deviations from the norm. So it was with Greece and Rome. But the Christians were shocked by such widespread immorality found in the highest places. No wonder they regarded Rome as "the whore of Babylon." Our story, however, requires one more chapter. For into the West in which Christianity began and grew there flowed a third stream—from the East.

THE ORIENT

Prior to the conquests of Alexander the Great, the West had been more or less insulated from the cultures of the East—Egypt, Mesopotamia, and India—by a sort of arrogance which is apparent in Herodotus, who wrote of these regions somewhat as though they contained Hottentots. To the Greeks, all foreigners were "barbarians," a prejudice fully shared by the conquering Alexander. Although a Macedonian himself, he had been tutored by Aristotle and was a passionate devotee of Hellenism. He sought to bring Greek enlightenment to the dark and superstitious Orient, the first self-appointed carrier of "the white man's burden." What Alexander did not reckon with was the destructive effects of his own hegemony imposed upon the Greek city-states, coming so soon after the devastation of the Peloponnesian War. Nor did he foresee that the missionary enterprise upon which he embarked was destined to open a two-way street. Into a West grown weary, disillusioned, and even cynical about the futility of the search for the good life in this world came the cults and the faiths of men and nations who had long ago abandoned hope for a material world and turned their eyes to an eternal realm of the spirit.

The Hellenistic Age, which began with the death of Alexander in 323 B.C., witnessed a heightening of a sense of sin, a growing otherworldliness, a hunger for salvation from a meaningless existence. The old ideals of rationality, of self-sufficiency, of balance and harmony and moderation, crumbled and vanished. Fulfillment and self-realization could not be found in time, in the world of visible, material objects. Salvation was attainable only through escape into another world, into eternity. The motif of the time was sounded in the Orphic pun, *soma sema,* "The body is a tomb." Four types of religious attitudes made themselves manifest in the Hellenistic Age, all of them imports from the East. First, there was the worship of Fate. All things were ruled by this blind and careless principle. Even the gods were subject to it. *Que sera sera—*"Whatever will be, will be," and one could do nothing but accept what Fate had in store for him. "The moving finger writes, and having writ, moves on, nor all your piety nor all your wit shall cancel half a line, nor all your tears wash out a word of it." Second, certain astral cults made their appearance, deifying the stars and the planets. Each man had his destiny determined by the cosmic sign under which he was born. He was a slave to his stars, and astrological consultation of horoscopes was essential to happiness and success. Third, the Hellenistic Age witnessed widespread deification of men.

Olympian religion had humanized the gods; the cults of the Hellenistic Age made gods out of men. Not alone the Roman Caesars were apotheosized, but any hero or puppet-king who possessed a *charisma*. Great deeds were possible only to deities; ordinary men were helpless and without worth.

By all odds the most important religious development of the times, however, was the fourth, the rise of the mystery cults. There had been from earliest times in Greece certain of these cults, such as the Dionysian or Orphic-Eleusinian mysteries, but they were small, prohibitively expensive, rigidly exclusive, and culturally of limited appeal. In the years after Alexander's death, many of these religious groups were imported into the Graeco-Roman world from the Orient, and they grew to positions of immense power and influence. The most significant of the Eastern mysteries were the cult of Cybele, the great mother of the gods, and Attis, with its origins in Asia Minor; the worship of Isis and Osiris, which came from Egypt; the rites of the Syrian Baals and Adonis; the cult of Sabazios from Phrygia; and of Mithras from Persia. The initiates of these mysteries were sworn to the strictest secrecy, and we know with certainty very little about them. It is necessary to piece together hints gleaned from remnants of liturgical texts and scattered references among the writings of the Christian fathers.

The cult of Cybele, the great Mother Earth, and her lover Attis, who was the spirit of vegetation, was, like the Greek Eleusinian mystery, centered in the cycle of the seasons, celebrating the birth and death of spring and autumn. Attis died each year and rose again, bringing new life with him. The worship of Cybele involved wild and frenzied dances during which the priests of the cult castrated themselves and threw their genitals upon the altar of their goddess. The apostle Paul apparently had this custom in mind when he wrote his Epistle to the Galatians, saying of those who insisted upon circumcision as necessary for Gentile converts to Christianity, "I wish those who unsettle you would mutilate themselves!" (Galatians 5:12). The worshipers of Cybele also practiced an initiation rite known as the taurobolium, in which the new convert was placed in a pit covered with a grating. A bull was slaughtered, allowing its blood to wash over the devotee, cleansing him of sin and mortality, giving him eternal life.

We have already mentioned the Egyptian cult of Isis and Osiris, another nature religion, mythically celebrating the annual cycle of death and rebirth of vegetation. Isis was, like Cybele, the earth-mother, while Osiris was the counterpart of Attis, though he was brother to the goddess as well as her husband. Their divine child Horus was frequently portrayed in his mother's arms, and the early Christian Madonnas with child bear striking resemblance to these Egyptian pictures and sculptures. The early form of the cult emphasized the fertility of the earth and the abundance of crops, but it gradually took on a more intimately personal significance, bringing individual redemption and immortality to its devotees. The resurrection of Osiris symbolized not only the new life in nature but also the rebirth of those united to him and to Isis in faith. The Ptolemies encouraged this mystery religion and assisted its spread through the Mediterranean world. Osiris was replaced as the consort of Isis by Serapis, a more cosmopolitan god; and the similarities of the divine couple to other Hellenistic deities, such as Cybele and Attis, were stressed.

Mithras was originally a god of the ancient Aryans who migrated into India and into Persia. From Persia the cult of Mithraism spread into Asia Minor, where the soldiers of Pompey encountered it in 67 B.C. The religion became highly popular in the Roman army, preaching as it did the sterner virtues of courage and self-discipline. Only men were eligible for initiation, a rite which bore close resemblance to the taurobolium of Cybele. Mithras was a god of the sun, and he was often portrayed as a bull-slayer, plunging his dagger into its throat, while a scorpion grasped its genitals and other animals waited to drink its blood. The winter solstice played an important role in the cult, symbolizing the annual triumph of the sun over darkness. Beginning about December 21, the sun, having since June been sinking daily lower on the horizon, bringing longer nights and shorter days, starts to climb once more, and the process is gradually reversed until the summer solstice when daylight reigns supreme. The Roman festival of Saturnalia celebrated the same phenomenon in December, and the worshipers of Mithras rejoiced in the birthday of their god on December 25. In the third century A.D. Mithraism was the strongest rival of Christianity in the Mediterranean world, and it is no accident that the Christmas festival, which was unknown in the first two centuries of the Christian era, was placed also on December 25.

This is not the only parallel between Christianity and the mystery cults of the Roman Empire. There were in certain of the cults sacramental meals, which has led some observers to assume that the church adapted the Eucharist to prevailing custom. It is clear, however, that the real source of the Christian communion was the Jewish Passover Seder. There was genuine danger in the first centuries of the Christian era that Christianity might become another mystery religion. Some of the classic heresies moved perilously in this direction. The church steadfastly maintained its rootage in Judaism, however, which gave to the faith a historical character which set it apart from all its rivals, excepting only Judaism itself. The mysteries were admittedly based upon myths. No one seriously claimed that Osiris or Cybele or Mithras had actually lived. They were symbols of cosmic powers. Christianity rested solidly within history, claiming that the Word became flesh, that Jesus of Nazareth lived and died, "crucified under Pontius Pilate." In general, it can also be said that the mysteries were indifferent to the morality of their members, while the church showed active concern for the daily conduct of her people. Mithraism, however, also preached and practiced a stern moral code.

The Hellenistic Age showed a growing contempt for and suspicion of the life of the body, and nowhere was this more manifest than in a movement known as Gnosticism, which posed a serious threat for the church in the first two centuries of her life. This was an eclectic philosophy, with roots in the Orient, which gathered to itself elements from a multiplicity of sources, using strands from many different religious and philosophical schools. The Gnostics shared the prevailingly pessimistic view of the material, historical world and sought salvation in escape from it through divine illumination and superior knowledge (*gnosis*) or wisdom. Some of them were attracted to Christianity by the magnetic personality of Jesus, whom they saw as an embodiment of the savior principle which they so eagerly sought. They could not, however, believe either that the material world had been created by God or that the Christ, the Savior, had actually become flesh, been incarnated. They therefore substituted an elaborate scheme of emanations from the Divine, the last and lowest of which was Yahweh, the God of the Old Testament who made the evil world and imprisoned therein the immortal souls of heaven. The first and highest emanation from the Divine, the Logos, agreed to come to earth on a rescue mission, but he only appeared to be a man, Jesus, only seemed to suffer and die. The Divine must at all costs be protected from contaminating contact with either the material world or human flesh.

So far as sex is concerned, the Gnostics were divided into two camps: extreme asceticism and extreme libertinism. The motivation to the former seems obvious enough and has its analogues throughout the Hellenistic world. If the flesh was evil, the less one had to do with it the better. It was a part of the realm of the devil, and those who fell prey to its tempting wiles suffered death of the soul as well as death of the body. This school of Gnostics preached virginity and celibacy, and looked upon marriage as an inferior estate. All sex suffered from a dual liability. It aroused material lusts and it resulted in imprisoning further souls in bodies through procreation. This was a viewpoint not confined to the Gnostics, and the New Testament reflects both Christian attraction and Christian hostility to such an attitude. The other approach, that of libertinism, is harder to comprehend, but it had its own logic. A passage from Irenaeus, a second century church father, is instructive at this point:

> To us [that is, the members of the church], therefore, they [that is, the Gnostics] maintain a moral life is necessary for salvation. They themselves, however, according to their teaching, would be saved absolutely and under all circumstances, not through works but through the mere fact of their being by nature "spiritual." For as it is impossible for the earthly element to partake in

> salvation, not being susceptible of it, so it is impossible for the spiritual element (which they pretend to be themselves) to suffer corruption, whatever action they may have indulged in. As gold sunk in filth will not lose its beauty but preserve its own nature, and the filth will be unable to impair the gold, so nothing can injure them, even if their deeds immerse them in matter, and nothing can change their spiritual essence. Therefore "the most perfect" among them do unabashed all the forbidden things. . . . Others serve intemperately the lusts of the flesh and say you must render the flesh to the flesh and the spirit to the spirit.[3]

There are several layers of Gnostic thought in this area. The first represented a sort of moral indifferentism, in which the "spiritual" man was freed from all restraints, inhibitions, or taboos, since these things belonged to the realm of the physical or material. The second not only permitted but positively enjoined the "spiritual" to violate conventional moral standards, either to show their contempt for the concerns of this world or to burn out the sensual passions of the flesh. There was at this point an occasional suggestion that the souls of men must pass through all experiences before attaining final salvation, and if one could pass through them all in one lifetime, so much the better! A third layer went so far as to say that he who allowed himself to be bound by conventional morality was enslaving himself to the demons in control of this mate-

---

[3] Irenaeus, *Adversus Haereses*, W. W. Harvey, ed. (Cambridge, England, 1857), I:6, 2–3.

rial world. Whatever layer one touched, therefore, one was under necessity to live in violent intemperance, sating the lusts of the body to the full. Thus one was given not only a convenient rationalization for any sexual act he cared to indulge in; it became a positive religious duty, the *sine qua non* of salvation!

THE EARLY CHURCH

Christianity in its early stages found itself, then, set in a context of extremes in sex attitudes and practices. Much of the ancient world regarded sex as a matter of relative indifference. *Chacun à son goût,* "Each to his own taste," as the French say. If one chose to practice homosexuality, to seek his satisfaction with prostitutes or in a series of adulterous liaisons, or in numerous temporary marriages or states of concubinage, few would say him nay. Liberty was synonymous with license. Others in antiquity rejected all contact with matter and retreated into asceticism, exalting celibacy and virginity at the expense of marriage and children. The church operated at considerable peril between these two poles and found itself pulled now in one direction, now in the other. In the end, however, she maintained a dialectical tension in between them that was, like radioactivity, both dangerous and powerful. Indeed, the New Testament word for power is *dynamis,* from which we derive our word "dynamite." That is a commodity which can be either creative or destructive, depending on its use. So the early church saw the force of sexuality.

It is clear from the passage in Paul's Epistle to the Romans with which this chapter opened, and from other epistles as well, that the New Testament took a stern stand on libertinism. The prevalent practices of prostitution, divorce, and homosexuality came in for strong condemnation, as we shall see in subsequent chapters. While it is true that, in the Gospels, Jesus associated with harlots and forgave a woman taken in adultery, scandalizing the Pharisees, this is not to say that the New Testament looked upon such acts with moral indifference. The "tax collectors and harlots" who were to enter the kingdom before the scribes and Pharisees did so on the basis of their repentance (Matthew 21:31), and the woman taken in adultery was told to "go, and do not sin again" (John 8:11). The early church would not in this matter set itself against the example of its Lord; and while it knew that libertines were not beyond the hope of salvation, that they, too, must have the gospel preached to them, still such persons, *continuing* in their sensual ways, could not be tolerated within the household of faith. "I wrote to you in my letter," said Paul to the Corinthians, "not to associate with immoral men; not at all meaning the immoral of this world . . . since then you would need to go out of the world. But rather I wrote to you not to associate with anyone who bears the name of brother if he is guilty of immorality . . . not even to eat with

such a one. For what have I to do with judging out-
siders? Is it not those inside the church whom you
are to judge? God judges those outside. Drive out the
wicked person from among you" (1 Corinthians 5:9–15).
"Put to death therefore," he wrote to the Colossians,
"what is earthly in you: immorality, impurity, passion,
evil desire, and covetousness, which is idolatry. On account of these the wrath of God is coming. In these
you once walked, when you lived in them. But now
put them all away" (Colossians 3:5–8).

Even the immoral who were excommunicated from
the church for their sins were not utterly lost. The door
of repentance was still open to them, as it was to the
Gentile world at large. Paul would not have the church
too stiff-necked about forgiveness. His serious break
with the Christian community at Corinth came over
their initial failure to obey his instruction and cast out
of their fellowship one member who lived openly in
defiance of moral conventions. When the church finally
yielded, Paul could conciliate: "But if anyone has
caused pain, he has caused it not to me, but in some
measure—not to put it too severely—to you all. For
such a one this punishment by the majority is enough;
so you should rather turn to forgive and comfort him,
or he may be overwhelmed by excessive sorrow. So I
beg you to reaffirm your love for him" (2 Corinthians
2:5–8). Nonetheless, those who persisted in "the works
of the flesh," which included "immorality, impurity,
licentiousness," were warned "that those who do such

things shall not inherit the kingdom of God" (Galatians 5:19–21). "Be sure of this, that no immoral or impure man . . . has any inheritance in the kingdom of Christ and of God" (Ephesians 5:5). The church as the community of those who were already living in the kingdom had to keep its life pure.

But if the early church set its face against the libertine attitudes and practices of the Graeco-Roman world, it also opposed the dualism and extreme asceticism which characterized some of the Gnostics and many others of the age. The Christian community had its roots sunk deep into Jewish soil, and the material world was affirmed as the creation of God, and therefore good. Jesus even broke with the Pharisees, who saw some foods as clean and unclean. "Not," he said, "what goes into the mouth defiles a man, but what comes out of the mouth, this defiles a man. . . . Do you not see that whatever goes into the mouth passes into the stomach, and so passes on? But what comes out of the mouth proceeds from the heart, and this defiles a man. For out of the heart come evil thoughts, murder, adultery, fornication, theft, false witness, slander. These are what defile a man" (Matthew 15:11–20). Again, Peter's vision on the housetop suggested the essential goodness of all created things, even those forbidden by dietary laws. "What God has cleansed, you must not call common" (Acts 10:9–16). The whole of the Johannine literature represents an answer to Gnosticism, insisting that "the Logos became flesh and dwelt among us" (John

1:14), and that "every spirit which confesses that Jesus Christ has come in the flesh is of God, and every spirit which does not confess Jesus is not of God. This is the spirit of antichrist" (1 John 4:2–3). It was the Gnostics also who were clearly referred to in 1 Timothy 4:1–5: "Now the Spirit expressly says that in later times some will depart from the faith by giving heed to deceitful spirits and doctrines of demons, through the pretensions of liars whose consciences are seared, who forbid marriage and enjoin abstinence from foods which God created to be received with thanksgiving by those who believe and know the truth. For everything created by God is good, and nothing is to be rejected if it is received with thanksgiving; for then it is consecrated by the word of God and prayer." There are numerous references to the marriages, not only of members of the church but also of ministers and even of the apostles. The apostle Paul expressly warned married couples against too long a period of sexual continence, lest they be tempted to adultery (1 Corinthians 7).

It is true that celibacy and virginity were regarded as possible vocations for the Christian, especially in times of persecution and in view of the imminence of the coming of the kingdom. But the motivation was apocalyptic and not dualistic. "The New Testament knows nothing of the very considerable depreciation of marriage which the influence of an ascetic dualism is to introduce later on into the Church."[4] Paul clearly had

---

[4] J. J. von Allmen, ed., *A Companion to the Bible.*

to deal in Corinth with those who regarded all sexuality as wicked and sinful, as well as with those who looked upon it as morally indifferent. He refused to sanction either extreme. Sex, like everything else in life, was to be consecrated to the service of God. It could be given up by those who sought to please the Lord, devoting the whole of their energies to that enterprise. But it could also be used in the household of faith without sin if it was carried on in love and fidelity. Thus, the early church stood between the two opposite poles of the Graeco-Roman world—libertinism and asceticism—seeking to hallow sexuality not to extirpate it, as the church sought to do with the whole of existence. Christians were to be in the world but not of the world. They could use all things so long as those things were consecrated by the Word of God and prayer, so long as they did not become idols, or ends in themselves.

7

PREMARITAL

SEX RELATIONS

IN THE

BIBLE

T HE QUESTION OF SEX RELATIONS before marriage is one of the most pressing problems confronting the younger generation. As one young man attending a religious conference said in all earnestness to one of the leaders, "This is the rawest concern we have." The sap rises early and strong in young bodies at the spring of life, and consciences are troubled. Our times are confused

230

and the morality of modernity offers little clear counsel. Few among the most puritanical find evil in holding hands or in a chaste good-night kiss. Nor are there many serious souls who hold any brief for sheer lechery, for unbridled gratification of animal passion without affection or responsibility. But between these two poles there is ample space for difficulty and for difference of opinion. Roman Catholicism speaks unequivocally on the basis of natural law, carefully delineating the fields of sin, both venial and mortal, from the areas of acceptability. But Protestantism appears torn between opposing camps. On the one side, a legalistic moralism occupies terrain with little to distinguish it from Rome; while on the other, a group pitches its tents on the ground of love and raises a banner carrying the inscription *"Amor omnia vincit"*—love conquers all. Professor John MacMurray of Edinburgh University has declared his belief that the ethic of Jesus is indifferent to all external circumstances and controls.[1] If a couple are deeply and genuinely in love, they require no further justification for their sexual union. An executive of a national church agency doing much premarital counseling announced that it is their practice to commend couples contemplating matrimony who reveal that they have already consummated their union sexually. The agency does not go so far as to advise premarital relations where they have not occurred; it only indicates

---

[1] In an essay entitled "The Virtue of Chastity," in his book *Reason and Emotion* (New York: D. Appleton-Century Co., 1936).

approval where they have already taken place. To the young in love, it appears that life is long and love brief —or at least opportunities for the expression of their love.

Out of the welter of conflicting opinions, one fact emerges with relative clarity. Man is the one living creature whose psychosexual development creates such a problem for himself.

> Man is the only animal who arrives at sexual maturity before he achieves social maturity, so that every society develops codes that are designed to prevent a man's becoming a grandfather before he can vote. There are many variations in the specific means used to attain this goal in the mores of various cultures, and the more complex the society the greater is the hiatus between the two levels of maturity. The Polynesian adolescent is ready for social responsibility long before the American or European, and Polynesian sexual morality is correspondingly less rigid. But whatever the differences, the primary concern of every society with sex is bound closely to procreation. Morality, in this sense, means that sex is used responsibly by persons who are prepared to face the consequences of their union, that is, parenthood.[2]

The fact that two hundred thousand young women in the United States annually produce babies out of wedlock, and that Kinsey's statistics reveal a widespread practice of premarital intercourse in both sexes, sug-

[2] William Graham Cole, *Sex in Christianity and Psychoanalysis* (New York: Oxford University Press, 1955), p. 22.

gests that society's concern for responsibility weighs rather lightly, in the scales of decision, against individual desire.

No one can deny that we face a problem of serious proportions. Our culture is divided into two strenuously opposed parties. On one side is arrayed the pomp and power of traditional morality, surrounded with the aura of ecclesiastical authority, hurling impressive anathemas against a wicked and adulterous generation. On the other is to be found the forces of "liberty," arrayed in the shining armor of what they regard as science and enlightenment, marching against the Bastille of reaction and restraint. Perhaps the most colorful of the legions in this army of revolt is the band of the so-called "Beatniks," the bearded Bohemians who read Jack Kerouac, who divide their time between drinking in the bars of San Francisco and being "on the road." Theirs is a religious quest for meaning and significance, as they seek to drain the last drop of sensation from each cup that life proffers to them. But in this army they do not fight alone. At their side stand the writers and essayists who want Western moral standards revised to conform to prevailing practice as revealed by Kinsey and others. Here are to be found anthropologists who brandish spears pointed with sharp facts concerning the sex life of countless other societies, primitive and advanced. The ranks are strengthened by experimental psychologists who draw the strong-bows created in their research laboratories and send arrows of potent data on the sex life of mammals against the ramparts of reaction. The heavy guns of psychotherapy boom with broadsides of neuroses produced by sexual repression, by guilt and shame and sense of sin. And ranging round the camp is the cavalry, the light-horse of novelists, poets, playwrights, who harass the enemy with swift attack and quick withdrawal. Against such a foe the strongest heart might faint, but firm stand the bastions of respectability. They fight for home and mother, for the sanctity of the family and the purity of love. The blessing of the church is upon them and they stand assured that the gates of hell shall not prevail. We who occupy the no man's land between the warring camps quietly take out the Bible and by the flickering firelight search its pages for guidance. Shall we join the fray? And if so, on which side?

THE OLD TESTAMENT

This is a book purported to be a blockbuster in the arsenal of the church, but regarded by the rebels as a dud, a weapon long obsolete. It does, to be sure, reflect a culture far different from our own, with different problems, different concerns. But it has, like all great literature, nourished souls in ages far removed from its own, and countless generations have heard its pages speaking to them with the voice of God. On many of the questions which perplex us it is maddeningly silent. There is nothing to be found here on the proprieties of kissing, on the problems of the nature and duration of embraces of various kinds between unmarried persons. If one seeks enlightenment on necking or petting, light or heavy, he will pore over this literature in vain. The ancient Hebrews simply did not think in these terms. Sex was not to them a mere amorous dalliance, a game to be played part way and then abandoned. They took their sex seriously, as an activity involving pleasure and peril, recreation and responsibility. The daughters growing up in the clan or the village were strictly protected by stern laws. And the protection was against their own impulses as well as against those of marauding males. "If there is a betrothed virgin, and a man meets her in the city and lies with her, then you shall bring them both out to the gate of that city, and you shall stone them to death with stones, the young woman because she did not cry for help though she was in the city, and the man because he violated his neighbor's wife; so you shall purge the evil from the midst of you. But if in the open country a man meets a young woman who is betrothed, and the man seizes her and lies with her, then only the man who lay with her shall die. But to the young woman you shall do nothing; in the young woman there is no offense punishable by death, for this case is like that of a man attacking and murdering his neighbor; because he came upon her in the open country, and though the betrothed young woman cried for help there was no one to rescue her" (Deuteronomy 22:23–27). A betrothed virgin approached within the city had thus the strongest incentive to cry out for help.

But suppose the young woman engaged in premarital relations without detection—perhaps in the open country. She still had to face a fearful test at the hands of her future husband. "If any man takes a wife, and goes in to her, and then spurns her, and charges her with shameful conduct, and brings an evil name upon her, saying, 'I took this woman, and when I came near her, I did not find in her the tokens of virginity,' then the father of the young woman and her mother shall take and bring out the tokens of her virginity to the elders of the city in the gate; and the father of the young woman shall say to the elders, 'I gave my daughter to this man to wife, and he spurns her; and lo, he has made shameful charges against her, saying, "I did not find in your daughter the tokens of virginity." And yet these are the tokens of my daughter's virginity.' And they shall spread the garment before the elders of the city. Then the elders of that city shall take the man and whip him; and they shall fine him a hundred shekels of silver, and give them to the father of the young woman, because he has brought an evil name upon a virgin of Israel; and she shall be his wife; he may not put her away all his days. But if the thing is true, that the tokens of virginity were not found in the young woman, then they shall bring out the young woman to the door of her father's house, and the men of her city shall stone her to death with stones, because

she has wrought folly in Israel by playing the harlot
in her father's house; so you shall purge the evil from
the midst of you" (Deuteronomy 22:13–21). All of this
seems to us from our modern perspective frightfully
primitive and even barbarous. The public display of
"the tokens of virginity," clearly a sheet or under-
garment stained with the blood of the broken hymen,
is scarcely a tasteful spectacle, and the capital punishment for fornication is terribly severe.

All of this must be seen, however, against the background of two facets of Hebrew life. In the first place,
this was a people originally nomadic and then agricultural in their economy. In both types of society all
children, male and female, represented an augmented
labor supply. The daughter was therefore an economic
asset to the father. She was a part of his property and
must be respected as such. In the second place, a major
concern of the Hebrews was their posterity. With life
beyond death somewhat dubious and at best shadowy,
one's only solid hope for survival lay in his progeny.
The greatest shame of a wife, therefore, short of adultery, was to prove barren. It was grounds for divorce.
Sarah bemoaned her inability to give Abraham a son
and encouraged her husband to make use of her own
handmaid, Hagar, for this purpose. Leah and Rachel
entered a fertility contest with their husband Jacob,
using not only their own wombs but those of their
maidservants as well. Jacob's twelve sons testify to the
success of their competitive enterprise. The Levirate

marriage, which guaranteed at least a putative offspring
to a man dying childless, is further testimony to the importance with which the Israelites regarded progeny.
A daughter, therefore, was not only an economic asset
to her father as a worker with flocks or in fields but
also as a prospective wife and mother for whom some
young man would pay a good price. If she were damaged goods, she lost her merchandise value and both
she (if she permitted herself to be damaged) and her
violator had to pay the penalty. If a young woman were
not betrothed, that is, promised to a man, with the
bargain sealed by at least a down-payment, then her
seduction was somewhat less serious. Death was not
the punishment, but marriage. "If a man meets a virgin
who is not betrothed, and seizes her and lies with her,
and they are found, then the man who lay with her
shall give to the father of the young woman fifty shekels
of silver, and she shall be his wife, because he has violated her; he may not put her away all his days" (Deuteronomy 22:28–29). A father who chose not to marry
his daughter to her seducer had the alternative of keeping her at home and collecting "money equivalent to
the marriage present for virgins" from the man (Exodus
22:16–17).

No provision was made for the punishment of a
young woman who lay with her husband before marriage, so long as their act was undiscovered. Presumably
he would not be concerned about the tokens of her
virginity, since he had earlier destroyed these himself.

But these were the only possible circumstances under which a girl could engage in voluntary fornication without risking death. Betrothal was tantamount to marriage, for the law was absolutely silent on sexual relations between a betrothed couple; no prohibitions were set up and no punishments provided. The daughters of Israel were not to be harlots, either secular or sacred. "Do not profane your daughter by making her a harlot, lest the land fall into harlotry and the land become full of wickedness" (Leviticus 19:29). "There shall be no cult prostitute of the daughters of Israel, neither shall there be a cult prostitute of the sons of Israel. You shall not bring the hire of a harlot, or the wages of a dog [that is, a Sodomite], into the house of Yahweh your God in payment for any vow; for both of these are an abomination to Yahweh your God" (Deuteronomy 23:17–18). So strong was the prejudice against cult prostitution, which was in such favor among the neighbors of Israel, that "the daughter of any priest, if she profanes herself by playing the harlot, profanes her father; she shall be burned with fire" (Leviticus 21:9), the most terrible penalty the Old Testament prescribed. Here the concern was as much for cultic purity as for sexual purity. Temple prostitution was idolatrous and therefore utterly opposed to the spiritual monotheism of Israel. In order to make doubly sure that the cult of Yahweh was uncontaminated by such abomination, "the priest who is chief among his brethren . . . shall take a wife in her virginity. A

widow, or one divorced, or a woman who has been
defiled, or a harlot, these he shall not marry; but he
shall take to wife a virgin of his own people, that he
may not profane his children among his people; for I
am Yahweh who sanctify him" (Leviticus 21:10–15).
No woman with previous sexual experience could be
allowed to dwell with the priest in charge of the shrine,
lest there be danger of her infidelity. A virgin was less
of a risk.

The law was clear on premarital sexual relations for
women—only with one's future husband could they be
carried on without considerable risk, and if a betrothal
had been arranged, then no real difficulties stood in the
way. There was no religious or civil ceremony of marriage in Israel in any case. An agreement was concluded, usually between the two sets of parents. The
betrothal was arranged, including the payment of the
mohar or bride-price (normally fifty shekels of silver)
to the father of the bride, and then after a feast the
groom went to the dwelling of his wife and brought
her home with him. Thus, fornication for a maiden
was virtually impossible without the severest penalties.
But what of the man? Were similar difficulties and
punishment imposed upon him? Obviously he approached a married or betrothed woman at his peril.
The penalty upon disclosure was death by stoning. If
he lay with an unbetrothed virgin and was caught, he
was forced to marry her and to keep her for life. He
could not divorce her. But there was no law against a

man's going to harlots, though the wise men of Proverbs warned against the enslaving ways of such women. The keeping of God's commandment would "preserve you from the evil woman, from the smooth tongue of the adventuress. Do not desire her beauty in your heart, and do not let her capture you with her eyelashes; for a harlot may be hired for a loaf of bread, but an adulteress stalks a man's very life" (Proverbs 6:24–26). Here the harlot was preferable to an adulteress, but "a harlot is a deep pit; an adventuress is a narrow well. She lies in wait like a robber and increases the faithless among men" (Proverbs 23:27–28); and "one who keeps company with harlots squanders his substance" (Proverbs 29:3).

Thus, wisdom's better part was the avoidance of such connections, but whatever sin might be involved was at worst venial. Judah, the son of Jacob, while on the road to Timnah, saw a woman he thought was a harlot and promised her a kid from his flock in payment for "coming in to her" (Genesis 38:12–19). His commerce in this fashion was reported without any moral judgment. The Old Testament reveals considerable suspicion against traffic with the cult prostitutes of Canaan, but this prejudice extended even to marriages with the pagan families of the land. The Israelites were commanded to tear down the altars of the Baals "lest you make a covenant with the inhabitants of the land, and when they play the harlot after their gods and sacrifice to their gods and one invites you, you eat of his sacrifice, and you take of their daughters for your sons, and their daughters play the harlot after their gods and make your sons play the harlot after their gods" (Exodus 34:15–16). This was not so much a fear of sex as of idolatry. There was no clear law against an unmarried man's having sex relations with a woman not belonging to someone else. There is evidence that sacred prostitution flourished in the Temple in the days of King Josiah, of whom it was said: "He broke down the houses of the cult prostitutes which were in the house of Yahweh" (2 Kings 23:7).

A woman taken captive could be used as a concubine by her master or given to his son for his pleasure, but an Israelite woman sold into slavery by her father in financial straits had certain rights. "When a man sells his daughter as a slave, she shall not go out as the male slaves do. If she does not please her master, who has designated her for himself, then he shall let her be redeemed; he shall have no right to sell her to a foreign people, since he has dealt faithlessly with her. If he designates her for his son, he shall deal with her as with a daughter. If he takes another wife to himself, he shall not diminish her food, her clothing, or her marital rights. And if he does not do these three things for her, she shall go out for nothing, without payment of money" (Exodus 21:7–11). In general, few restraints were placed upon man's sexual urges. He could not violate the rights of another man: the father, the betrothed, or the husband of a woman; but no limit was placed upon the number of women he might keep in his household as wives or concubines or slaves. If progeny were his guarantee of continued existence after his own death, the more offspring he could produce, the safer was his future. Unlike the woman, his market value was not diminished by the loss of his virginity. In marriage, his father lost nothing, but gained a daughter to help carry on the family line. Such dowry as came later with a bride was in compensation for the increased financial burden of her support, but it remained at least partially in her control and was to be refunded if she were divorced. The real compensation was the *mohar*, the price paid to the woman's father whose loss was real. The fathers of daughters required protection of their investment, and this the law supplied. The father of sons incurred no such liability, and the law was correspondingly silent. The double standard is very ancient indeed, with roots in biology and economics. John Calvin, in his commentary on the commandment against adultery, remarked on the divine oversight in virtually granting license to fornication to men, and tried to supply what God forgot, extending the sense of the commandment to all sexual impurity.

In summary, we can say that the Old Testament reveals little prejudice against sex as such. There was considerable concern to protect the purity of one's bloodline, to guarantee one's posterity. There was likewise strong prohibition against cultic prostitution, so closely was this institution attached to pagan idolatry. But beyond that, the motivation behind the legislation on pre-

marital sex relations seems to have been largely economic rather than puritanical. It was the rights of the
maiden's father which were paramount, equaled only by
the rights of the betrothed into whose care she was to
be given. A man seducing or violating a maid was guilty
of trespassing on another man's territory. There seemed
little concern over the girl herself as a person. Beyond
the respect which the male owed to his neighbor's property, few restraints were placed upon his sexual drives
and desires, so long as they followed normal, heterosexual lines.

What, then, shall we say to these things? Does this
material furnish us with guidance in our questioning
stance between the two warring camps? Does it provide potent ammunition for the hosts of righteousness,
or is it, as the "sons of liberty" maintain, obsolete? In
order properly to answer this query it is necessary to
look more closely at the Hebrew conception of the family, the community, which represents a perspective far
different from our modern conception of individualism.
To us, it is the individual who is all-important. His
rights, his liberties, must not be infringed save in cases
of gravest emergency. Erich Fromm is eloquent in his
writings on the necessity of severing the umbilical cord
binding the individual to his family, to his past. He even
cites Scripture to his purpose, "A man leaves his father
and his mother and cleaves to his wife" (Genesis 2:24).
The Hebrews saw it from another angle of vision. For
them, the family was far more fundamental than the in-

dividual, who occupied a decidedly secondary position in society until well after the Babylonian exile, when Ezekiel tore down the ancient fabric of solidarity and communal responsibility. No individual was anything apart from his family, his clan, his tribe. He was bound within its common life, flesh of its flesh and bone of its bone. His sins were its sins and his triumphs theirs. If there were any weakness in the family, it was his weakness; and if there were any strength, it was his strength. Cain paid for his question, "Am I my brother's keeper?" by being cut off from the source of his identity and his security. And he cried out, "My punishment is greater than I can bear!"

The Hebrews knew what modern man has forgotten —that no man is unto himself an island. When an individual member of a family suffers dishonor or disgrace, are not all wounded, all hurt? When a man marries a girl, he joins his destiny not alone to her but to her parents and to her brothers and sisters, and she binds her life into the community of his blood relatives. Thus, premarital relations are not the sole concern of the couple involved. His family is involved and so is hers, whether either of them likes it or not. If a pregnancy ensues, they must share the onus, the shame, and they must share in the responsibility for shaping the life of the child. Those who inveigh against the restraints of sexual morality usually speak from the perspective of youth, frustrated and denied the fulfillment of strong desire. But what of the elders? When impatient young

men perform an exercise of the imagination and project
themselves twenty years into the future, seeing themselves as the father of a seventeen-year-old daughter,
they are brought up sharp. They realize the short-
sightedness and the selfish individualism of their present
impetuosity. They know that they will be concerned for
their daughter in a way that it has not been possible for
them to see, and that the object of their present affection
and desire also has a father who is concerned for her.
The Old Testament turns out, then, to be a mine,
planted deep beneath the defenses of the libertines,
threatening their entire position. Its explosion may be
delayed, waiting for years of maturity and parenthood,
but it ticks away ominously.

The Old Testament threatens the other camp as well,
for it stands clearly against all efforts to depreciate or
ignore sexuality as a potent force in life. Sex is good; it
is the creation of God, and all men are expected to enjoy it. No prudishness or squeamishness is appropriate.
Sex is not an occasion for shame or embarrassment. All
members of a family must learn to use their sexual drives
responsibly, but they do so by facing the facts openly,
not by hiding behind blinders, pretending that life is
asexual, that such matters are never discussed in polite
society. One thing these conservatives need to learn:
it is not the open treatment of sex in our society that is
wrong; it is the context of that treatment. Nothing is to
be gained by a conspiracy of silence. Our so-called sex-
saturated society needs as its antidote not a return to

repression and ignorance but a discussion of sex in its proper context. The Hebrews saw all of life as one, as related to and governed by the Lord of the covenant. There were no watertight compartments sealed off from his sovereign rule. There was, in short, nothing secular anywhere in existence. All of life was hallowed by his presence and his will. What our own times require is what the Old Testament possessed—a full, frank, and open facing of the facts of sexuality in human life, but in the context of divine sovereignty. Sex is sacred, as all human existence is sacred. It cannot be used selfishly or irresponsibly without serious damage to the very structure of one's being, to the whole network of one's interpersonal relationships. The Old Testament is in itself an arsenal of weapons, useful perhaps to both sides of the battle—and it is certainly no dud!

THE NEW TESTAMENT

The New Testament is in some respects even less helpful than the Old if one is looking for direct reference to premarital sex relations and specific advice on the problems thereof. It is perfectly plain in its condemnation of what the Greek calls *porneia,* which is translated variously as "fornication" or "whoredom." Fornication means to us sex relations between unmarried persons, but its Latin root *fornicare* meant to patronize a brothel, or whoredom. The verb was derived

from the noun *fornix,* meaning arch or vault, and as
Roman brothels were located in underground vaults,
the connection is clear. The Revised Standard Version
of the Bible translates *porneia* simply as "unchastity,"
which is wise, since the term obviously covers more
than mere traffic with prostitutes, though it does include that. By New Testament times polygamy and
concubines had begun to disappear from Jewish life,
and monogamy had almost become the rule. Divorce
and remarriage were still possible, but the rabbis and
the oral tradition sought to confine sexual relations for
both men and women strictly within matrimony. Prostitution was condemned by the Jewish religious leaders, as was all premarital or extramarital intercourse.
This is not to say that harlots were unknown in Palestine. Quite clearly they were in evidence, as the
Gospels make abundantly plain, but they enjoyed no
toleration from the moral and religious standards of
the nation.

The pious Jews were shocked at the laxness of sexual
customs among the Gentiles of the Graeco-Roman
world and prided themselves on their own purity.
Hence, when Paul set out on his mission to the Gentiles, one of the conditions the Jerusalem community
made for the inclusion of these converts in the Christian Church was that they should abstain from all
porneia. The activities of Paul and Barnabas in preaching to Gentiles and bringing them into the fellowship
of the church stirred up a considerable controversy.

Those in Jerusalem were inclined to believe that before one could become a Christian, he must first become a Jew, i.e., submit to circumcision. And being a Christian did not deliver a man from the necessity of observing the Jewish law; on the contrary, it made him even more zealous in obedience. Paul viewed the gospel as the end of the Law and freedom from its precepts. The disagreement created the necessity for a Council, which was called in Jerusalem to hear both sides. The matter was settled, apparently, by an agreement that the apostles in Palestine, led by James and Peter and John, should confine their mission to the Jews, while Paul and Barnabas were given "the right hand of fellowship, that we should go to the Gentiles" (Galatians 2:9). According to the account in Acts, James declared, "My judgment is that we should not trouble those of the Gentiles who turn to God, but should write to them to abstain from the pollutions of idols and from unchastity (*porneia*) and from what is strangled and from blood" (Acts 15:19–20). A letter to this effect was drawn up and sent off with Judas and Silas to the Pauline churches where trouble had been stirred up. The account in Acts differs sharply from Paul's own description in his Epistle to the Galatians, where the only condition laid upon him was the remembrance of the poor, "which very thing I was eager to do" (Galatians 2:10). Whatever the controversy over circumcision, the pollution of idols, and refraining from things strangled or from blood, there was no disagreement between Paul and

Jerusalem about unchastity. He regarded it as seriously as did they.

All of his letters reflect the difficulties he had with his Gentile converts at this point. Inured as they were to a casual view of sexual morality, it seemed difficult for them to grasp the demands of their new faith. This was especially true because many of the early converts had been among the so-called "God-fearers." These were Gentiles who surrounded the Jewish synagogues of the Graeco-Roman world, attracted by the monotheism, by the high moral standards of the Jews. But the pain of circumcision and the inconvenience of ritual purity kept most of these God-fearers from becoming full converts to Judaism. Many were permitted to sit in the gallery of the synagogue and witness the worship, if not to take part. Wherever Paul went on his travels, he visited first the synagogue in the city and preached his gospel of freedom there. For the most part, the Jews rejected him, but many of these God-fearers were eager to hear more. Here was an opportunity to enjoy all of the advantages of Judaism, with none of its liabilities. The Law had been set aside. Circumcision, dietary laws, ritual purity—all these were as nothing. So, many of the Gentiles converted and were baptized. But some of them obviously misunderstood what Paul meant by freedom. He referred to freedom from the ceremonial laws; they thought he meant freedom from moral laws. It is not surprising, then, that the apostle found it necessary to include in almost every epistle some word of clarification on this matter.

To the Thessalonians he wrote: "For you know what instructions we gave you through the Lord Jesus. For this is the will of God, your sanctification: that you abstain from immorality; that each one of you know how to take a wife for himself in holiness and honor, not in the passion of lust like heathen who do not know God; that no man transgress, and wrong his brother in this matter, because the Lord is an avenger in all these things, as we solemnly forewarned you. For God has not called us for uncleanness, but in holiness. Therefore whoever disregards this, disregards not man but God, who gives his Holy Spirit to you" (1 Thessalonians 4:2–8). In this passage the Revised Standard Version renders *porneia* as "immorality," and the context clearly indicates that it was sexual immorality which the apostle intended. Those who had sexual urges were not to satisfy them outside the bonds of matrimony but were to take a wife. Nor were they to enter a series of temporary marital liaisons "in the passion of lust like heathen who know not God." Their relationships were to be characterized by "holiness and honor." The same point was made to the church at Corinth, where Paul counseled: "Because of the temptation to immorality (*porneia*), each man should have his own wife and each woman her own husband. The husband should give to his wife her conjugal rights, and likewise the wife to her husband. . . . To the

unmarried and the widows I say that it is well for
them to remain single as I do. But if they cannot exercise self-control, they should marry. For it is better to
marry than to be aflame with passion" (1 Corinthians
7:2–9). No sexual relations outside of marriage were
justified in the apostle's eyes. Marriage represented for
him a kind of medicine for immorality, a prevention
against unchastity or fornication.

He was explicit in his condemnation of prostitution.
"Do you not know," he asked the Corinthians, who
lived in the most celebrated center of harlotry in the
Mediterranean world, "that your bodies are members
of Christ? Shall I therefore take the members of Christ
and make them members of a prostitute? Never! Do
you not know that he who joins himself to a prostitute
becomes one body with her? For, as it is written, 'The
two shall become one.' But he who is united to the
Lord becomes one spirit with him. Shun immorality.
Every other sin which a man commits is outside the
body; but the immoral man sins against his own body.
Do you not know that your body is a temple of the
Holy Spirit within you, which you have from God?
You are not your own; you were bought with a price.
So glorify God in your body" (1 Corinthians 6:15–20).
This represents a rather curious extension of the Old
Testament concept of "one flesh," rendered in the
Greek as *henosis*. The apostle here indicated that *any*
union of two bodies in the sexual embrace, no matter
how casual or commercial, established the state of one

flesh. There is no such interpretation to be found in the Old Testament, which saw the state as characterizing a married couple who had bound the totality of their lives together until death. Paul perhaps went too far in this respect, but he did see that sex represents a depth of personal existence which is unique. It is the most intimate of all interpersonal relationships, expressing the essence of one's attitudes toward others. If one's personal orientation is exploitative and grasping, this is reflected in his sexual attitudes and practices. He cannot insulate his sex life from the rest of his existence. Whatever he does in this area affects what he is, and what he is in turn affects what he does sexually.

Thus Paul argued vehemently against those who claimed that sex was purely a physical appetite to be satisfied without respect to the circumstances. The man who is thirsty wants water; he does not care much whether he drinks it from a glass or a cup. The apostle apparently agreed that gluttony or drunkenness can be pursued without permanent effects in the personality. "Every other sin which a man commits is outside the body." This is not to be taken literally, since all sins of sensuality are obviously in some sense in the body. What he was trying to say was that all other sins are transitory, though one cannot help but wonder how murder fits such a theory. Stolen goods can be returned; lies can be retracted and replaced by the truth; covetousness can be overcome. Even idolatry can be undone and forgiven.

But the sex act once committed with another person cannot be undone. The interpersonal relationship has undergone a radical change, and the couple involved can never return to where they were before. Something indelible has stamped them both. Even with a prostitute, sexual connection leaves its mark and its memory. It is a spot which will not out, not with all the perfumes of Araby. "The immoral man sins against his own body." This is a truth the modern world cannot see. Many a young man regards premarital sexual experiences as helpful, if not essential, to a satisfactory adjustment in marriage. And a surprising number of young women confess that they almost hope that their husband-to-be will prove "experienced." Thus far have the marriage manuals and books on sex technique led us down the road with their dire warnings about the terrible consequences of a blundering wedding night. Some even believe that sexual relations before marriage with one's intended are necessary to guarantee sexual compatibility. What such attitudes fail to recognize is what Paul was trying to say. Sexual intercourse with a prostitute is the worst possible preparation for marriage. There are no similarities between such an encounter and the marital embrace, except in the crudest physical sense. What bride wants her husband to regard her as a whore, to be used, paid, and left? And what kind of test of sexual compatibility is a clandestine, guilty connection, snatched from beneath the nose of the watchdog of society? There is no comparison

between such a brief encounter and the relaxed, trust-
ful commitment of a wedding night. Paul may appear
to be a Puritan, but he was in fact profounder than all
mere moralists. He saw to the depths of personal
existence with a clarity that blazed with insight.

"Your body is a temple of the Holy Spirit," and the
Holy Spirit is redemptive, selfless, outgoing in generous
and sacrificing concern for others. How, then, can such
a temple be used for activities that are selfish, exploit-
ing, abusing, treating another human soul as a mere
body to be callously mauled and grasped and thrown
aside? The man in whom the Holy Spirit dwells regards
all men as his brothers to be served and loved and, if
possible, saved. They are, like himself, sinners for
whom Christ died. As he is a member of Christ's body,
he has the responsibility to preach the gospel to all,
seeking to bring them also into the holy community
of which Christ is the Head. This he cannot do if he
is constantly seeking to get rather than to give. Of such
a one people say, "What you are speaks so loudly that
I cannot hear what you are saying." This is why Paul
was so desperately concerned to maintain the purity
of the church's life. He knew, as C. S. Lewis has observed, the truth of the reverse of the wartime poster's
warning: "Careless talk costs lives." Careless lives also
cost talk. And to those who would justify premarital
relations on the basis of love and intention to marry,
Paul also had a word to say: "If anyone thinks that he
is not behaving properly toward his betrothed, if his

passions are strong, and it has to be, let him do as he wishes: let them marry—it is no sin" (1 Corinthians 7:36).

Modern youth, whose passions are strong, may argue that it was easy for Paul to say, "Let them marry." He did not know what it means to contend with the necessity for prolonged education, for economic security, for a home and a future. These are they who plead that they must have each other. Their love is too imperious to be denied any longer. And to the query, "Why not get married?" they reply indignantly, "We *can't* get married!" There is college to be finished or money to be saved or a job to be found. And then, paradoxically to the further inquiry, "What if a pregnancy occurs?" they respond blithely, "Oh, then we'll get married." Of course, one can always get married if one has to, and far better to have to because of strong passions than because of an unwanted child. "Let them marry —it is no sin." Fortunately, many modern parents understand the problems of youth and are making it possible for their children to marry earlier. College campuses today are witnessing a sharp increase in the numbers of married students. Some of these unions are doubtless "in the passion of lust," but many of them are "in holiness and honor."

The church is a community of the Spirit. As such, it must be kept pure from selfishness and irresponsibility of all kinds. "Be imitators of God, as beloved children. And walk in love, as Christ loved us and gave himself up for us, a fragrant offering and sacrifice to God. But immorality and all impurity or covetousness must not even be named among you, as is fitting among saints. Let there be no filthiness, nor silly talk, nor levity, which are not fitting; but instead let there be thanksgiving. Be sure of this, that no immoral or impure man, or one who is covetous (that is, an idolater), has any inheritance in the kingdom of Christ and of God. Let no one deceive you with empty words, for it is because of these things that the wrath of God comes upon the sons of disobedience. Therefore do not associate with them, for once you were in darkness, but now you are light in the Lord; walk as children of light (for the fruit of light is found in all that is good and right and true), and try to learn what is pleasing to the Lord. Take no part in the unfruitful works of darkness, but instead expose them. For it is a shame even to speak of the things that they do in secret; but when anything is exposed by the light it becomes visible, for anything that becomes visible is light" (Ephesians 5:1–13).

The dictum, "Do not associate with them," may seem to contrast with Jesus' example of mingling with harlots and publicans, but the Pauline word already quoted in the last chapter must be remembered: "I wrote to you in my letter not to associate with immoral men; not at all meaning the immoral of this world, or the greedy and robbers, or idolaters, since then you would need to go out of the world. But rather I wrote to you not to associate with any one who bears the name of brother if he is guilty of immorality" (1 Corinthians 5:9–11). Those within the church must keep themselves free from wickedness of every kind. The doors to salvation were by no means closed to those in the world who were immoral. The gospel was preached precisely to them, and Paul said specifically to his Corinthian converts, "Such were some of you," that is, the immoral, idolaters, adulterers, homosexuals, thieves, the greedy, drunkards, revilers, and robbers. "But you were washed, you were sanctified, you were justified in the name of the Lord Jesus Christ and in the Spirit of our God" (1 Corinthians 6:9–11). Therefore, such acts must now be abandoned, and all that is earthly must be "put to death in you" (Colossians 3:5).

Paul and the Flesh

There are numerous passages in the Pauline Epistles where the apostle contrasted the Spirit and the flesh in such a way that he sounded like a Gnostic, or a Hellenistic dualist. It appears as though all the evils of human life were centered in the material body. But this is grossly to misunderstand Paul's meaning. The clearest illustration of the falsity of such an interpretation is to be found in the third chapter of the letter to the Galatians, where the apostle asked, "Having begun with the Spirit, are you now ending with the flesh?" (Galatians 3:3). He was writing here not to sensualists at all, but rather to those who were in danger of being persuaded by the Judaizers that strict observance of the Jewish law was essential to salvation as a Christian. Thus, to be zealous for the Law was "fleshly," which scarcely sounds like indulgence of the body. Actually, Paul meant by "the flesh," which is a translation of the Greek *sarx*, the whole realm of human potentiality, of worldly power. To live according to the flesh meant to live in the illusion that one had his own life at his disposal, to believe that one was self-sufficient. For the Jew, this manifested itself in the conviction that a man could earn his salvation by obedience to the Law. For the Gentile, it took the form of boasting in human wisdom. It could appear in sensuality, in preoccupation with sex or food or drink. But that was only one possible symptom of an underlying malady. And the disease was far more serious than mere physical lust; it was the total orientation of the personality. The Pharisees and Judaizers walked after the flesh, and yet they had their passions under the strictest control. The opposite of life in the flesh was not asceticism at all but life in the Spirit, which was the surrender of one's attempts to control his own destiny and a complete trust in God. The man who lived according to the flesh was one whose existence was determined by that which was visible and controllable, by that which he could manipulate and use as he chose. He who lived according to the Spirit had his existence determined by what God had done in Christ and was doing in the church. Such a man gave up all efforts to control his life and became a slave of God or Christ. This is what it meant to be in

Christ, to walk or live in the Spirit. It emphatically did
not mean to reject the world of the body, of matter. Paul
was much too good a Jew to be guilty of such an
essentially Oriental viewpoint.

Law and Gospel

This brings us to the final and in some respects the
most important word of the New Testament on sex,
which applies not alone to premarital relations, but to
the whole of human sexuality. Neither Jesus nor Paul
was asking for a rigid, moralistic control of one's desires
by the sheer exertion of will power. The life of the
kingdom was not to be entered by "being good" in
spite of strong desires to do otherwise. This would in
no wise distinguish the gospel from Judaism or Stoicism
or moralism in general. Jesus explicitly rejected such an
understanding in his word, "You have heard that it was
said, 'You shall not commit adultery.' But I say to you
that every one who looks at a woman lustfully has already committed adultery with her in his heart" (Matthew 5:27–28). The sheer suppression of lustful desires
represented the righteousness of the scribes and Pharisees, which must be exceeded by those who would enter the kingdom. What the New Testament was seeking
was not so much a transformation of behavior as a radical change in attitude, represented by the symbol,
"being born again." The Christian was one who had
abandoned all efforts to earn his salvation by being
good, recognizing that God's claim upon him was such

that he could never fulfill all that was demanded of him. He might be able to refrain from the more obvious sins of commission, but God's will is positive and the sins of omission accumulate daily. Furthermore, God claims not only a man's acts but his heart and mind and soul, and who can pretend to himself that he has a purity of heart that can stand before the divine gaze which probes to the depths? Jesus' word cited above makes adulterers of us all. Yes, and murderers too, for who has not known what it means to hate?

The good news of the gospel is not that we should be good. That, as Reinhold Niebuhr has observed, is not good news at all. It is bad news. For the fact of the matter is that none of us is good. Jesus himself declared that none is good save God. The good news of the gospel is that God loves us in spite of the fact that we are unlovable, that God forgives us in spite of the fact that we are unforgivable, that he accepts us in spite of our unacceptability. When this truth is seen and grasped in the depth of a man's soul, he has become a new creature. He gives up his anxious and fretful attempts to save his own life and loses it—to God. He finds his life by throwing it away. In becoming a captive, he is set free. He is liberated from all of the concerns of the world, including the Law. He loves the God who has spoken to him the saving word in Jesus Christ and trusts utterly in the divine grace. The Spirit is now the determining power in his life, and there is no longer a strenuous struggle with one's inner lusts, desperately striving to hold them in check. Rather, one's inner desires are transformed. Where previously one sought out of his own emptiness selfishly to use others as a means of reassuring the self or augmenting the self, he now seeks to serve, to give—not out of his own resources, but out of what has been given to him in Christ. He is no longer a pauper, impoverished and grasping. To him have been given the riches of Christ and he has become a philanthropist, scattering the coins of God's goodness in prodigal extravagance.

Paul did not mean, any more than Jesus, that the Christian becomes a plaster saint, that henceforth he will never do anything wrong. Nor did he mean that once one has made the decision for Christ, he has finished the course and need trouble himself no longer. The decision must be made daily, even hourly—moment by moment. Paul commented that he died daily to the old man and rose daily to newness of life in Christ. Even so, he did not become perfect. "Not," he said, "that I have already attained." He knew better than that. Freedom from sin means simply that one is free from the compulsion to sin, the compulsion to live anxiously and selfishly. Of course, one will err, will make mistakes. That is inescapable so long as one is human. But the Christian no longer is determined by his worldly or fleshly concerns. A new dimension has been added to his existence, and he is open to the possibilities of the future, where before he was the prisoner of the past.

There is a striking analogy to this in contemporary

psychotherapy. The neurotic is one who suffers from what Seward Hiltner has called "dated emotions," from the compulsion to act and to feel according to patterns established early in life. He suffers from reminiscences, as Freud put it. He cannot respond to new situations in the present or future with spontaneity and creativity. He is rigidly bound by his past. Successful therapy does not render him a superman, a paragon of virtue and wisdom. It does not guarantee him against error or pain. It only sets him free from compulsion, free to live in the "now" of the present and the "not yet" of days to come. Nor is therapy a "once-for-all." Analysis is both terminable and interminable, according to Freud. Terminable in the sense that the patient need no longer lie on the couch for his daily hour. Interminable in the sense that the processes of self-understanding and insight set in motion by the therapy continue throughout the rest of a man's life. So the Christian, as the New Testament sees him, is set free to make his own choices, really to make his own decisions instead of being driven by subterranean forces beyond his control. But he must go on making his decisions every day. He will go wrong, of course. He will misjudge and misunderstand. But he will not waste his energies in vain regrets. His failures are not decisive in his existence. He presses on to the high mark of his calling in Christ Jesus.

This means, concretely, that the Christian is set free from moralistic legalism, from "other-directed" efforts to win the approval or avoid the censure of society by suppressing his desires and conforming to some arbitrarily set standard of behavior. Whatever he does is not to please men at all but to please the Lord, to the glory of God. He is free from all externally imposed laws, including even the biblical law. The apostle Paul would be horrified to discover what the church has done with his epistles. He who battled so strenuously against the Judaizers and the exaltation of the Torah would struggle today against ecclesiastical efforts to impose conformity to his writings. The time has come when we need a new Epistle to the Galatians to free us from the legalism of the New Testament. Luther broke the shackles of medieval moralism, but Protestantism has only cast the irons into a melting pot, remolded them and fastened them again upon the limbs of Western Christendom. To this extent, the armies of sexual liberty are right in their war against the defenders of the *status quo,* who include within their ranks the churches, both Catholic and Protestant. To be sure, the former confuse liberty with libertinism, and therefore must be resisted. But the resistance must come not in the name of tyranny. That is why, in our present situation, a victory for either side in the struggle would be a calamity. Either to silence the opposition to traditional sexual standards or to destroy those standards for the sake of individual license would be a serious error. "Behold," said the apostle Paul, "I show you a more excellent way."

The New Testament maintains a dialectic of tension between the moralism of Jewish legalism on the one hand, and the libertinism of Graeco-Roman paganism on the other. To the former, the gospel was a scandal, and to the latter it was foolishness. The Pharisees, against whom Jesus had to contend, and the Judaizers, the enemies of Paul, are still with us. They set up their standard of law, strictly forbidding any and all sexual relations outside of marriage. Nor are the Gentiles of Hellenistic days no more to be seen. Still there are the apostles of license, of sexual *carte blanche*, who argue for the freedom of the individual to act as he chooses, pointing to the wide variations of sexual behavior not only in other mammals, other societies, but even within our own society. As the pagans of old, they remark with a shrug, "Each to his own taste." All else is a moralistic violation of individual liberty. They do not defend violence or the seduction or perversion of the young; but between two partners who are willing and responsible, anything goes. To the Jews of today, the gospel of liberty is scandalous, for it refuses to deal with human beings as bound by laws; and to the contemporary Gentiles, the gospel is foolishness because it insists that "you are not your own."

The heirs of the Torah, the defenders of the right, are frightened that Christian freedom will lead young people astray, that premarital relations will multiply, grown in a culture of rationalization. The only alternative seems to them to utter a clear, unequivocal "Thou

shalt not." Anything else is to open the doors to moral
chaos. What they do not seem to realize is the growing
futility and failure of all their earnest endeavors. They
refuse to take the Kinsey reports seriously. The clock
cannot be turned back. The young cannot be kept
down on the farm after they've seen Paree. The only
direction open now is forward. The question, realisti-
cally, is only whether we shall move forward to responsible liberty or to irresponsible license. The gospel of
license has its apostles in considerable numbers, but
where are the prophets of Christian freedom? Those
few who are bold enough to raise their voices are
haled before the Sanhedrin of the present and accused
of blasphemy, encouraging immorality, attacking the
very foundations of the Temple. The command to
silence is loud and imperious. Thus the young are left
with but two choices: to remain within the gates of
propriety or to desert to the pagans, to frolic with the
Gentiles, to pet, to play, to fornicate, slowly burning
out all pangs of conscience until sexual pleasure becomes an end in itself without regard to considerations
of personality.

The New Testament offers a third choice, a way out
of this dilemma. The gospel of Christian liberty offers
escape from a rigid legalism which says implicitly, if not
explicitly, what the young know to be false—that sex is
shameful. Biblical faith proclaims the goodness of all the
created world, including sexuality. It also declares, however, that man is more than an animal, that he is his

brother's keeper, that he has a responsibility for his neighbor. He who loves the God revealed in Jesus Christ also loves all those in whose midst God has set him down. In every human encounter he meets God, who demands of him a response. Each encounter is absolutely unique, defying calculation or prescription by law. To walk through life according to the rules is to live by the letter which kills. One must walk in the Spirit which gives life. One must trust in the Spirit and his guidance, "proving all things" and doing all things to the glory of God. Should a young couple kiss good-night? Should they engage in prolonged necking in the back seat of a car? Should they pet? Where should they stop; how far is it "all right" for them to go? The Law has its answers, but it kills. The life-giving Spirit never speaks in abstractions. Only in the concrete event, only in the personal encounter, is his voice to be heard. And he liberates from the lower levels of law, enabling the Christian to climb the heights of love. And one need not be anxious, for "love is patient and kind. . . . Love does not insist on its own way . . . it does not rejoice at wrong but rejoices in the right. Love bears all things, believes all things, hopes all things, endures all things . . . and the greatest of these is love."

8

SEX

IN

MARRIAGE

❧

THE MAJOR PROBLEM of our time in marital sex relations appears to be one of technique. There are numerous volumes on the market which instruct couples, who either are married or are about to be married, in the arts and skills of making love to each other. This is not a new subject matter for authors. Ovid, as we saw in Chapter 6, produced a poetic treatise for his own age on the mysteries of Eros, and India has long known a document called the *Kamsutra* (barred from circulation in the proper West) which describes the various postures and possibilities of coitus in incredible detail. Our own literature is somewhat more reticent, or at least more coldly scientific, but the aim is the same: the initiation of the reader into the cult of successful sexual performance.

Recently some heretics have suggested that such literature is almost entirely useless. Persons whose psychosexual development and orientation enable them to perform adequately do not need these aids, and those whose warped personalities distort their sexual capacities will find that no books of any kind can help them. Indeed, one psychoanalyst[1] points to the paradox that the very people who eagerly pore over books on sex technique are usually the ones whose sex adjustment is most unsatisfactory. Some of the literature may be worse than useless; it may do positive harm. So alarmist is it in describing the dangers of the wedding night, so sentimental and romantic in singing the joys of love, that it awakens needless anxieties and tensions as well as false expectations in those who follow the guidebook to the marriage bed. A growing consensus regards sexual incompatibilities in marriage as symptoms of a deeper, more fundamental disturbance in the interpersonal relationship. When the latter is worked through and re-

---

[1] Milton Sapirstein, *Paradoxes of Everyday Life* (New York: Random House, 1955).

solved, the former takes care of itself. Sex in marriage, in
other words, is a symbol of the union as a totality. A
good marriage produces a good sex life; a bad marriage
results in an unsatisfactory sex life. And in both cases,
a circular situation is set up where the sexual life rein-
forces and deepens the patterns, either for good or for
ill. This understanding of the place of sex in marriage
is remarkably close to the biblical view.

THE OLD TESTAMENT

It is important first of all to know what the Old Testament means by marriage. There are two stories of creation in the opening chapters of Genesis. The first (Genesis
1:1–2:4a) is comparatively late in composition, dating
from the period in Israel's history after the Babylonian exile. Its priestly authors represented the Deity and
his creative activity in a highly sophisticated fashion.
God sends his Spirit upon the face of the waters and
creates by simple *fiat*. He speaks and it is done. Man
stands at the climax of the six days' work. "Then God
said, 'Let us make man in our image, after our likeness;
and let them have dominion over the fish of the sea, and
over the birds of the air, and over the cattle, and over all
the earth, and over every creeping thing that creeps
upon the earth.' So God created man in his own image,
in the image of God he created him; male and female he
created them. And God blessed them, and God said to
them, 'Be fruitful and multiply, and fill the earth and

subdue it.'" (Genesis 1:26–28.) This narrative has become so much a part of the Western cultural heritage
that its uniqueness is obscured in its being taken for
granted. Most primitive peoples, it is true, have some
form of creation myth or legend, but there are two important respects in which Genesis differs from the stories
which have grown out of other cultures.

In the first place, not all peoples have universally regarded creation as a good thing. The Orient has characteristically tended to view it as an accident or a
calamity, a fall out of pure spirituality into illusion or
Maya. The Genesis story repeats the refrain like a chant,
"And God saw that it was good." The material world
does not stand opposed to the divine purpose and plan
but is a part of it. In the second place, there are numerous creation myths which represent man as having been
created not as male and female but rather as androgynous, a sort of hermaphrodite containing both sets of
reproductive organs. The split into two sexes is seen as
the result of a fall, a divine punishment visited upon human pride or sin. Such a view is presented with great
imagination and beauty by Aristophanes in Plato's *Symposium* and is used there to explain the driving force of
love and sexuality. Those who were originally one strive
feverishly to reunite their bodies. This is a myth also
widely popular in Oriental cultures. As Sandor Rado has
commented, observing that sexual partners sometimes
feel curiosity and even envy at the capacity for enjoy-
ment possessed by the other, this fact "may have in-

spired one Hindu mystic of antiquity to invent the doctrine of bisexuality; to be both male and female, a pair
by oneself, is a perfect dream; it leaves nothing to be
envied and nothing to be feared."[2] In contrast to this,
the Old Testament sees sexuality as a fact of creation.
It is not the result of a fall, a rupture in the created
order, but a feature of the divine will. "Male and female
he created them." Thus the Bible stands eternally opposed to any and all efforts to make of sex something
evil or subspiritual. It is God's word and God's work
that are responsible for human sexuality, which is therefore good.

Genesis 2:4b–24 contains a second account of creation, which dates in composition from the ninth century
B.C., but is unquestionably based upon an oral tradition
much older than that. Long before the story was written
down, it was passed by word of mouth from parents to
children through countless generations. Far less sophisticated and more primitive than the account in Genesis
1, the story depicts God forming man from the dust of
the ground, breathing life into the nostrils of this lump of
clay, casting a deep sleep upon him and removing a rib
which is transformed into woman. The Hebrew word
for man as distinct from woman is *ish*, while the term
for man as a generic term, distinct from animals, is *adam*.
The term for woman is *ishshah*. Here again man (*adam*)

---

[2] Sandor Rado, "An Adaptational View of Sexual Behavior," in
Psychosexual Development in Health and Disease, Hoch and Zabin,
eds. (New York: Grune & Stratton, 1949), p. 162.

is created male (*ish*) and female (*ishshah*), but now something new has been added. In the first place, the two
sexes are not created simultaneously but in sequence, a
symbol (or so it has been used) of the ontological priority and hence superiority of the male. So the apostle
Paul could write, "For man was not made from woman,
but woman from man. Neither was man created for
woman, but woman for man" (1 Corinthians 11:8–9).
And in the second place, the reason why woman was
created is because "it is not good that the man (*adam*)
should be alone" (Genesis 2:18). God tried first to find
a helper for man by creating the beasts of the field and
the birds of the air, and the man gave names to them
all, "but for the man there was not found a helper fit
for him." Only out of himself, only that which is "bone
of my bones and flesh of my flesh" could be a companion
to him. "She shall be called Woman (*ishshah*) because
she was taken out of Man (*ish*)" (Genesis 2:23). And the
narrative concludes with the profound observation that
"a man leaves his father and his mother and cleaves to
his wife; and they become one flesh."

This narrative points to the fact that woman, according to the biblical view, is the doorway into community.
Without her there is only *ish*, there is no *adam*. Full
humanity is not "alone"; it demands relatedness not
simply to the Other that is God but also to the other
that is the partner. Thus at the very beginning of the
Bible, marriage is instituted by God as a symbol of man's
need for the companionship of at least one other person

in order really to be man. A baby isolated from all human contact will not, if it survives, grow up to be a human but an animal. Human nature is not something that develops automatically, as does monkey nature or bird nature or fish nature. It requires the nurture of other humans to bring it out. Without community it remains an unrealized potentiality. This is the ontology of man. Robinson Crusoe is possible because he grew up in society and experienced isolation later, but Tarzan of the Apes is an utter impossibility, for he was isolated from birth and would be only an ape without as much body hair or pigmentation of the skin as his companions in the jungle. Marriage in the Old Testament is the symbol of community, and for this reason every Hebrew was expected to enter wedlock. Jeremiah was an object of curiosity because of his single state. Adam without Eve is not really *adam*.

In Hebrew life a man did not in fact leave his father and his mother and cleave to his wife. This verse may represent an echo of a time when the wife remained in the home of her parents and was visited there by her husband. But no man ever left his father and mother entirely. He remained a part of his father's household and family so long as his father was alive, when the leadership passed to the eldest brother. Occasionally an unusually strong or gifted individual might by his outstanding accomplishments establish a "house" of his own, as Joseph or David, both of whom were younger brothers, comparatively low on the totem pole of succession. But Joseph remained the son of Jacob, as David was forever the son of Jesse. Neither ever imagined that he was leaving his father's "house." In practice, it was rather the wife who forsook her family to join her destiny to her husband's forbears and descendants. This is the significance of the *mohar,* the bride-price, which was compensation to the woman's father for his loss. Her family continued to exercise interest in her and responsibility for her, in the event that her husband should mistreat her or take unfair advantage of her. Naomi, left without husband or sons in distant Moab, returned to her father's house.

But regardless of who left whose parents, it is clear that the Hebrews saw marriage as a cleaving together which created one flesh, perfectly symbolized in the children which were to be expected. They are indeed the blending of two into one in an absolutely indissoluble way. One can say, "he has his mother's eyes, or his father's nose," but can the child be divided? He is to both parents equally "bone of my bones and flesh of my flesh." The sexual union of man and wife itself creates one flesh between them, and the children are the symbol and the fruit of that union. No religious ceremony took place in Israel; no marriage license was issued. The "state," such as it was, never intervened, nor did the "church." Marriage was a family affair, arranged by the two sets of parents and consummated by the couple themselves in the sexual act. Sex was itself the ceremony, as the law makes abundantly clear. A man lying with an unbetrothed maiden made her his wife by that act. He was compelled to pay her father the *mohar* and to keep her in his household for life. So the apostle Paul argued that a man lying with a prostitute became "one flesh" with her.

The Old Testament uses the verb "to know" (*yada*) frequently to indicate sexual relations. This usage was by no means confined to marital coitus, though it is clear that such "knowledge" belonged ideally in marriage. The Hebrew was not being delicate about sexuality, substituting the phrase "he knew her" for some expression more direct or coarse. The choice of words was deliberate, as Otto Piper has pointed out in his book *The Christian Interpretation of Sex*. What is, in fact, conveyed in sexual intercourse is a knowledge both of one's self and of another. No man really knows what it means to be a man until he has experienced sex with a woman; and every woman is similarly innocent until she has had relations with a man. This is the knowledge about which youth expresses insatiable curiosity. Not simply "the facts of life," the familiar and agonizing parental lecture on the birds and the bees and the flowers. That is merely words, an abstraction from life. What the young seek is firsthand knowledge, the experience itself. So Professor Piper places great emphasis upon the first act of coitus, for it is there that the secret is unlocked, the knowledge attained. Now at last one knows the essence of masculinity and femininity. Here the two become "one flesh." But the Old Testament does not confine the use of "knowing" to first coitus, and this again deliberately, with the unconscious profundity so often displayed. For there are always deeper levels of knowledge to be plumbed, knowledge of one's self and of another.

If, as we suggested at the beginning of this chapter, sex is in some sense central to and symbolic of the marriage relationship, then as a man and his wife grow in mutual understanding and ability to communicate themselves to one another, this growth is expressed in and deepened by their sexual intercourse. The word intercourse itself means communication. Carried to its highest level, this reaches the point when the man and his wife are naked and unashamed. They know one another fully and accept each other completely. This is the essence of the marital union, symbolized in the perfection of Eden before the Fall. It is this knowledge which is sought through all of the existential distortions of marriage as it is experienced in the world of sin and estrangement. Hosea traced the sins of Israel, who had been a faithless wife to Yahweh, to her lack of knowledge of God. She had never known him properly and had therefore gone astray in her national life. This viewpoint is amazingly Freudian. The good Doctor Sigmund believed that neurosis was caused by a disturbance in the sex life. Hosea declared Israel's iniquities traceable to her failure to know God aright. Freud asserted that no neurosis is possible with a normal *vita sexualis*. Hosea promised Israel forgiveness and restoration if only she would truly know her God. Sex symbolizes selfhood. As goes a man's interpersonal relations in general, so goes his sexual orientation. Insofar as a marriage is sound, its sexual aspect will also prove sound and satisfying to both partners. Any disturbance in the marriage will quickly reflect itself in a disturbed sexual relationship. Not that marital harmony can be attained through the direct pursuit of sexual harmony, through consulting books on technique. That is to place the horse behind the cart. Sexual happiness follows marital happiness, not vice versa, though certainly a basically good relationship between husband and wife is deepened and reinforced by their sexual sharing.

But even on a superficial level, in a shaky marriage, or outside of marriage, sex does communicate knowledge. One always learns something about another in shared sexuality. Where the knowledge is without guilt or shame, as in marriage, it leads to trust and the willingness to explore and to communicate further. Where the knowledge is acquired clandestinely or illicitly, it leads to putting on "aprons," to hiding even levels of the personality which have been revealed before. A man and woman who have been close friends frequently find that an adulterous episode raises barriers between them that did not previously exist, though they have known each other more intimately than ever. One of the problems with sexuality in our own age is its association with status and self-esteem. It has become extraordinarily important in our society to be able to perform sexually, and not just to perform but to perform well. There is

widespread anxiety about frigidity in women and im-
potence in men. Both of these conditions are relative, to
be sure. Their extremes are pathological and seldom encountered, but fear of partial affliction is widespread in
both sexes. To enter a sexual liaison with another is
therefore to know and to be known in one's erotic capacities. That is why "the chase" in premarital or extramarital affairs is so often more exciting than the fulfillment, for the latter involves a revelation and a risk.
Flirtation is safe. One is not required to stand and deliver, to submit to being known. One can maintain an
aura of mystery, a promise of things to come. The reality
may prove to be far less satisfying than the anticipation.
This is the insight of Philip Wylie, who remarked in one
of his novels that illicit sexual affairs prove in the majority of cases to be disappointing when they enter the
realm of reality and leave the realm of the imagination,
which is their legitimate place.

So far as techniques of coitus are concerned, the Old
Testament is almost silent. Sex was to be reserved for
marriage, if one was a woman, though the man had
somewhat greater freedom, as we have seen. But there
are no directions as to how or when a married couple
should copulate—with a few exceptions, presently to be
noted. Nor, with similar exceptions, are there prohibitions as to manner or posture of intercourse. The laws
of many states rendering it a crime to engage in certain
variations of position have no biblical warrant. They
represent a *consensus gentium* of Western civilization

rather than a Judeo-Christian prejudice. The Old Testament does regard a menstruating woman as "unclean," as it also looks upon a woman newly delivered of a child and a man who has had an emission of semen. But the Law was not entirely consistent at this point. Leviticus 20:18 declares: "If a man lies with a woman having her sickness, and uncovers her nakedness, he has made naked her fountain, and she has uncovered the fountain of her blood; both of them shall be cut off from among their people." Exile or death was the punishment decreed for sexual relations during menstruation. But Leviticus 15:19–24 was far less severe. "When a woman has a discharge of blood which is her regular discharge from her body, she shall be in her impurity for seven days, and whoever touches her shall be unclean until the evening. . . . And if any man lies with her, and her impurity is on him, he shall be unclean seven days; and every bed on which he lies shall be unclean." The only penalty here was the attribution of a week's ceremonial defilement from which one could be ritually purified. This may represent a later softening of the earlier law which proved in practice to be too harsh.

"If a man has an emission of semen, he shall bathe his whole body in water, and be unclean until the evening. And every garment and every skin on which the semen comes shall be washed with water, and be unclean until the evening. If a man lies with a woman and has an emission of semen, both of them shall bathe themselves in water, and be unclean until the evening" (Leviticus

15:16–18). The text is unclear at this point as to what was meant. Was this a spontaneous emission, the so-called "wet dream"? Or was it premature ejaculation or even *coitus interruptus?* The Roman Catholic interpretation of the sin of Onan (Genesis 38:1–10) would emphatically rule out the last-named possibility, but this is a passage much in dispute, and no light is shed elsewhere. It is perfectly apparent that the Old Testament regards sexual emissions as what the French call *sacré,* which means both sacred and taboo. In men *and* women sexual discharges from the body rendered the person ritually "unclean." But this is not to suggest that sex was itself regarded as impure or contaminating. There is no indication in the Law that a married couple were rendered unclean by their coitus. No cleansing or purifying ceremony was required after sexual relations, although Exodus 19:14–15 directed that the people shall prepare for their solemn covenant with Yahweh by washing their garments and refraining from sex. Moses said to the people: "Be ready by the third day; do not go near a woman." Only where some bodily discharge was involved, whether of semen, of menstrual blood, or of the waters surrounding the foetus in the womb, was impurity incurred. And such a defilement was by no means confined to sexual substances. A bodily discharge of any sort rendered the person unclean and suspect as a carrier of contamination. He must be isolated until the discharge cleared up completely, and then go through an elaborate ritual for purification. In the Near East, where skin diseases that are highly infectious abounded, where leprosy was a common affliction, such precautionary measures were altogether sensible.

The awe and fear of menstrual blood and of semen probably had another origin than mere hygienic concern. The Hebrews always regarded blood as the source of life, and placed the strongest taboos around the eating of blood. "The life of every creature is the blood (*dam*) of it; therefore I have said to the people of Israel, You shall not eat the blood of any creature, for the life of every creature is its blood; whoever eats it shall be cut off" (Leviticus 17:14). Some of Israel's neighbors, whose religion consisted of nature cults, as we have seen, practiced the eating of raw flesh and the drinking of blood as a part of their orgiastic rituals. This is a phenomenon widely encountered in primitive religions worshiping nature and fertility. The thought behind the act seemed to be that he who ate the flesh and drank the blood of an animal took into himself the life, the power, and the strength of the sacrificial victim. Totemism, i.e., the worship of an ancestor-animal and a ritual meal, is clearly indicated here, and vestiges of cannibalism are by no means out of the question. Whatever the background, Israel was to have no part in such practices. The blood was to be offered to Yahweh. It was a link between God and man. Every bloody discharge, therefore, whether a normal menstrual flow or not, rendered a woman unclean, as it did everything she touched (Leviticus 15:25–30).

It does not require any forcing at all to extend the taboos surrounding blood as the locus of life to semen as a similar source. The male discharge rendered one impure only for the rest of the day, while the female contamination lasted a week. Was this the prejudice of a patriarchal society, equivalent to the disparity of defilement incurred by the mother of a female as against a male child? "If a woman conceives, and bears a male child, then she shall be unclean seven days; as at the time of her menstruation, she shall be unclean. And on the eighth day the flesh of his foreskin shall be circumcised. Then she shall continue for thirty-three days in the blood of her purifying; she shall not touch any hallowed thing, nor come into the sanctuary, until the days of her purifying are completed. But if she bears a female child, then she shall be unclean for two weeks, as in her menstruation; and she shall continue in the blood of her purifying for sixty-six days" (Leviticus 12:2–5). As the delivery of a female child meant greater impurity than that of a male, so menstrual blood was more taboo than semen. But it may be that this prejudice was merely that attached to blood in general. Or there may have been an economic factor involved. The male simply could not afford to spend so much time in purification rites.

That Israel's superstitious fear of sexual discharges did not at all lessen her appreciation of sex as a gift of God to be enjoyed is obvious. The permission of polygamy, the Levirate marriage, the expectation of

marriage and children, all point to a positive attitude
toward sexuality. If Israel was to go to war, the question was asked, "What man is there that has betrothed
a wife and has not taken her? Let him go back to his
house, lest he die in battle and another man take her"
(Deuteronomy 20:7). This privilege was extended still
further in Deuteronomy 24:5. "When a man is newly
married, he shall not go out with the army or be
charged with any business; he shall be free at home
one year, to be happy with his wife whom he has
taken." The King James Version is even more pictur-
esque here, reading "and shall cheer up his wife whom
he has taken."

However, there are two passages in the books of
Samuel which point to the connection between war
and sexual self-denial. The first of these comes in
1 Samuel 21, where David, in his flight from Saul,
paused at Nob and asked for bread for the young men
of the army with whom he indicated he had an appoint-
ment. Ahimelech the priest replied, "I have no common
bread at hand, but there is holy bread; if only the
young men have kept themselves from women." And
David answered the priest, "Of a truth women have
been kept from us as always when I go on an expedi-
tion; the vessels of the young men are holy, even when
it is a common journey; how much more today will
their vessels be holy?" The other passage is found in
2 Samuel 11:11–13. Uriah, the husband of Bathsheba,
refused to oblige the king by going to the arms of his

wife and covering her adultery. To David's urgings, Uriah replied, "The ark and Israel and Judah dwell in booths; and my lord Joab and the servants of my lord are camping in the open field; shall I then go to my house, to eat and to drink, and to lie with my wife? As you live, and as your soul lives, I will not do this thing." And even David's making him drunk failed. "In the evening he went out to lie on his couch with the servants of his lord, but he did not go down to his house." This may have been simple loyalty to his comrades-in-arms, refusing to indulge himself in pleasures denied to them. But it may also have been a conviction that the soldier on a campaign must "keep himself from women." But these were exceptions to the rule that sex is the command of God.

The primary purpose of sex in marriage is a question of considerable dispute between Roman Catholic and Protestant churches, with particular implications for family planning and contraception. We shall return to this problem at the close of the chapter, trying to assess it from the perspectives of both Testaments of the Bible. Suffice it to say here only that the Old Testament throughout expected marriage of all, assumed that marriage means sexual intercourse and that both pleasure and offspring would result. Aside from the few prohibitions and taboos noted, Hebrew law and lore were silent on questions of sex technique in marriage. For that one must look elsewhere.

THE NEW TESTAMENT

As in the preceding section, before examining the few words the New Testament contains concerning sex in marriage, it is necessary to look first at marriage itself and its meaning. To begin with, the new age which had been inaugurated by the life and death and resurrection of Christ had radically called into question all human institutions, marriage among them. It was no longer necessary or even "normal" that all the chosen people of God should marry. It was no longer a calamity to be a virgin or childless wife. Celibacy was in the new aeon a gift of God, as was marriage. Some men, said Jesus, will make themselves eunuchs for the sake of the kingdom (Matthew 19:12), and Paul expressed the wish that all Christians were as he, that is, single (1 Corinthians 7:7). No man in the church was "alone," as Adam was, and therefore did not require a wife. Nor did he require offspring to carry on his name and line, to continue the chosen people of God so that their "name should not be blotted out." One's community was no longer his family; it was the church, wherein all who do the will of God were his brothers and sisters, father and mother, husband and wife. When the kingdom finally comes, there will be neither marriage nor giving in marriage. But as we saw in the previous chapter, the New Testament in no way disparages matrimony. On the contrary, it exalts it to a new state of sanctity.

The Epistle to the Ephesians stands at this point to the New Testament as the book of Hosea does to the Old. As the anguished prophet saw an analogy between his own relationship to his wife and that of God to Israel, so Ephesians saw marriage as a great mystery, reflecting the union between Christ and his Church. "Wives, be subject to your husbands, as to the Lord. For the husband is the head of the wife as Christ is the head of the church, his body, and is himself its Savior. As the church is subject to Christ, so let wives also be subject in everything to their husbands. Husbands, love your wives, as Christ loved the church and gave himself up for her, that he might sanctify her, having cleansed her by the washing of water with the word, that the church might be presented before him in splendor, without spot or wrinkle or any such thing, that she might be holy and without blemish. Even so husbands should love their wives as their own bodies. He who loves his wife loves himself. For no man ever hates his own flesh, but nourishes and cherishes it, as Christ does the church, because we are members of his body. 'For this reason a man shall leave his father and mother and be joined to his wife, and the two shall become one.' This is a great mystery, and I take it to mean Christ and the church; however, let each one of you love his wife as himself, and let the wife see that she respects her husband" (Ephesians 5:22–32).

The word "mystery" here is in the Greek *"mysterion."* Jerome rendered it into the Latin as *sacramentum* in his Vulgate Bible, with the result that Catholicism regards marriage as a sacrament, while Protestantism does not. But this is a semantic quarrel, depending on one's understanding of what makes a sacrament. If it is a "means of grace," then certainly marriage "in the Lord" (1 Corinthians 7:39) or "in the name of the Lord" (Colossians 3:17) fits the definition very well indeed. If it is "an outward and visible sign of an inward and invisible state," again the terminology is appropriate. This is one point at which Protestantism could well afford to surrender its traditional stiff-necked attitude toward Rome and move in the direction of a partial rapprochement. It is a curious irony that a celibate hierarchy should exalt matrimony to the position of a sacrament, while a married clergy, acquainted at first hand with the joy, the love, and the divine grace which flow through one's relationship with a beloved wife, should insist that matrimony is only an "ordinance." Eastern Orthodoxy and Anglicanism have found a *via media,* maintaining both a married clergy and a sacramental view of marriage.

Marriage was to be monogamous and for life. "A married woman is bound by law to her husband as long as he lives; but if her husband dies she is discharged from the law concerning the husband. Accordingly, she will be called an adulteress if she lives with another man while her husband is alive. But if her

husband dies she is free from that law, and if she
marries another man she is not an adulteress" (Romans
7:2–3). Paul made the same point in the First Epistle
to the Corinthians, though there with a qualification.
"If the husband dies, she is free to be married to whom
she wishes, only in the Lord. But in my judgment she
is happier if she remains as she is. And I think that I
have the Spirit of God" (1 Corinthians 7:39–40). The
Pastoral Epistles are the subject of some scholarly dispute on this point, touching on the question as to
whether bishops (*episcopoi*), presbyters (*presbyteroi*),
and deacons (*diakonoi*) have the right to marry a second time in the event of their being widowed. The
phrase "the husband of one wife," as the Greek has it,
appears three times in the Pastorals (1 Timothy 3:2, 12;
Titus 1:6), and the Revised Standard Version translates,
"married only once." The meaning is obviously somewhat opaque as to the privileges of the widowed clergy,
but it is clear that the clergy were to be monogamous
as long as their wives were alive. Nor could marriages
be contracted with just anyone. The various barriers
to incest still held (1 Corinthians 5:1); a second marriage was possible only if the first partner were dead,
unless that partner should be "an unbeliever" and wish
to separate (1 Corinthians 7:12–16); one should not
marry outside the church but "in the Lord" (1 Corinthians 7:39). This question of divorce and remarriage
will be discussed more fully in the next chapter.

Marriages were to be holy: everything that the Chris-

tian did was to be "to the glory of God," and the
marriage of Christians was no exception. They were in
their relationship to show forth the new life which had
been bestowed upon them, living together in love and
mutual devotion and sacrifice. Their love was not to be
purely sensual, "like the heathen who do not know
God," but rather self-renunciatory for the sake of the
other, even as Christ gave himself to and for the
church. When Paul directed that women were not permitted to "speak" in the churches, the Greek verb he
used was *lalein,* which means literally "to gossip"
(1 Corinthians 14:34). He wanted Christian marriages
to be examples to the Gentile world—examples not of
strife, jockeying for position and power, but of a well-
ordered and happy relationship. Each couple had, then,
a missionary function to perform; to display marriage
as God intended it should be. This meant that the man
was the head of the household and the woman accepted
his leadership. But his authority was always exercised
in love, even as Christ's authority over the church was
expressed by his love. In her submission, the woman
emulated Christ who "humbled himself and became
obedient" (Philippians 2:8). Wives were to "be subject
to your husbands, as is fitting in the Lord," but husbands were enjoined, "Love your wives, and do not be
harsh with them" (Colossians 3:18–19).

Marriage is thus exalted by the New Testament to
heights of significance and sanctity unknown in the old
covenant. "Let marriage be held in honor among all,

and let the marriage bed be undefiled; for God will judge the immoral and adulterous" (Hebrews 13:4). Jesus sought to restore matrimony to its state as intended by God at creation. "What therefore God has joined together, let not man put asunder" (Mark 10:9). So lofty a view did the Master put forth that even the disciples responded with some trepidation. "If such is the case," they said, "of a man with his wife, it is not expedient to marry." And Jesus responded, "Not all men can receive this precept, but only those to whom it is given" (Matthew 19:10–11). Adultery was not merely the violation of another man's household, the trespass upon the rights of a fellow male, threatening the security of his bloodline, but a violation of his own unity with his wife, a breaking of his state of "one flesh" (*henosis*). And adultery was not of the body only but also of the heart, "for out of the heart come evil thoughts, murder, adultery, fornication" (Matthew 15:19). Since this was true, adultery had already been committed by a lustful look or a libidinous desire (Matthew 5:27–28).

But the heights to which the New Testament rises in its visions of the possibilities of marriage "in the Lord" do not block its view of the realities of sex. The apostle Paul revealed a healthy realism in his counsels to married couples. "It is well," he said, "for a man not to touch a woman. But because of the temptation to immorality, each man should have his own wife and each woman her own husband. The husband should give to his wife her conjugal rights, and likewise the wife to her husband. For the wife does not rule over her own body, but the husband does; likewise the husband does not rule over his own body, but the wife does. Do not refuse one another except perhaps by agreement for a season, that you may devote yourselves to prayer; but then come together again, lest Satan tempt you through lack of self-control. I say this by way of concession, not of command. I wish that all were as I myself am. But each has his own special gift from God, one of one kind and one of another. To the unmarried and the widows I say that it is well for them to remain single as I do. But if they cannot exercise self-control, they should marry. For it is better to marry than to be aflame with passion" (1 Corinthians 7:1–9).

On the one hand, this passage appears to present a somewhat negative attitude toward sex. A man is told that it is better for him not to touch a woman, that the apostle wished that all were single as he was, and if one had been unfortunate enough to get married and been left alone by the death of the spouse, then he or she should take advantage of this good fortune and remain alone. There is no blinking away Paul's prejudices. They are there. But it is important to recognize why they are there. Paul was no Gnostic, no Hellenistic dualist, counseling asceticism and self-denial out of contempt for the body. His advice about marriage was set against the background of what he called "the impending distress. . . . the appointed time has grown

very short. . . . the form of this world is passing away"
(1 Corinthians 7:26–31). Paul believed firmly that the
end of the world was at hand and that the end would
be preceded by a time of troubles in which "the man
of lawlessness, the son of perdition" would reign and
rage. Therefore, the fewer earthly concerns binding any
Christian, the freer he would be, the more single-
minded he would prove in the day of decision.

And Paul realized that not all men were in fact as
he was. "Each has his own special gift from God, one
of one kind and one of another." Some do possess the
ability to remain single, to dedicate themselves to celibacy. But others have the gift of love and marriage.
To such as these, Paul gave sound advice. If, he said,
you want to refrain from sexual relations for a time, by
all means feel free to do so. But be careful not to let
such conjugal vacations last too long. You are, after
all, only human, with understandable human appetites
and needs. And if you deny those over an extended
period, you weaken your resistance to temptation. Remember that the city of Corinth in particular abounds
in temptation, in constant opportunities and induce-
ments to satisfy sexual desires. Therefore, you wives,
if your husbands are obviously in need of sexual expression, do not deny them. And you husbands, show
a like consideration for your wives. You are both far
better off to give your sexual needs satisfaction in your
marital relationship than to be guilty of adultery with

another, either in action or in inner thought and desire.
And if you are "aflame with passion," it is clear that
you cannot "please the Lord." So if your libidinal urges
are strong, you had better maintain a vigorous sex life
within your marriage. In doing this, you do not sin.

Here the apostle reveals the dialectical position he
occupied between the two extremes of Corinth in particular and the Graeco-Roman world in general. He did
not agree with those who regarded all sexuality as sinful, counseling celibacy for everyone. But he did not,
on the other hand, share the prevailing moral indifferentism which was blithely unconcerned about the
nature and circumstance of sexual activity. Sex for the
Christian, he said, belongs in marriage, in a context of
love and fidelity. He was unequivocal in his opposition
to prostitution (1 Corinthians 6:15–20), to homosexuality (Romans 1:26 ff., 1 Corinthians 6:9–10), to adultery,
to sexual impurity (*porneia*) of any kind. But in marriage, sex was no sin. It had its legitimate place as an
expression of love and as a symbol of the way in which
man and wife continually minister to one another's
needs. A false prudery is dangerous, opening the doors
of temptation.

SEX AND PROCREATION

This brings us to the thorny question of the biblical
view of the purpose of sex in marriage. The ways of

Roman Catholicism and Protestantism sharply divide at this crossroads, and the way of God's truth is obscured by the mists of human finitude. From the end of the first century, when the rift between Judaism and the new faith became complete, and Christianity found itself a totally Gentile movement, the force of asceticism became increasingly strong. Virginity and celibacy were exalted, for which, it must be confessed, there was some warrant in the Pauline Epistles, especially First Corinthians. There were numerous attempts to sever the church altogether from its Jewish roots and to make it essentially another Hellenistic mystery cult. This involved, among other things, a depreciation of the material world, including the body and sexuality. The church for the most part successfully resisted these efforts and continued faithful to its Hebrew heritage, retaining the Old Testament as sacred Scripture. But by the time of Augustine in the fourth century A.D. two points had been firmly established within the Christian tradition: first, that virginity and celibacy were superior to marriage; and second, that the only religious justification for sex was procreation. That sex and reproduction go hand in hand, both Judaism and Christianity had believed, but Augustine went one step further and insisted that each and every act of sexual intercourse ought to be procreative in intention. Otherwise, sin was incurred. If a husband made love to his wife without the conscious desire to impregnate her,

his sin was venial,[3] covered by the sacramental grace
of matrimony but nonetheless a sin. The wife who
allowed herself to be loved on such terms was without
sin, since she merely rendered the so-called "marriage
debt." According to Paul, her body was not her own
but her husband's. Therefore she must allow him to
use it even with impure motivation, lest he be tempted
to worse sins, sins which might be mortal rather than
merely venial. This "marriage debt" was a double indemnity, applying equally to both sexes, for the husband's body was not his own either, and a wife also
was capable of venial sin.

Sex without intent to impregnate was therefore
grudgingly permitted, but sex which in any way pre-
vented or blocked the possibility of fertilization was
intolerable. *Coitus interruptus* or contraception was
strictly forbidden. This Augustinian principle was elaborated by medieval scholasticism, and remains the basis
for Roman Catholic opposition to all forms of birth
control which are "unnatural." The so-called "rhythm
method," which Augustine explicitly condemned, is
permitted for serious reasons, i.e., the frail health of
the mother or financial straits of the family, and Catholics are encouraged to consult their confessors to as-
sure their consciences that the reasons are weighty and

---

[3] In 1 Corinthians 7:6 Paul wrote, "I say this by way of concession,
not of command." The Greek for "concession" is *sungnomen,* or "allowance for individual differences." Jerome translated this into Latin
as *veniam,* meaning "necessitating pardon," whence comes the whole
concept of venial sins.

not selfish or trivial. Such a use of the regular menstrual cycle is not unnatural and therefore is not against God's law. But either *coitus interruptus* or the use of mechanical or chemical devices is contrary to the dictates of nature and therefore also forbidden by divine law. Modern Roman Catholicism teaches that there is a secondary purpose for sex in marriage: the expression of love or the quieting of lust, and that this secondary purpose is legitimate and right. But it must never be pursued in such a way that it blocks or interferes with the primary purpose, which is procreation.

The scriptural basis for all of this rests upon two fundamental passages: Genesis 38:1–11 and 1 Corinthians 7:2–6. The former of these is the story of Onan and his faithlessness to his obligation to his dead brother Er, who proved to be "wicked in the sight of Yahweh," and was therefore slain. "Then Judah [the father of Er and Onan] said to Onan, 'Go in to your brother's wife, and perform the duty of a brother-in-law to her, and raise up offspring for your brother.' But Onan knew that the offspring would not be his; so when he went in to his brother's wife he spilled the semen on the ground, lest he should give offspring to his brother. And what he did was displeasing in the sight of Yahweh and he slew him also." The text is not clear as to whether Onan practiced *coitus interruptus* or spilled his semen by masturbation. Roman Catholic interpreters extend the passage to cover both acts, which are regarded as mortal sins. They point to the fact that Onan paid for his deed with his life, while the penalty for refusing the responsibilities of the Levirate marriage was far milder. Such a man merely had his sandal removed and was forced to submit to being spat upon in the face before all the elders of the village. The Corinthian passages we have already quoted, where Paul called upon both husband and wife to give to one another the "conjugal rights," rendered in the Latin as "the marriage debt." This was advanced "because of the temptations to immorality" and by way of concession (*veniam*), not of command. But Roman Catholicism is rarely content to rest its moral teaching upon the single pillar of Scripture. It usually searches also for foundation in nature, in the "natural law." To Thomas Aquinas, the "Angelic Doctor" of Catholicism, it appeared clear that nature's primary concern in sex is with procreation, with an extravagant spawning of life in order to ensure survival. Therefore, any interference with nature's work is clearly to rebel against nature's Author, God himself.

This is the Roman Catholic position on sex and procreation. There is no single Protestant position on the question, since no one can speak with authority for all Protestants. Broadly speaking, however, one may say that many non-Roman Christians read both Scripture and nature in a different light. To begin with, there is no quarrel over the text in Genesis which conveys the divine command, "Be fruitful and multiply." It is clear from both nature and the Bible that God intended man to use sex to produce offspring. Protestantism does not advocate a selfish use of sex for purely sensual purposes. The phrase which has been widely adopted is "planned parenthood," not no parenthood. Sometimes in polemics with their Roman brethren, Protestants have appeared to be anti-family, to attempt to persuade people that they should not have children. But this is not characteristic. All Christians share the belief that love always moves out from itself. Even God was not content to remain in his lone perfection, but created the world and man out of his love. There are serious questions to be raised about the love of any man and wife who fearfully hoard their affection for one another, unable or unwilling to share what they have, afraid that a child might prove to be a rival. Such persons do not know the parable of the talents, do not understand the meaning of the story of the feeding of the five thousand. He who jealously and anxiously clings to what he has been given loses it in spite of all his care, while he who risks his talent upon the open market of life, who gives it away, even if it is only a few loaves of bread and a handful of fish, finds that the supply is inexhaustible and that at the end he gathers up more than he had at the beginning. So it is with all love, human and divine; and the ontology of the family suggests that it is an organism which grows. Every married couple who have found themselves in their relationship naturally seek to be fruitful and multiply their love in and for their children. So Protestants and Catholics alike

believe in the family and alike frown on a selfish use
of sexuality which is purely for pleasure.

But the ontology of sexuality is by no means ex-
hausted by the "be fruitful and multiply" text. There
is also the word "and they became one flesh." This, as
we have seen earlier in this chapter, is the beginning
of community. The man and woman unite themselves
into one living organism, symbolized and deepened by
the mingling of their bodies in coition. Sexuality stands
for and contributes to community. It is the very antith-
esis of being "alone." Neither man (*ish*) nor woman
(*ishshah*) make man (*adam*) but only the two together.
Man alone is not man. Therefore sex has another aim,
another purpose, than procreation. Here also there is
agreement between Protestants and Catholics. The controversy arises over the relative importance of the two
ends of sex. The Catholic Church exalts procreation to
primacy, while Protestantism (or at least some of it)
either reverses the order, insisting that sex as the creator
of community is self-justifying and does not require procreation to justify it, or that the two ends are of equal
status, and neither has claim to priority.

A Protestant reading of the two basic biblical passages produces sharply different results. The sin of
Onan is seen as a violation of his responsibility to the
memory and the posterity of his dead brother. True,
he was killed, but directly by Yahweh himself without
any human intermediary, and the story is not made the
occasion for the origin of any law. The fact that Deu-

teronomy prescribes a far milder penalty for evasion of the Levirate marriage is not in itself significant, since several centuries had elapsed between the legends of Genesis and the law code composed in the days of King Josiah, providing ample occasion for the later softening of earlier penalties that proved in practice far too harsh. The 7th chapter of First Corinthians is read with emphasis on different syllables. The word "concession" is seen not in its Latin rendition, as *veniam,* pardon or indulgence, but in the original Greek, *sungnomen,* allowance for individual difference. And the fact that the apostle Paul positively forbade married couples with normal libidinal urges to abstain from sex for long periods "because of the temptation to immorality" is placed side by side with the absence of any mention of procreation at all. Indeed, the only such reference in the entire New Testament is found in 1 Timothy 2:9–15; "Women should adorn themselves modestly and sensibly in seemly apparel, not with braided hair or gold or pearls or costly attire but by good deeds, as befits women who profess religion. Let a woman learn in silence with all submissiveness. I permit no woman to teach or to have authority over men; she is to keep silent. For Adam was formed first, then Eve; and Adam was not deceived, but the woman was deceived and became a transgressor. Yet woman will be saved *through bearing children* [italics added], if she continues in faith and love and holiness, with modesty."

This passage from the Pastoral Epistles illustrates the

contention of New Testament scholars that these letters, while they may contain fragments of Pauline writing, are not actually by the apostle himself. In 1 Corinthians 11:5 Paul made it clear that women as well as men might be called to prophesy and to speak in the church. Phoebe was specifically called a "deaconess of the church at Cenchreae" (Romans 16:1), and the other letters abound in references to women at work in the new community in various capacities. Paul's view of sex in marriage was clearly illumined by his concern to prevent adultery or unchastity. Nowhere did he say anything about the connection of sex with procreation. He urged Christians to sacrifice their sexuality because of the impending distress, so that they might please the Lord, consecrating all of their energies to this task. Rome, of course, stresses the passage as a justification of a celibate clergy, and Protestantism has sometimes been injudicious in its attacks upon this institution. There is no reason why individuals should not choose religious celibacy as a vocation. There is nothing "unnatural" about such a choice. But Protestants would insist that neither is there anything unnatural about a family's spacing its children in such a way that they can be given the best possible nurture "in the Lord." A family overburdened with offspring is scarcely in a position to devote its energies to the affairs of the Lord.

The essential thing about Christian family life, from the Protestant perspective, is not its quantity but its quality—the community, the love, and the understanding that characterize the common life. If the financial resources are adequate, a couple may choose to raise numerous children and find themselves able to give the requisite love and care to all of their progeny. But a couple pressed for the bare necessities may find that additional offspring seriously deprive the children they already have, and the parents owe a responsibility to them. Even Rome recognizes the legitimacy of such a claim, permitting the rhythm method where circumstances warrant it. What the quarrel boils down to, then, is the question of method. Roman Catholicism allows family limitation by continence or by the rhythm method but forbids contraception. Protestantism sees nothing unnatural in devices or chemicals which have been medically tested and approved as doing no harm to either parents or prospective offspring. There is still serious question about the side effects or long-range dangers of the pills that are being tried, and premature endorsement of them is a dubious wisdom. But there is nothing unnatural about contraceptive devices any more than about tranquilizing drugs or pain killers or medicine in general. Anything can be misused, even the rhythm method itself, as Rome recognizes. The decisive question is as to motive rather than means. If a Christian couple is morally responsible and unselfishly devoted to their family responsibilities, they are free to choose whatever method they prefer to plan their family, or at least so Protestantism sees it. Sex as an expression of love and companionship is at least as important in the sight of God as sex for procreation, and numerically it is incalculably more significant. Even in the largest families, the number of sexual acts resulting in impregnation is tiny beside the figure counting the acts which have no such result either in fact or in intention.

Finally, there is one overriding consideration in this whole discussion: the present population explosion going on all over the world today. The demographers of all nations are seriously alarmed. The total number of humans on the globe is presently doubling itself in a little less than half a century. The introduction of Western medicine and sanitation into the so-called underdeveloped countries of Asia and Africa has sharply lowered their death rates, which formerly balanced a tremendously high birth rate. Infant mortality alone has decreased at a fantastic rate, and life expectancy has climbed rapidly. Certainly no Christian could possibly advocate returning to the old balance, allowing millions to suffer and die needlessly when they could be saved. But if some control is not placed upon conception, there will soon be a crisis of global proportions. It is not simply a question of enough food. Science may be able to develop new sources of energy. Rather, the crucial problem is one of space. Given a century or two at present rates, the world's population will be of such a size as to allow one square yard for

every living human being! From the Protestant standpoint, therefore, birth control is not only permissible
and natural, it is imperatively necessary. To ignore
the mammoth dimensions of this problem is to be
guilty of social irresponsibility of a highly dangerous
kind.

9

PROSTITUTION,

ADULTERY,

AND

DIVORCE

᪥

THE PRECEDING TWO CHAPTERS have discussed sex before and in marriage. The present chapter will be devoted to extramarital sexual relations and their consequences. As we have seen, the two Testaments of the Bible differ somewhat at this point. The Old Testament, while strictly prohibiting adultery and frowning on prostitution (though not altogether forbidding male recourse to harlots) does permit divorce for the man whose wife has found no favor in his eyes because he has found some indecency in her (Deuteronomy 24:1). And the privilege of divorce carries with it the permission of re-marriage. The New Testament, on the other hand, places an equal prohibition on all forms of extramarital sex re-lations, including a second marriage after divorce; and the restrictions apply to both sexes. It will be helpful to consider each of these three topics in turn, as it is treated in the two sections of the Bible.

PROSTITUTION

The prophet Hosea saw in his own marriage to an un-faithful wife a parable of Yahweh's marriage to the faith-less Israel, and this is a metaphor which appears again and again in the Old Testament. Not alone in the Song of Songs is this relationship portrayed in sensuous sym-bol, but in many another passage as well. Ezekiel, for example, spoke of it thus: "You grew up," says Yahweh to Israel, "and became tall and arrived at full maiden-hood; your breasts were formed, and your hair had grown; yet you were naked and bare. When I passed by you again and looked upon you, behold, you were at the age for love; and I spread my skirt over you, and covered your nakedness; yea, I plighted my troth to you and entered into a covenant with you, says Yahweh, and you became mine" (Ezekiel 16:7–8). The same point is made in Ezekiel 23, where the northern kingdom is

symbolized by the woman's name, Oholah, and the
southern kingdom by Oholibah. They are two daughters of the same mother, both belonging to Yahweh,
who says, "she was mine" (23:5). But both played the
harlot, turning elsewhere for their security. Oholah
"doted on her lovers the Assyrians, warriors clothed in
purple, governors and commanders, all of them desirable young men, horsemen riding on horses. She bestowed her harlotries upon them, the choicest men of
Assyria all of them; and she defiled herself with all the
idols of every one on whom she doted. She did not give
up her harlotry which she had practiced since her days
in Egypt; for in her youth men had lain with her and
handled her virgin bosom and poured out their lust
upon her" (23:5–8).

Oholibah proved to be even worse. She failed to profit
by the example of her sister's punishment. Not only did
she dote upon the desirable young men of Assyria; she
also became enamored of the Babylonians, whose pictures she saw upon walls, "and sent messengers to them
in Chaldea. And the Babylonians came to her into the
bed of love, and they defiled her with their lust" (23:16–
17). She, too, had in the days of her youth "played the
harlot in the land of Egypt and doted upon her para-
mours there, whose members [sexual organs] were like
those of asses, and whose issue [ejaculation] was like
that of horses. Thus you longed for the lewdness of your
youth, when the Egyptians handled your bosom and
pressed your young breasts" (23:19–21). No one can ac-

cuse the Old Testament of prudery about sex. It knows
what to call a spade!

Quotations such as these could fill an entire chapter.
Jeremiah, Isaiah, Hosea, Nahum, all used the metaphor
of the wife who played the harlot. Even the Psalms sing
in these terms. The books of Judges, which celebrates
the cycle of apostasy-punishment, repentance-deliver-
ance, remarks sadly, "Then Yahweh raised up judges,
who saved them out of the power of those who plun-
dered them. And yet they did not listen to their judges;
for they played the harlot after other gods and bowed
down to them" (Judges 2:16–17). Now, all of this must
be seen against the background of the nature cults of
Israel's neighbors in the Fertile Crescent where sacred
prostitution was almost universal. That the practice
penetrated Israelite life in Canaan is abundantly clear
from the Old Testament. In 1 Samuel, we read that the
sons of Eli, the priest of Yahweh at the sanctuary at
Shiloh, "lay with the women who served at the entrance
to the tent of meeting" (1 Samuel 2:22). The suggestion
is strong that these women who served at the entrance
were cult prostitutes, and it is strengthened by references in both Amos and Hosea. "A man and his father
go in to the same maiden, so that my holy name is profaned; they lay themselves down beside every altar upon
garments taken in pledge; and in the house of their God
they drink the wine of those who have been fined"
(Amos 2:7–8). Here the connection between the drinking of wine in the house of God with going in to the

same maiden points to the cultic link between sex and
alcohol. And Hosea declared, "Wine and new wine take
away the understanding. My people inquire of a thing
of wood, and their staff gives them oracles. For a spirit
of harlotry has led them astray, and they have left their
God to play the harlot. They sacrifice on the tops of the
mountains, and make offerings upon the hills.
. . . Therefore your daughters play the harlot, and your
brides commit adultery. I will not punish your daughters
when they play the harlot, nor your brides when they
commit adultery; for the men themselves go aside with
harlots, and sacrifice with cult prostitutes, and a people
without understanding shall come to ruin" (Hosea 4:11–
14). These cult prostitutes (*kedeshoth*) were "holy"
women with whom the priests shared in sacred sexual
intercourse as a part of a fertility rite. Micah said that
all the images and idols were paid for "from the hire of a
harlot" (Micah 1:7), indicating that a price of some sort
was exacted from the men who went in to these women.
Thus, as Pedersen has written, "We receive the impression that sexual rites dominated the Israelite cultus
throughout the monarchic period."[1]

It is not surprising that the Hebrews adopted these
Canaanitish customs, untutored as they were in the ways
of agriculture, and dependent upon their former neighbors for instruction and assistance. Nor was the Hebrew
understanding of sexuality or ethics such that a man

---

[1] Johannes Pedersen, *Israel*, III-IV (London: Oxford University
Press, 1947), p. 470.

could not have intercourse with a woman other than his wife. Therefore it was perfectly natural for Israel to imitate the Canaanites in their nature worship, including the sacred sexual acts. What was not so natural was the strong reaction of the religious leaders of the covenanted people against these rites. The protest was made not against sex as such, for that would have been altogether inconsistent with the total view of Hebrew religion. Rather, the basis for the objection to this cult prostitution was its connection with idolatry and with the worship of the fertility gods. To the judges and prophets of Israel this was apostasy and idolatry, unfaithfulness to their own tribal god Yahweh. To cite Pedersen once more:

> The utterances of the prophets would seem to indicate, however, that the sexual cult in itself struck them as non-Israelitish and inimical to their traditions. They regarded it as a sin that Israelite women, who were to serve the purity of the race, gave themselves to any man who visited them. Hence they called it all fornication and adultery; and even though they did not condemn men's intercourse with women other than their wives, they could not reconcile it with the character of their ancestral God that such acts should be considered holy ones. Precisely because the sexual rites affected the most intimate part of their nature, they could not on that point allow themselves to be transformed by the customs and feelings of Canaanite agriculture. The sexual cult was not only useless, it was sacrilegious.[2]

---

[2] *Ibid.*, p. 472.

This is why the Law was so strict with regard to the purity of the priests of Yahweh. There must be no slightest taint of sacred sexuality about them. "They shall not marry a harlot or a woman who has been defiled; neither shall they marry a woman divorced from her husband; for the priest is holy to his God. . . . And the daughter of any priest, if she profanes herself by playing the harlot, profanes her father; she shall be burned with fire. . . . And he [the priest] shall take a wife in her virginity. A widow, or one divorced, or a woman who has been defiled, or a harlot, these he shall not marry" (Leviticus 21:7, 9, 13–14). This is also why the prejudice is strong against an Israelite daughter's serving as a prostitute. "Do not profane your daughter by making her a harlot, lest the land fall into harlotry and the land become full of wickedness" (Leviticus 19:29).

The connection between prostitution and religious apostasy is made abundantly clear in a rather bloody narrative in the book of Numbers. The people, so the story has it, began to commit whoredom with the daughters of Moab, obviously in a sexual cult. This apparently resulted in a plague, interpreted as a punishment from Yahweh. Moses received instructions to slay all those who had "yoked themselves with Baal of Peor," the god in whose worship these fertility rites were celebrated. Then, "one of the people of Israel came and brought a Midianite woman to his family, in the sight of Moses and in the sight of the whole congregation of the people of Israel, while they were weeping at the

door of the tent of meeting. And when Phinehas the son
of Eleazar, the son of Aaron the priest, saw it, he rose
and left the congregation, and took a spear in his hand
and went after the man of Israel into the inner room, and
pierced both of them, the man of Israel and the woman,
through her body. Thus the plague was stayed from
the people of Israel" (Numbers 25:6–9). Actually the
two stories, that of the sexual relations with the women
of Moab and that of the Israelite who brought home the
Midianite woman, come from different sources, the
former from the Yahwist and the latter from the Priestly
writers, and they are linked in the text somewhat artifi-
cially. In both cases, however, the fear of sexual connections with foreign women (cult prostitutes) is clear. The
106th Psalm celebrates the act of Phinehas, crediting
him with punishing the apostasy of Israel to Baal of
Peor and thus delivering Israel from the plague.

Deuteronomy contains three references to prostitution, and two of the three illustrate the same association
with idolatry. "There shall be no cult prostitute (*kedeshah*) of the daughters of Israel, neither shall there be a
cult prostitute (*kadesh*)[3] of the sons of Israel. You shall
not bring the hire of a harlot, or the wages of a dog, into
the house of Yahweh your God" (Deuteronomy 23:17–
18). The two Hebrew terms used here refer specifically
to sacred prostitutes, not to ordinary, secular harlots,
and the prohibition against bringing "the hire" or the
money of the prostitute into the temple is clearly pointed

---

[3] *Kedeshah* is a female cult prostitute; *kadesh* is a male.

at the pagan practice of supporting religious institutions with such funds. "The wages of a dog" apparently mean those of a male prostitute, known as a "dog." In Yahweh's final words to Moses at the end of Deuteronomy, he warned the old man that his people would "play the harlot after the strange gods of the land" (Deuteronomy 31:16), underlining once more the familiar metaphor.

That there was little or no prejudice against purely secular prostitution in Israel seems relatively clear. We have already seen how Judah lay with Tamar, thinking she was a harlot (Genesis 38). Rahab, the whore of Jericho, was singled out for remembrance and praise. Jephthah, the judge in Israel, was the son of a harlot, who, despite evil treatment from his half brothers who were of legitimate birth (Judges 11), rose to prominence in Israel and was used by Yahweh. Proverbs warns young men against the wiles of whores after the manner of fatherly advice in every generation. Especially in chapter 7 is there a vivid description of the dangers to be encountered in such company. But the allurements are not minimized, either. The old wise man sees a youth accosted on the street by a harlot. "She seizes him and kisses him, and with impudent face she says to him . . . 'I have decked my couch with coverings, colored spreads of Egyptian linen; I have perfumed my bed with myrrh, aloes, and cinnamon. Come, let us take our fill of love till morning; let us delight ourselves with love. For my husband is not at home; he has gone on a long journey.' . . . With much seductive speech she persuades him;

with her smooth talk she compels him." Then the wise
man warns against her evil ways: "Her house is the way
to Sheol, going down to the chambers of death" (Proverbs 7). But the prejudice is not against sexuality as
such, but against squandering one's substance.

The New Testament has comparatively little to say
about prostitution, which is surprising in view of the
prevalence of the practice in the Graeco-Roman world.
Jesus mentioned harlots several times in the Gospels,
linking them with the publicans, those whose lives were
centered in their own pleasure and profit. These were
to enter the kingdom before the scribes and Pharisees,
because the latter were guilty of the worst of all sins—
pride and self-righteousness. There was little danger
that the harlot would feel either proud or complacent.
She walked constantly close to penitence, and therefore
personal redemption. This is not to say that Jesus con-
doned prostitution or recommended it as a path to salvation! This would be of a piece with Paul's question,
"Shall we then say, 'Let sin abound that grace may the
much more abound?' Nay, God forbid!" But no sins of
the flesh were such that they banished the sinner beyond
the realm of God's forgiving love. Even he who makes
his bed in hell finds that God is there. Jesus taught and
exemplified the willingness of God to receive all those
who come in repentance and in faith. He did not, as all
too many of his subsequent followers have done, draw
his skirts in righteous horror away from the contaminating touch of the whore. He came to seek and to save

those who are lost, who know themselves to be in need of a physician, and he did seek them out. Remote waiting was no policy of his, but rather active search. It must be said in justice to the Christian community that it has always been more or less prepared to welcome the penitent sinner, but the initiative has for the most part been left to him. Seldom has the church followed its Lord in its ministry to misfits. What minister could risk going into the red-light district of a community? To hear the gospel, whores must come to the church; the church does not go to them. And coming to the church means risking shocked rejection from the pews and moralistic denunciation from the pulpit. The gentler "Neither do I condemn thee" finds small echo in the corridors of the centuries.

We have already quoted the apostle Paul's remarks on commerce with a prostitute in 1 Corinthians 6, where he says that "he who joins himself to a prostitute becomes one body with her," which means to take "the members of Christ and make them members of a prostitute," an unthinkable act. This extension of the Old Testament concept of "one flesh"—which obviously applies to marriage—to any sexual union is, in the eyes of many New Testament commentators, highly questionable. One cannot help but wonder in this context whether Paul was not thinking of the sacred, ritual prostitution so common in Corinth, rather than of the purely secular variety. Such an understanding would be in accord with the Old Testament outlook, which regarded

union with the priestesses of the fertility cults as idolatry
and infidelity to Yahweh. If Paul was operating within
such a frame of reference, he would not be overextend-
ing himself at all. The relationship between Israel and
Yahweh was conceived metaphorically as a marriage
bond, a state of "one flesh" between God and his covenanted people. So Christ and his Church were, symbolically, groom and bride (Ephesians 5) and also "one
flesh." Sexual relations with a cult prostitute, then, either
for Jew or Christian, might symbolize union with the
deity of the shrine and therefore also a state of "one
flesh." Such a view would seem more applicable than to
regard a casual, commercial intercourse with a woman
of the streets as creating such a unity. Not that Paul
would therefore regard secular prostitution lightly. He
stood in unequivocal opposition to any and all extramarital sexual relations, but his language in 1 Corinthians 6 makes more sense if one thinks in terms of the
temple of Aphrodite in Corinth and its sacred sexuality,
rather than of nonsacred brothels. In Ephesians 5:5,
"one who is covetous" is explained as meaning an idolater, and is linked with a whoremonger and an unclean
person. The reference here to the Old Testament conception of the worship of the Baals as adultery is inescapable. If, in the Old Testament, idolatry equaled
adultery, then, perhaps for Paul also, adultery or intercourse with cult prostitutes equaled idolatry.

There are numerous references in the book of Revelation to whores and whoredom, but these are mostly sym-

bolic, referring to Rome as a whole rather than to the
specific institution of prostitution in the Empire. "The
great harlot" of chapter 17, the "mother of harlots" who
sits upon a beast with seven heads is "the great city
which has dominion over the kingdoms of the earth."
"The seven heads are seven hills on which the woman is
seated," and one could scarcely ask for a more obvious
reference to the Eternal City. The same reference is
found in 19:2, when God "has judged the great harlot
who corrupted the earth with her fornication." Those
who had been guilty of whoredom, or *porneia,* were to
share in the punishment of the wicked, the cowardly,
the faithless, murderers, sorcerers, and all liars. "Their
lot shall be in the lake that burns with fire and brimstone, which is the second death" (Revelation 21:8).
Outside the city of salvation were "the dogs [sodom-
ites?] and sorcerers and fornicators and murderers and
idolaters" (Revelation 22:15). Thus the whole of the
New Testament condemns prostitution or sexual activity
of any kind outside of marriage, which is considerably
more sweeping than the Old Testament, wherein the
male is allowed a certain limited freedom.

ADULTERY

The Old Testament viewed adultery as a serious sin,
oriented as it was toward a concern for progeny and the
purity of the family's bloodline. Not only was it forbidden in both versions of the Decalogue, in Exodus 20:14

and Deuteronomy 5:18, where it is simply listed, along with killing, stealing, bearing false witness, and coveting, but also Leviticus specifically prescribed the death penalty as its punishment. "If a man commits adultery with the wife of his neighbor, both the adulterer and the adulteress shall be put to death" (Leviticus 20:10). The law codes were somewhat obscure about the exact nature of an adulterous act. Any married woman guilty of sexual relations with another man, married or not, was clearly adulterous, as was any man, married or not, involved with another man's wife. But there was no prohibition against a married man's sexual intercourse with an unmarried woman, unless she was the daughter of an Israelite, in which case he wronged her father. But his punishment in such a case was not death but marriage. He must take the girl to wife.

The patriarchal prejudice is apparent. One's male rights as husband or father were jealously and zealously guarded, while the rights of the wife to the fidelity of her husband were ignored. No harm was done to a willing woman who was not under the sovereignty of her father or her husband, for she had no progeny to protect. Apparently neither she nor her male bedfellow, even if he had a wife at home, was guilty of adultery. That was an act defined by the law as violating the rights of another male, more especially a husband. In a polygamous society, the father's interests can be safeguarded by requiring the seducer to marry the girl. If he is already married, he can, after all, take still another wife. But the man who cuckolds a husband threatens the sanctity of the family line and must be killed, together with the unfaithful wife. In procreation there is never any question of a child's mother. The only uncertainty attaches itself to the father. Therefore the husband was zealous to protect his wife's purity, and by extension of his own concern he had a certain empathy for other husbands. He need not, however, be unduly concerned about the paternity of a child born to some woman unclaimed and unowned. He had no responsibility to her or to his neighbor.

A curious and bizarre ceremony enabled a suspicious husband to test the fidelity of his wife by a kind of ordeal. "If any man's wife goes astray and acts unfaithfully against him, if a man lies with her carnally, and it is hidden from the eyes of her husband, and she is undetected though she has defiled herself, and there is no witness against her, since she was not taken in the act; and if the spirit of jealousy comes upon him, and he is jealous of his wife who has defiled herself; or if the spirit of jealousy comes upon him, and he is jealous of his wife, though she has not defiled herself; then the man shall bring his wife to the priest, and bring the offering required of her, a tenth of an ephah of barley meal; he shall pour no oil upon it and put no frankincense on it, for it is a cereal offering of jealousy, a cereal offering of remembrance, bringing iniquity to remembrance. And the priest shall bring her near, and set her before Yahweh; and the priest shall take holy water in an

earthen vessel, and take some of the dust that is on the
floor of the tabernacle and put it into the water. And
the priest shall set the woman before Yahweh, and un-
bind the hair of the woman's head, and place in her
hands the cereal offering of remembrance, which is the
cereal offering of jealousy. And in his hand the priest
shall have the water of bitterness that brings the curse.
Then the priest shall make her take an oath, saying, 'If
no man has lain with you, and if you have not turned
aside to uncleanness, while you were under your husband's authority, be free from this water of bitterness
that brings the curse. But if you have gone astray,
though you are under your husband's authority, and if
you have defiled yourself, and some man other than your
husband has lain with you, then' (let the priest make
the woman take the oath of the curse, and say to the
woman) 'Yahweh make you an execration and an oath
among your people, when Yahweh makes your thigh fall
away and your body swell; may this water that brings
the curse pass into your bowels and make your body
swell and your thigh fall away.' And the woman shall
say, 'Amen, Amen.' Then the priest shall write these
curses in a book, and wash them off into the water of
bitterness; and he shall make the woman drink the water
of bitterness that brings the curse, and the water that
brings the curse shall enter into her and cause bitter
pain. And the priest shall take the cereal offering of
jealousy out of the woman's hand, and shall wave the
cereal offering before Yahweh and bring it to the altar;

and the priest shall take a handful of the cereal offering, as its memorial portion, and burn it upon the altar, and afterward shall make the woman drink the water. And when he has made her drink the water, then, if she has defiled herself and has acted unfaithfully against her husband, the water that brings the curse shall enter into her and cause bitter pain, and her body shall swell, and her thigh shall fall away, and the woman shall become an execration among her people. But if the woman has not defiled herself and is clean, then she shall be free and shall conceive children. This is the law in cases of jealousy, when a wife, though under her husband's authority, goes astray and defiles herself, or when the spirit of jealousy comes upon a man and he is jealous of his wife; then he shall set the woman before Yahweh, and the priest shall execute upon her all this law. The man shall be free from iniquity, but the woman shall bear her iniquity" (Numbers 5:11–31).

The one-sided understanding of adultery in the Old Testament law was not specifically broadened in the prophetic writings, which were not altogether silent on the subject. Hosea had numerous references to adultery, with respect both to Gomer's infidelity and to Israelite life as a whole. The faithless wife of the prophet was warned to "put away her harlotry from her face, and her adultery from between her breasts; lest I strip her naked and make her as the day she was born, and make her like a wilderness, and set her like a parched land, and slay her with thirst" (Hosea 2:2–3). Hosea was com-

manded to "go again, love a woman who is beloved of
a paramour and is an adulteress; even as Yahweh loves
the people of Israel, though they turn to other gods and
love cakes of raisins" (Hosea 3:1). But the prophet listed
adultery among the indictments which Yahweh directed
against the whole nation, and not only symbolically, in
their worship of pagan gods. "There is no faithfulness
or kindness, and no knowledge of God in the land; there
is swearing, lying, killing, stealing, and committing adultery; they break all bounds and murder follows murder.
. . . My people inquire of a thing of wood, and their
staff gives them oracles. For a spirit of harlotry has led
them astray, and they have left their God to play the
harlot. They sacrifice on the tops of the mountains, and
make offerings upon the hills, under oak, poplar, and
terebinth, because their shade is good. Therefore your
daughters play the harlot, and your brides commit adultery. I will not punish your daughters when they play
the harlot, nor your brides when they commit adultery;
for the men themselves go aside with harlots, and sacrifice with cult prostitutes, and a people without understanding shall come to ruin" (Hosea 4:1–2, 12–14). Here
is even-handed justice, an equal treatment of both sexes
—both culpable, both guilty of participation in the fertility cults of Canaan, so that "they are all adulterers"
(Hosea 7:4). But notice that the real force of this passage
lies in God's refusal to punish the brides and daughters
of Israel for their harlotry and adultery, a judgment
surely to be expected, because the men themselves are

involved in idolatry. It was not so much the sexual aspect of their activity which was condemned as it was their religious apostasy. Sexual promiscuity in women was in itself heinous and deserving of punishment, but Yahweh would let it pass because of the men's paganism.

Isaiah's condemnation was directed at cult prostitution; seeing adultery in this light, Yahweh calls upon those in Israel who have visited the shrines of the local Baals on the high places. "You, draw near hither, sons of the sorceress, offspring of the adulterer and the harlot. Of whom are you making sport? . . . you who burn with lust among the oaks, under every green tree; who slay your children in the valleys, under the cleft of the rocks?" This is apparently a reference to the custom of infant sacrifice rather than abortion. "Upon a high and lofty mountain you have set your bed, and thither you went up to offer sacrifice. Behind the door and the doorpost you have set up your symbol [probably the phallic symbol of the Asherah, or sacred pillar]; for, deserting me, you have uncovered your bed, you have gone up to it, you have made it wide; and you have made a bargain for yourself with them, you have loved their bed, you have looked on nakedness" (Isaiah 57:3–5, 7–8). The adultery here was with the prostitutes of the pagan shrines, but it was also infidelity to Yahweh.

Jeremiah again and again used the symbol of adultery for Israel's apostasy. "You have played the harlot with many lovers; and would you return to me?" says Yah-

weh. "Lift up your eyes to the bare heights, and see!
Where have you not been lain with? By the waysides
you have sat awaiting lovers like an Arab in the wilderness. You have polluted the land with your vile
harlotry. . . . Have you seen what she did, that faithless one, Israel, how she went up on every high hill and
under every green tree, and there played the harlot?
And I thought, 'After she has done all this she will
return to me'; but she did not return, and her false
sister Judah saw it. She saw that for all the adulteries
of that faithless one, Israel, I had sent her away with
a decree of divorce; yet her false sister Judah did not
fear, but she too went and played the harlot. Because
harlotry was so light to her, she polluted the land,
committing adultery with stone and tree (Jeremiah
3:1–2, 6–9). "How can I pardon you?" asks Yahweh,
"Your children have forsaken me, and have sworn by
those who are no gods. When I fed them to the full,
they committed adultery and trooped to the houses of
harlots. They were well-fed lusty stallions, each neigh-
ing for his neighbor's wife. Shall I not punish them for
these things?" (Jeremiah 5:7–9).

The mixture in these passages of adultery as a symbol
of faithlessness to the God of the covenant and adultery
as a literal act, relations with other women, is striking.
"Will you steal, murder, commit adultery, swear falsely,
burn incense to Baal, and go after other gods that you
have not known, and then come and stand before me in
this house, which is called by my name?" (7:9). "O

that I had in the desert a wayfarer's lodging place, that
I might leave my people and go away from them!
For they are all adulterers, a company of treacherous
men" (9:2). Jerusalem was to be destroyed "because
they have committed folly in Israel, they have committed adultery with their neighbors' wives, and they
have spoken in my name lying words which I did not
command them" (29:23). These false prophets were
themselves guilty of sexual sins. "Both prophet and
priest are ungodly; even in my house I have found
their wickedness, says Yahweh. . . . In the prophets
of Jerusalem I have seen a horrible thing: they commit
adultery and walk in lies" (23:11, 14). And, God
threatened, because "I have seen your abominations,
your adulteries and neighings, your lewd harlotries, on
the hills in the field. . . . I myself will lift up your
skirts over your face, and your shame will be seen"
(13:27, 26).

Ezekiel spoke entirely of adultery in reference to
the nation as a whole, though the symbolism is such
that cult sexuality was obviously in the prophet's mind.
"You were not," said Yahweh to his people, "like a
harlot, because you scorned hire. Adulterous wife, who
receives strangers instead of her husband! Men give
gifts to all harlots; but you gave your gifts to all your
lovers, bribing them to come to you from every side
for your harlotries. So you were different from other
women in your harlotries: none solicited you to play the
harlot; and you gave hire, while no hire was given to

you; therefore you were different" (Ezekiel 16:31–34). The two sisters Oholah (Israel) and Oholibah (Judah) "have committed adultery, and blood is upon their hands; with their idols they have committed adultery; and they have even offered up to them for food the sons whom they had borne to me. Moreover this they have done to me: they have defiled my sanctuary on the same day and profaned my sabbaths. For when they had slaughtered their children in sacrifice to their idols, on the same day they came into my sanctuary to profane it. And lo, this is what they did in my house. They even sent for men to come from far, to whom a messenger was sent, and lo, they came. For them you bathed yourself, painted your eyes, and decked yourself with ornaments; you sat upon a stately couch, with a table spread before it on which you had placed my incense and my oil. The sound of a carefree multitude was with her; and with men of the common sort drunkards were brought from the wilderness; and they put bracelets upon the hands of the women, and beautiful crowns upon their heads. Then I said, 'Do not men now commit adultery when they practice harlotry with her?' For they have gone in to her, as men go in to a harlot. Thus they went in to Oholah and to Oholibah, to commit lewdness. But righteous men shall pass judgment on them with the sentence of adulteresses, and with the sentence of women that shed blood; because they are adulteresses, and blood is upon their hands" (Ezekiel 23:37–45). The significant sentence here is the question, "Do not *men* now commit adultery?" which suggests that the male visiting a harlot was guilty of sin, but the symbolism confuses the issue and it remains obscure.

Proverbs makes it clear that adultery as intercourse with a married woman was a crime, but still the question as to the status of the married man remains. "The commandment is a lamp and the teaching a light, and the reproofs of discipline are the way of life, to preserve you from the evil woman, from the smooth tongue of the adventuress. Do not desire her beauty in your heart, and do not let her capture you with her eyelashes; for a harlot may be hired for a loaf of bread, but an adulteress [some man's wife] stalks a man's very life. Can a man carry fire in his bosom and his clothes not be burned? Or can one walk upon hot coals and his feet not be scorched? So is he who goes in to his neighbor's wife; none who touches her will go unpunished. Do not men despise a thief if he steals to satisfy his appetite when he is hungry? . . . He who commits adultery has no sense; he who does it destroys himself" (Proverbs 6:23–32). The implication is that a harlot was easily accessible and relatively safe, but the neighbor's wife was exceedingly dangerous. Thus, the Old Testament views adultery not primarily as marital infidelity, but as trespassing upon the rights of the male.

The New Testament views the relationship differently. All marital infidelity, male or female, was adulterous. The whole sexuality of man was internalized and placed in the context of motivation. Anyone who had lustful desires toward a person of the opposite sex outside of marriage was already guilty of adultery (Matthew 5:27–28). This is because the things that defile come from within, from the heart. "Out of the heart come evil thoughts, murder, adultery, fornication, theft, false witness, slander" (Matthew 15:19). Or, as Mark put it, "All these evil things come from within, and they defile a man" (Mark 7:23). The apostle Paul said the same thing in his appeal to the Jews in Romans: "You then who teach others, will you not teach yourself? While you preach against stealing, do you steal? You who say that one must not commit adultery, do you commit adultery?" (Romans 2:21–22). "Therefore you have no excuse, O man, whoever you are, when you judge another; for in passing judgment upon him you condemn yourself, because you, the judge, are doing the very same things" (Romans 2:1). It was not so much an outward act, or the mere omission of a sinful deed, that was important as it was the inner feeling. "He who loves his neighbor has fulfilled the law. The commandments, 'You shall not commit adultery, You shall not kill, You shall not steal, You shall not covet,' and any other commandment, are summed up in this sentence, 'You shall love your neighbor as yourself.' Love does no wrong to a neighbor; therefore love is the fulfilling of the law" (Romans 13:8–10). There was no distinction between the sexes here. The principle applied equally to men and women, demanding a positive, outgoing concern for one's neighbor, not a merely negative restraint upon wrongdoing.

So far does the New Testament extend the understanding of marriage and its binding force that "whoever marries a divorced woman commits adultery" (Matthew 5:32), and "every one who divorces his wife and marries another commits adultery" (Luke 16:18). We shall have occasion in the next section, on divorce, to examine the implications of this more fully. Suffice it to say here that sex relations were clearly to be confined to monogamous marriage. Paul permitted remarriage to those bereaved, though he advised remaining single. "If the husband dies, she is free to be married to whom she wishes, only in the Lord. But in my judgment she is happier if she remains as she is" (1 Corinthians 7:39–40). The Pastoral Epistles, as we have seen, are not altogether clear whether they deny remarriage after the death of the partner to officers of the church or are simply enjoining monogamy, but even if the former was true, the counsel was limited to bishops, priests, and deacons, and not extended to all. Any married person, however, was bound to sexual fidelity to his spouse for life. Any other sexual activity was impurity, which, unrepented, barred one from entrance into the kingdom. "God will judge the immoral" (Hebrews 13:4). Christians especially must beware of falling into adultery, for they then became like the dog returning to its vomit or the washed sow wallowing in the mire, and "the last state has become worse for them than the first" (2 Peter 2:22, 20). Once more, the New Testament sweeps aside the old double standard and applies the same requirement to both sexes, as it does also in the case of divorce.

DIVORCE

The classical Old Testament passage dealing with divorce is Deuteronomy 24:1–4. What is sometimes overlooked in discussions of this text is the conditional character of the first three verses. These are not setting up the conditions of divorce, as it might appear, but rather leading up to the legislation in the last verse. "*When* a man takes a wife and marries her, *if* then she finds no favor in his eyes because he has found some indecency in her, *and* he writes her a bill of divorce and puts it in her hand and sends her out of his house, *and* she departs out of his house, *and if* she goes and becomes another man's wife, *and* the latter husband dislikes her and writes her a bill of divorce and puts it in her hand and sends her out of his house, *or if* the latter husband dies, who took her to be his wife, *then* her former husband, who sent her away, may not take her again to be his wife, after she has been defiled; for that is an abomination before Yahweh, and you shall not bring guilt upon the land which Yahweh your God gives you for an inheritance." There is, curiously, no law in the Old Testament instituting divorce itself, which was simply taken for granted. The custom was

ageless among the Hebrews and required no legislation
to justify it. The law was simply trying to regulate
divorce, setting up certain restrictions upon it, primarily
for the protection of the woman. The Deuteronomic
passage indicates that a man must have good cause to
put away his wife, that he must go before a public
official and set forth his grounds, which must then be
written out in an official document and given to the
woman. All of this mitigated against hasty and uncon-
sidered action. But the initiative lay solely with the
husband, and Jewish interpreters differed widely about
what constituted sufficient grounds for divorce, ranging from restriction to adultery to extension to the most
trivial displeasure. The school of Hillel, for example,
said that a wife's burning her husband's bread constituted good reason for divorce.

There were, however, certain protections for a wife.
A husband forced to marry a girl by reason of having
seduced her, could not put her away. "If a man meets
a virgin who is not betrothed, and seizes her and lies
with her, and they are found, then the man who lay
with her shall give to the father of the young woman
fifty shekels of silver, and she shall be his wife, because
he has violated her; he may not put her away all his
days" (Deuteronomy 22:28–29). A man who falsely accused his wife was likewise bound to her for life. He
was to be fined one hundred shekels of silver (twice the
mohar or bride-price) and "he may not put her away
all his days" (Deuteronomy 22:13–19). Any woman

divorced by her husband was free to remarry, but not
her former husband nor a priest, who was required to
marry a virgin (Leviticus 21:14). Jeremiah referred to
the prohibition against remarrying a former husband,
asking, "If a man divorces his wife and she goes from
him and becomes another man's wife, will he return to
her? Would not that land be greatly polluted? You
[Judah] have played the harlot with many lovers; and
would you return to me? says Yahweh" (Jeremiah 3:1).

These restrictions show that there was an uneasy feeling in Israel that divorce was fundamentally abnormal.
Malachi voiced this with conviction and vehemence.
"You cover Yahweh's altar with tears, with weeping
and groaning because he no longer regards the offering
or accepts it with favor at your hand. You ask, 'Why
does he not?' Because Yahweh was witness to the
covenant between you and the wife of your youth, to
whom you have been faithless, though she is your
companion and your wife by covenant. Has not the
one God made and sustained for us the spirit of life?
And what does he desire? Godly offspring. So take heed
to yourselves, and let none be faithless to the wife of
his youth. 'For I hate divorce,' says Yahweh the God of
Israel, 'and covering one's garment with violence,' says
Yahweh of hosts. So take heed to yourselves and do not
be faithless" (Malachi 2:13–16). It should not be forgotten, either, that the early Yahwist account of creation
in Genesis 2 speaks of a married couple as "one flesh,"
of a man's leaving his father and mother to cleave to

his wife, which indicates that even in the Old Testament there are those strands which look upon divorce with genuine misgivings. In general, however, divorce was possible if not praiseworthy, and once again the man's privileged position prevailed. He held the right solely in his hands.

The New Testament again destroyed the male prerogative and banished divorce altogether, precisely as in the cases of prostitution and adultery. If the Old Testament's *locus classicus* on divorce is Deuteronomy 24:1–4, its New Testament counterpart is Mark 10:2–10, with parallels in Matthew 19:1–9 and Luke 16:18. "And Pharisees came up and in order to test him asked, 'Is it lawful for a man to divorce his wife?' He answered them, 'What did Moses command you?' They said, 'Moses allowed a man to write a certificate of divorce, and to put her away.' But Jesus said to them, 'For your hardness of heart he wrote you this commandment. But from the beginning of creation, "God made them male and female." "For this reason a man shall leave his father and mother and be joined to his wife, and the two shall become one." So they are no longer two but one. What therefore God has joined together, let not man put asunder.' And in the house the disciples asked him again about this matter. And he said to them, 'Whoever divorces his wife and marries another, commits adultery against her; and if she divorces her husband and marries another, she commits adultery.'" Matthew substantially duplicated Mark's account, with one small but highly significant change. "Whoever," Matthew had it, "divorces his wife, *except for un-chastity,* and marries another, commits adultery" (Matthew 19:9). The same insertion, "except on the ground of unchastity," appears in Matthew 5:32. Luke, however, copied Mark's version, leaving the statement absolute. Many New Testament scholars regard Matthew's addition as much later, edited by someone seeking to soften a too harsh dictum. Both Mark and Luke were closer to the spirit of Jesus' ethic, which was absolutist throughout.

Paul followed his Lord, writing, "To the married I give charge, not I but the Lord, that the wife should not separate from her husband (but if she does, let her remain single or else be reconciled to her husband)— and that the husband should not divorce his wife" (1 Corinthians 7:10–11). But Paul went beyond this, confessing, "To the rest I say, not the Lord, that if any brother has a wife who is an unbeliever, and she consents to live with him, he should not divorce her. If any woman has a husband who is an unbeliever, and he consents to live with her, she should not divorce him. For the unbelieving husband is consecrated through his wife, and the unbelieving wife is consecrated through her husband. Otherwise, your children would be unclean, but as it is they are holy. But if the unbelieving partner desires to separate, let it be so; in such a case the brother or sister is not bound. For God has called us to peace. Wife, how do you know whether

you will save your husband? Husband, how do you
know whether you will save your wife?" (1 Corinthians
7:12–16). The Christian married to an unbeliever was to
make every effort to convert the spouse, but if there
were no peace in the home, and the unbelieving one
wanted out, then the Christian was free to marry again,
only this time "in the Lord." It is significant that Paul
made this his own exception and not the Lord's, as it is
also significant that he appears to have known nothing
of Matthew's exception "on the ground of unchastity."

Even if we grant authenticity to Matthew's word,
the text is not clear as to whether the wronged partner
was free to remarry. Roman Catholicism has traditionally given a negative answer to that question, restricting
the privilege of remarriage only to those separated
from an unbelieving spouse. Luther and Calvin took
the position that an adulterous wife or husband severed
the marriage bond and thus set the innocent partner
free. They also permitted a long-deserted married
person to remarry, regarding this as an extension of the
so-called "Pauline privilege." In recent times some
Protestant churches have considerably softened the
traditional ban against the remarriage of divorced persons. Some have agreed to marry the innocent party to
a divorce "on scriptural grounds," while others have
become even more lenient than that, wishing to avoid
the appearance of Pharisaic legalism. They will marry
virtually anyone who appears to them truly desirous of a
Christian ceremony. The alarming increase in the di-

vorce rate in the twentieth century has caused some
second thoughts on this problem, and a general tighten-
ing up is manifesting itself in many circles.

It is perfectly clear that the New Testament is utterly
opposed to divorce. Jesus' word on this was absolute.
The real question, however, is whether the church
should take this particular word as literally as it does.
Maude Royden, writing in 1923 in *The Atlantic
Monthly,* remarked:

> The Church again and again has sanctioned war and
> capital punishment. Every bishop on the bench, every
> incumbent of a living, every witness in a court of law
> takes oaths. No country executes a man for murder be-
> cause he admits he hates his brother, nor literally re-
> gards a lustful glance as adultery. Neither does the
> Church excommunicate Christians who refuse loans or
> gifts to those who ask. Yet it argues that Christians who
> have almost universally disregarded the *literal* meaning
> of every other principle enunciated in the Sermon on
> the Mount must *literally* obey the injunction against
> divorce on pain of disloyalty to their Lord!

Miss Royden was not arguing for ethical laxity in any of
these areas. She was simply pointing out that Jesus was
not legislating for our earthly society. He was no social
reformer, providing blueprints for Utopia. He was in
every case stating the absolute and uncompromising demand of God. His message is summed up in the command: "Be perfect as your Father in Heaven is perfect."

The early church, living as it did in the lively expectation of the second coming of Christ and the end of the present age, the beginning of God's eternal kingdom, took these counsels of perfection very seriously and refused to compromise with the demands of the world. Christians would not serve in the army or in the Roman government. The community in Jerusalem "had all things in common" and took little thought for the morrow, since the morrow could be expected to put an end to all worldly concerns. As time went on, however, and the hope of the second coming began to fade, more and more compromises became necessary. After Constantine, Christendom became a cultural unity and the church adapted itself widely to the demands and the responsibilities of power. Nonresistance to evil, clearly demanded by the Sermon on the Mount, became impractical in a real world. The taking of oaths, likewise forbidden, grew necessary, as did long-range planning for the future—the social, political, and economic demands of reality. One by one the "impossible possibilities" of Jesus' ethic were adapted and interpreted in such a way that the church could live with them. The prohibition against divorce, however, stood firm and remains so to this day.

Anyone who seeks to follow Jesus' teaching literally is regarded as a perfectionist. The Christian pacifist, whose conscience will not allow him to make use of violence, is told by the church that he must learn to choose the lesser of two evils: tyranny is worse than war. Some churches have taken the position that a similar

principle applies to marriage. Sometimes, divorce may
be a lesser evil than the continuation of a hopelessly
broken and hostile union. Even Roman Catholicism
will permit the separation of a couple between whom
peace proves impossible. But what of the future? May
such persons seek a new mate, a second chance at fulfillment and happiness? Rome answers negatively; Protestantism with a voice divided, yes and no. The issue
resolves itself ultimately into one of biblical interpretation. Those who refuse permission to remarry point to
the flat prohibition in the New Testament and regard it
as the will of God, with which man dare not tamper,
putting asunder what God has joined. Those who are
more liberal object to an unfair emphasis upon one passage in the New Testament, seeking to go beyond what
they regard as the letter of the law to the spirit. They
stress the note of forgiveness, of new opportunity, of
compassion, declaring that Jesus' word on the Sabbath
applies also to marriage. Neither is to be a strait jacket,
confining and imprisoning man. Both are intended for
his greater joy and fulfillment. "When the doctors differ,
who shall decide?"

One thing seems abundantly clear. If the churches
took more care with the first marriages they performed,
they would be less troubled with problems of the second
or the third. Fortunately two hopeful signs are on the
horizon, perhaps no larger than a man's hand at the
moment, but growing rapidly. First of all, the clergy are
increasingly being trained to deal with marital problems

with some knowledge as well as good intentions. Theological seminaries are introducing courses in pastoral counseling, utilizing some of the skills and tools derived from psychology and medicine. These courses are frequently taught jointly by pastors and psychiatrists, and include supervised clinical training. Second, the custom of giving premarital instruction and advice to couples planning matrimony is decidedly on the increase. Most marriages in trouble can be saved if the man and woman will seek competent professional help, and divorce rarely helps. The same inner tensions and problems that undermined the first marriage continue to operate and eat away corrosively at the second. The church needs desperately to provide the sort of atmosphere where couples with conflicts can come for trained and sympathetic assistance. They do not want or need moralizing sermons at such a time, but most of all an impartial and objective listener. Such a positive approach to preparing people for good marriages and then helping them to maintain their union through storm and stress will go a long way toward rendering the negative wails about divorce obsolete and unnecessary.

The Bible is rather stuffy, from the secular standpoint, about extramarital relations. The woman is throughout forbidden any such activities. The Old Testament gives to the man certain freedoms which the New Testament promptly snatches away from him. Polygamy, recourse to prostitutes (secular), sexual acts with unmarried women not under their father's care, divorce—of all these one might say, "The Lord hath given and the Lord hath taken away." Few secular moderns would go on to add, "Blessed be the name of the Lord!" But of course the permissiveness of the Old Testament represents some survivals from primitive paganism rather than concessions on the part of the Lord. The New Testament is closer to an understanding of the divine will, but then so was the Judaism of the first century. The point is that none of the prohibitions in either Testament is merely negative, motivated by a false prudery or rejection of sexuality. The Bible throughout is concerned with the personal qualities of life, with relationships between total human beings and not simply with "contacts," as Dr. Kinsey called them, between bodies. The Bible points to the highest possibilities, to love and commitment and fidelity, to a lifelong covenant which carries with it a depth of satisfaction and community that is simply unknown to those whose sexual experience is casual or commercial. The appeal is in the plus, in what marital sexuality as a covenant offers in joy and in love, rather than in the minus, in the moralistic threats and condemnations of infidelity. Those who understand, as Bishop Sheen has put it, that "it takes three to get married," who are aware of their responsibility to God as well as to each other, find a depth to their relationship which the world can neither give nor take away.

10

HOMOSEXUALITY

IN

THE BIBLE

OF ALL THE DEVIATIONS from sexual "normalcy," homosexuality is the most common. Apparently it has existed from earliest times, in all parts of the earth. Its popularity and acceptability have varied widely in different ages and different societies, ranging from a tiny "lunatic fringe" minority to rather broad appeal. Some societies have tolerated it, some have encouraged it,

342

and some have condemned and punished it severely. Both the Hebrews and the early church fall into the last category. Homosexuality was to them a sin and a crime, and that attitude has entered deeply into the texture of Western civilization. Why they should have reacted so violently to a practice obviously confined to a negligible part of the population is not clear. The early Hebrews struggled against a cruel nature and the threats of other nomadic tribes. Could it be that their population policy required that all sexual activity be directed to procreation? This would represent a kind of economic determinism, and there may be some truth in it. A somewhat more plausible theory, more plausible because there is some evidence for it in the Old Testament itself, traces the objection to homosexuality to religious roots. Israel's pagan neighbors in the Fertile Crescent used male cult prostitutes in their exaltation of sexuality as the creative principle in nature. This would associate homosexuality with idolatry in the minds of the religious leaders in the Hebrew nation and would be sufficient to condemn the custom.

The reader may express some surprise at this speculation, arguing that a natural revulsion against such perversions is innate, but cultural anthropology does not support this argument. We have already seen, in Chapter 6, that fifth century Athens knew no such revulsion, and other societies reveal a similar toleration, if not encouragement. Among many Indian and Eskimo tribes on the North American continent, for example, the homosexual was regarded as a shaman or holy man, not as a moral outcast or criminal. That the preference for one's own sex should be confined to a minority of any population we should expect, but extremes of social attitude, either enthusiastic endorsement or violent rejection, represent phenomena which require some explanation. Most cultures neither encourage nor punish; they simply accept the fact that people are not all the same. Striking differences, especially among primitives, are frequently interpreted as due to spirit possession, and insanity is akin to sanctity. Thus Greece with its exaltation of homosexual love represents one end of the spectrum and gives rise to some curiosity. Israel's stern prohibition and violent punishment stands at the other end and also raises questions of origin.

The earliest encounter with homosexuality in the Old Testament appears, appropriately, in the city of Sodom, which has bestowed its name upon the practice. The story in Genesis 19 is, in the minds of Old Testament scholars, clearly a mythological attempt to account for the destruction of a city which had once been located near the Dead Sea. This was a tale probably current among the indigenous inhabitants of the region and found by the Hebrews after their arrival. The city's destruction by fire and brimstone indicated volcanic activity, but there are no volcanoes in the region of the Dead Sea, which suggests that the story had been brought in from another locale. If the myth had grown up in the valley, the agent of destruction would doubtless have been water and not fire, an inundation by the Dead Sea itself—a supposition supported by the fact that Genesis traces the origin of the Sea to this event, the destruction of Sodom and Gomorrah.

After a quarrel between the herdsmen of Abraham and those of his nephew Lot, the patriarch offered the younger man his choice of territory, agreeing to accept what was left. "Let there be no strife between you and me . . . for we are kinsmen. Is not the whole land before you? Separate yourself from me. If you take the left hand, then I will go to the right; or if you take the right hand, then I will go to the left" (Genesis 13:8–9). Lot chose the Jordan valley where were located the cities of Sodom and Gomorrah. "Now," says the narrative, preparing the reader for what is to come, "the men of Sodom were wicked, great sinners before the Lord" (Genesis 13:13). But embedded in the book of Genesis is a curious narrative that comes from a source altogether strange and unknown, belonging to none of the main documents which make up the Hexateuch, not J or E or P. This strange chapter 14 paints the king of Sodom, at least, as far from a wicked sinner. He joined forces with his neighbors to strike for liberty from a distant overlord. His forces were defeated and many of the inhabitants of Sodom, including Lot, were taken captive. Abraham sped to the rescue and defeated the victors, releasing his nephew and all of the other prisoners and taking back the store of goods carried away. On Abraham's triumphant return, the king of Sodom went out to meet him, accompanied by Melchizedek, king of Salem and "priest of God most High." After Melchizedek's blessing upon the patriarch, the king of Sodom generously offered, "Give me the persons, but take the goods for yourself" (Genesis 14:21). Abraham refused, but it is clear that this was a monarch more concerned for his subjects than for his wealth.

The Yahwist narrator, however, repeated his theme that "the outcry against Sodom and Gomorrah is great and their sin is very grave" (Genesis 18:20). The cities, therefore, were to be destroyed, because not even ten righteous men could be found in them. This brought the "two angels," companions of Yahweh, into Sodom on a mission of investigating conditions in the city. Their original desire was to spend the night in the street, though their forcing Lot to coax them may have been simply a touch of Oriental courtesy. "The two angels came to Sodom in the evening; and Lot was sitting in the gate of Sodom. When Lot saw them, he rose to meet them, and bowed himself with his face to the earth, and said, 'My lords, turn aside, I pray you, to your servant's house and spend the night, and wash your feet; then you may rise up early and go on your way.' They said, 'No; we will spend the night in the street.' But he urged them strongly; so they turned aside to him and entered his house; and he made them a feast, and baked unleavened bread, and they ate. But before they lay down, the men of the city, the men of Sodom, both young and old, all the people to the last man, surrounded the house; and they called to Lot, 'Where are the men who came to you tonight? Bring them out to us, that we may know them.' Lot went out of the door to the men, shut the door after him, and said, 'I beg you, my brothers, do not act so wickedly. Behold, I have two daughters who have not known man; let me bring them out to you, and do to them as you please; only do nothing to these men, for they have come under the shelter of my roof.' But they said, 'Stand back!' And they said, 'This fellow came to sojourn, and he would play the judge! Now we will deal worse with you than with them.' Then they pressed hard against the man Lot, and drew near to break the door. But the men put forth their hands and brought Lot into the house to them, and shut the door. And they struck with blindness the men who were at the door of the house, both small and great, so that they wearied themselves groping for the door" (Genesis 19:1–11).

This incident sealed the doom of the city, which was destroyed the very next day, and Sodom bequeathed its name to those men who seek "to know" others of their own sex, the Sodomites. The entire episode is questionable historically—an earlier myth taken over by the Yahwist and made a vehicle of Hebrew religion. Whether the Israelites took over the opprobrious reference to Sodom and its inhabitants or created this reputation themselves is not clear. But the twofold affront, the homosexuality itself and the attempt to force their attentions upon unwilling guests, rendered the men of Sodom guilty of a terrible crime in the eyes of Israel. A similar story is found in Judges 19. A certain Levite from the remote hill country of Ephraim traveled to Bethlehem to fetch his concubine who had grown angry with him and returned to her father's house. On the way back home, they stopped for the night at Gibeah, which belonged to Benjamin. They "went in and sat down in the open square of the city; for no man took them into his house to spend the night." Fortunately, an old man returning from his work in the field came upon them and took them to his home. "As they were making their hearts merry, behold, the men of the city, base fellows, beset the house round about beating on the door; and they said to the old man, the master of the house, 'Bring out the man who came into your house, that we may know him.' And the man, the master of the house, went out to them and said to them, 'No, my brethren, do not act so wickedly; seeing that this man has come into my house, do not do this vile thing. Behold, here are my virgin daughter and his concubine; let me bring them out now. Ravish them and do with them what seems good to you; but against this man do not do so vile a thing.' But the men would not listen to him. So the man seized his concubine, and put her out to them; and they knew her, and abused her all night until the morning. And as the dawn began to break, they let her go. And as morning appeared, the woman came and fell down at the door of the man's house where her master was, till it was light" (Judges 19:22–26).

The similarities between this story and that of the Sodomites in Genesis are striking, so much so that one wonders whether the former has not been written with the latter in mind. At Gibeah the "base fellows," sons of Belial, were, however, satisfied with the Levite's concubine, whereas the men of Sodom refused the virgin daughters of Lot. Evidently the men of Gibeah were bisexual; the men of Sodom insisted on their homosexual desires. Both hosts took the responsibilities of Oriental hospitality so seriously that they were willing even to sacrifice their daughters to protect their guests. The Genesis narrative concerns pagans, while the Judges story involves Israelites, evidently corrupted by their Canaanite neighbors. The punishment visited upon the tribe of Benjamin for this terrible crime was swift and severe, but the rest of Israel relented and helped to provide wives for the Benjaminites from outside the nation, since the other tribes had sworn not to marry their daughters to these malefactors. In this case, the misdeed was primarily the violation of the Levite's concubine, but the homosexual designs on the Levite himself were reported with horror.

These two narratives are by no means isolated stories in Israel's history. In 1 Kings 14:22–24, for example, we read that during the reign of Rehoboam, son of Solomon, "Judah did what was evil in the sight of Yahweh, and they provoked him to jealousy with their sins which they committed, more than all that their fathers had done. For they also built for themselves high places, and pil-

lars [phallic symbols], and Asherim on every high hill
and under every green tree; and there were also male
cult prostitutes in the land. They did according to all the
abominations of the nations which Yahweh drove out
before the people of Israel." Here it is clear that sacred
homosexuality was being practiced, borrowed from the
Canaanite cults. Asa, grandson of Rehoboam, "put away
the male cult prostitutes out of the land, and removed
all the idols that his father had made. He also removed
Maacah his mother from being queen mother because
she had an abominable image made for Asherah; and
Asa cut down her image and burned it at the brook
Kidron. But the high places were not taken away"
(1 Kings 15:12–14). "And the remnant of the male cult
prostitutes who remained in the days of his father Asa,
he [Jehoshaphat] exterminated from the land" (1 Kings
22:46). That this did not altogether end the practice,
however, is clear from 2 Kings 23, which describes the
reforms of King Josiah after the "discovery" of the Deuteronomic Law in the Temple. He found "houses of cult
prostitutes" which had to be broken down.

It is against this background that the laws in the
Torah are to be understood. Evidently, male cult prostitutes were a common phenomenon throughout the years
of the monarchy, with some kings supporting them and
other kings exterminating them. They went hand in
hand with the phallic symbols of pillars and Asherim,
the worship on the high places, the exaltation of fertility
and sexuality. Deuteronomy makes the connection quite

specific. "There shall be no cult prostitute . . . of the sons of Israel. You shall not bring the hire of a harlot, or the wages of a dog [Sodomite], into the house of Yahweh your God in payment for any vow; for both of these are an abomination to Yahweh your God" (Deuteronomy 23:17–18). The laws in Leviticus do not mention the cult, but the prohibition is quite explicit. "You shall not lie with a male as with a woman; it is an abomination" (Leviticus 18:22). And the penalty was death. "If a man lies with a male as with a woman, both of them have committed an abomination; they shall be put to death, their blood is upon them" (Leviticus 20:13).

But strong as the Hebrew antagonism to homosexuality was on religious grounds, that is, its association with pagan idolatry, and although the economic or demographic factor was probably also involved, there was still a third element—the psychological or ethnic. We see just a clue to this in Deuteronomy 22:5. "A woman shall not wear anything that pertains to a man, nor shall a man put on a woman's garment; for whoever does these things is an abomination to Yahweh your God." This is not simply a passing pejorative comment on the aberration the psychologists call transvestism— the desire to dress like a member of the opposite sex. Rather, this points to something deeply embedded in the Hebrew consciousness: the conviction that a man was a man and a woman, a woman; and that all confusion between them was to be avoided. "Male and female created he them." There was no twilight zone of bisexuality or hermaphroditism. The man was the head of his household, the *baal* of his family. His strength and his power determined the character of all who belonged to him, and he communicated to them all that he was and did. If he was guilty of a crime, as Achan in Joshua 7, his whole household shared in his fate. "And Joshua and all Israel with him took Achan the son of Zerah, and the [stolen] silver and the mantle and the bar of gold, and his sons and daughters, and his oxen and asses and sheep, and his tent, and all that he had; and they brought them up to the valley of Achor. And Joshua said, 'Why did you bring trouble on us? Yahweh brings trouble on you today.' And all Israel stoned him with stones; they burned them with fire and stoned them with stones" (Joshua 7:24–26).

If a man was powerful and successful, then Yahweh was with him, and the honor and strength that were his were passed on to all members of his family, to his "house." The line of David reigned in the southern kingdom in unbroken succession until the Babylonian exile. Under such circumstances, it was a distortion for a man to act the role of a woman under any conditions. It was his function to lead, to rule, to be strong. Not that the woman was seen as weak or unimportant. She had her indispensable and honored role to play, and she alone could play it. Something in the created order was fundamentally out of joint when a man was not the *baal*, the lord of his family, when he played the part of a woman. Clearly this understanding of masculinity-femininity and their essential separation was neither unique with Israel nor sufficient to explain the ferocity of opposition to homosexuality, decreeing the death penalty for those afflicted with the deviant orientation. That probably stemmed from the connection with idolatry. However, it is striking how the Old Testament view coincides with a growing body of thought in contemporary psychoanalytic circles.

Sandor Rado, for example, the former director of the New York Psychoanalytic Institute, has sharply criticized Freud's whole theory of bisexuality, which has entered into many levels of modern culture and become the basis for much justification and rationalization of homosexuality. His argument is well worth recapitulation against the background of Hebrew psychology. As we have seen, the myth of the androgynes, of a bisexual creation, is a very ancient one, found in several cultures. In the nineteenth century, the myth received surprising and unexpected support from the science of embryology. Cellular material of both male and female gonads was discovered in the embryo, which pointed strongly to a rootage of bisexuality in nature. If both sexes contain cells belonging to the opposite sex, then an imbalance might produce homosexuality. Krafft-Ebing, the Viennese pioneer sexologist and psychiatrist, reasoned that the cellular evidence in the embryo indicated that not only is the peripheral sexual apparatus bisexually predisposed but also the central nervous system as well. The central cortex of the brain must contain male and female centers which determine the sexual inclinations and desires of the individual. Thus a human being can have a male body but an unusually strong feminine center in the cerebrum. Homosexuality is almost never accompanied by physical hermaphroditism or other genital abnormality, and this fact led Krafft-Ebing to assume the autonomy of the sexual centers of the higher nervous system, so that it is subject to developmental disturbances in no way connected with the sexual organs themselves. Sandor Rado argues that there never has been, either in the nineteenth century or at any other time, any neurological evidence to support such an assumption. Krafft-Ebing's hypothesis went far beyond the evidence of biological research. But his theory seemed to account for homosexuality better than any other and it became widely accepted.

Freud followed Krafft-Ebing's lead, describing the central as well as the peripheral part of the sexual apparatus as bisexual. He knew, however, that such a theory had not been physiologically substantiated, and that only biological research could substantiate it. He accepted it as one of his assumptions, borrowed from an outside source, and always recognized it for what it was, never confusing the assumption with established fact. Some of his followers, however, were not so discerning and regarded bisexuality as an established fact rather than as an hypothesis. They did not realize, as Freud did, that bisexuality cannot be proved or refuted by psychoanalysis, that such confirmation can come only from biology. Rado points out that contemporary biology renders the inescapable verdict that there is no such thing as bisexuality in man or any of the higher vertebrates. The double embryological origin of the genital system does not produce any physiological duality in reproductive function. There are individuals who possess parts of the genital organs of the opposite sex, semi-hermaphrodites, but this results in the impairment of sexual activity—sometimes rendering any activity impossible—not in a double reproductive capacity. Physiologically, there are only two sexes, male and female. The rare occurrence of hermaphroditism does not produce a third sex, but either no sex at all or else one or the other with some peripheral appurtenances of the opposite sex. The highly publicized "transformations of sex" by operation are either simply the castration of a male, who nonetheless remains a male, even without his genitals, or else the establishment of the truly dominant reproductive system, obscured and confused by physical anomalies. But there is always one sex or the other, never both.[1]

Karen Horney also voiced her criticism of the concept of bisexuality, maintaining that Freud sometimes sounded as though the male homosexual's mouth or anus had become so "vaginalized" that he derived the same feelings as a woman when those areas were erotically stimulated. But the fact of the matter is that all sexual pleasure has its final goal and climax in the orgasm

---

[1] William Graham Cole, *Sex in Christianity and Psychoanalysis*, pp. 268–269.

which is centered in the genitals. A man always experiences a male orgasm, no matter how desperately he may yearn or pretend to be a woman; and a woman always has a female orgasm, however she may act like a man. All sexual aberrations are deviant methods of stimulation, but irrespective of variety in those methods, the physiological orgasm reflex is the same. This is true of deviations both in aim and in object. One may derive sexual pleasure from attention paid to parts of the body other than the genital organs, and from association with persons or objects other than members of the opposite sex. But the sexual pleasure is centered in the genitals, not elsewhere. If the genitals are not involved, the pleasure is not sexual but alimentary or related to some other biological system. "Male and female created he them" remains a fact of nature.

But if homosexuality is not traceable to biology, then whence does it come? Rado argues that the male-female sex pattern is indicated both anatomically and culturally. Every child grows up with genitals clearly "intended" by nature to be joined with those of the opposite sex. And every child has before him the example of his parents and of society in general, crying out that heterosexuality is "normal." So powerful is this anatomical-cultural conditioning that the early childhood desires of homosexuals universally contain heterosexual elements, and even those who couple exclusively with their own sex attempt to approximate the standard coital pattern, as Rado calls it—the insertion of the penis into the vagina. The homosexual couple act as though there were two sexes, not one, pretending that one is the man, penetrating; the other the woman, being penetrated. But why? What is the attraction which compels the homosexual to violate the powerful taboos of society?

The answer given by all those who reject the biological basis of homosexuality is early experience. Although Kinsey was inclined to look upon all sexual predispositions as somehow innate, he did recognize the strong influence of the initial sexual contacts. Many homosexuals reported having been seduced while they were children by an older person of the same sex. One could, of course, retort that it was only a biological predisposition which made such a seduction possible, since many youngsters flee from all sexual advances in fear and horror. Furthermore, not all those initiated early into homosexual activity continue the practice into adult life. Many a schoolboy, more especially in Britain, has accumulated considerable homosexual experience in adolescence and grown out of it in maturity. Nor can the fact be ignored that some adult homosexuals have been entirely innocent of all sexual activity in their earlier years and have had relations with the opposite sex as their first encounter. Nonetheless the biological is rejected by many contemporary students in favor of the cultural. The predisposition to homosexuality is traced to a distortion in the psychosexual development. For some reason, usually rooted in the family relationships, the individual develops anxiety about the opposite sex and is rendered incapable of functioning normally. The growing child is unable to identify with the parent of the same sex, feeling that he cannot be like his father (or that she cannot be like her mother) and retreats into identification with the parent of the opposite sex.

The male homosexual incurs fears of the vagina. Incidentally, it is those same fears which underlie the phenomenon known as premature ejaculation. The man is able to insert the penis into the vagina, but he unconsciously desires to get out as quickly as possible, so that no matter how he may consciously long to be able to prolong the stimulation, he cannot. The orgasm occurs spontaneously and quickly. Premature ejaculation is a psychological, not a physiological problem. But what is only a partial difficulty with the sufferer from premature ejaculation is virtually a total one for the male homosexual. He cannot stand it even to insert the penis, let alone have an orgasm. This fear of the vagina makes it necessary for him to confine his sexual relations to someone of his own sex, someone without the fearful vagina and with the reassuring penis. A similar attitude prevails in the Lesbian, who fears the penetrating penis and can enjoy sex only with someone who does not possess such a frightening organ. The so-called castration complex seems to play an important role in this process. Popular prejudice against Freudian ideas should not prevent recognition of the fact that awareness of differences between the sexes is often gained by small children in an atmosphere of anxiety and tension. Questions asked by youngsters often reveal their assumption that females must at one time have had a penis and then lost it. Where there is a relatively happy and secure relationship between parents and children, recognition of sexual differences can be absorbed without trauma, and normal identification with the parent of the same sex can readily occur. It is only where the parent-child relationship is already disturbed that sexual differences heighten anxiety and distort development.

The homosexual is one whose psychosexual development has been warped not by his biological predisposition but by his environment. His fears block his ability to enjoy normal sexuality, but he discovers that he can obtain satisfaction and release from sexual tension through his association with those of his own sex. His patterns are compulsive and rigid, lying to a large extent beyond his conscious control. This type of homosexuality Rado terms "reparative," that is, motivated by the desire and the need to repair damage to the ego.

Not to be confused with the true, or reparative, homosexuality are Rado's "variational" or "situational" patterns. Some individuals may on occasion submit passively to the advances of an active homosexual. They may be motivated by curiosity, by the quest for variety, by the desire to try it out, to see what it is like. This probably accounts for the overwhelming majority of Kinsey's alarmingly high proportion of American males who had experienced homosexual contacts. The motive was variational and not reparative, and these individuals cannot properly be regarded as homosexuals. The situational pattern is set in motion by an isolation of the sexes—in prison, on prolonged service on sea or land, any enforced absence from access to heterosexual activity. Individuals so deprived may temporarily resort to sex play among themselves, as a substitute more satisfactory and less lonely than masturbation. But as soon as they are returned to normal society and its outlets, they promptly seek out the opposite sex. Neither can these be regarded as homosexuals. Only the reparative type, who is not free to engage satisfactorily with his opposites, is the true homosexual; and he is, by virtue of his loss of freedom, sick. He is not a vastly superior creature endowed by nature with greater creativity and sensitivity than the mass of normal clods. He is neurotic, and at the deeper levels of his being he knows it. The Old Testament is profoundly aware that the differences between the sexes are rooted in nature, in creation itself, and that diffusion and confusion are freaks.

The New Testament is, as in the case of prostitution, surprisingly silent on the subject of homosexuality—surprisingly, because the problem was so widespread in the Graeco-Roman world. Jesus had nothing to say about homosexuality, possibly because he never encountered it in the remote province of Palestine, whose life was so dominated by Jewish law and custom. The apostle Paul referred to the practice scathingly at several points. We have already noted his words in the opening chapter of his Epistle to the Romans: "The

wrath of God is revealed from heaven against all un-
godliness and wickedness of men who by their wickedness suppress the truth. For what can be known about
God is plain to them, because God has shown it to them.
Ever since the creation of the world his invisible nature,
namely, his eternal power and deity, has been clearly
perceived in the things that have been made. So they
are without excuse; for although they knew God they
did not honor him as God or give thanks to him, but
they became futile in their thinking and their senseless
minds were darkened. Claiming to be wise, they became
fools, and exchanged the glory of the immortal God for
images resembling mortal man or birds or animals or
reptiles. Therefore God gave them up in the lusts of
their hearts to impurity, to the dishonoring of their
bodies among themselves, because they exchanged the
truth about God for a lie and worshiped and served the
creature rather than the Creator, who is blessed forever!
Amen. For this reason God gave them up to dishonorable passions. Their women exchanged natural relations
for unnatural, and the men likewise gave up natural relations with women and were consumed with passion
for one another, men committing shameful acts with
men and receiving in their own persons the due penalty
for their error. And since they did not see fit to acknowl-
edge God, God gave them up to a base mind and to improper conduct" (Romans 1:18–28).

It is significant that in this passage the apostle traced
homosexuality to idolatry, to the failure to know God

aright. A false understanding of God leads to a distorted understanding of one's self and his proper role. This was curiously prophetic in its foreshadowing of current psychological thought, which sees the whole quest for personal identity as intimately related to one's relation to the cosmos, to one's sense of relatedness to purpose and meaning in life. Confusion in one leads inevitably to confusion in the other. Homosexuality is seen therefore, both by Paul and by contemporary psychotherapy, as a symptom of an inner disturbance in identity and relatedness. The apostle's other references to homosexuality were somewhat less extended, and were to the effect that such persons could not enter the kingdom and must therefore be excluded from the church, so long, that is, as they continued in their evil ways. If they would repent and amend their lives, of course salvation was available to them.

"Do you not know that the unrighteous will not inherit the kingdom of God? Do not be deceived; neither the immoral, nor idolaters, nor adulterers, nor homosexuals, nor thieves, nor the greedy, nor drunkards, nor revilers, nor robbers will inherit the kingdom of God. And such were some of you. But you were washed, you were sanctified, you were justified in the name of the Lord Jesus Christ and in the Spirit of our God" (1 Corinthians 6:9–11). The Revised Standard Version renders two Greek words by the one English term, "homosexual." Paul used both *arsenokoites,* which means the act of men lying with men; and *malakoi,* meaning those who are soft, effeminate, who are sensualists. The Eastern Orthodox churches extend the use of the latter term to cover all those who procure orgasm or sexual pleasure in ways other than normal intercourse, but this is an extension which goes beyond both the Greek of the New Testament and classical Greek. The King James Version translates *malakoi* as "effeminate" and *arsenokoites* as "abusers of themselves with mankind." Probably the Revised Standard Version is correct in joining the two words into the one, "homosexual." Notice here that Paul indicated to the Corinthians, "such were some of you." Some within the church had before their conversion been engaging in these practices but had abandoned them. Yet some, perhaps, were continuing; and this had raised questions in the church at Corinth, questions directed to Paul in a long letter from his converts in the isthmus-city. The fact that this passage occurs in the context of a discussion of the meaning of Christian liberty points to the probability that Paul's old problem was reappearing.

He had insisted on the freedom of the Christian from the law. "All things are lawful for me." Some of the newly won church members evidently misunderstood his meaning, regarding themselves as superior to any and all moral considerations. Possibly among these were some homosexuals who believed that their predilection was permissible under the rubric of liberty from the law. Against such a view Paul insisted that

although all things are lawful, not all things are wholesome, not all things contribute to community (1 Corinthians 6:12). "The body is not meant for immorality"
(1 Corinthians 6:13). To engage in sexual relations
with anyone other than one's wife was a sin against
one's body, which belonged to God and was a temple
of the Holy Spirit. This was to go beyond the Old
Testament, which saw sexual sin in terms of the horizontal dimension, wronging one's neighbor. The New Testament sees it also in the light of the vertical dimension,
sinning against God and also against one's self. Thus
"it is a shame even to speak of things they [the pagans]
do in secret." Perhaps this is why Paul had no more
to say, indeed the New Testament itself has no more to
say, on the subject of homosexuality. The indication
is clear that the practice was included in the numerous
references to "immorality" (*porneia*), but a modest
reticence carefully covers a multitude of sins with the
inclusive term.

But can we leave the matter there? Is it sufficient
from our present perspective simply to condemn homosexuality as against God and nature, to preach repentance to those unfortunate enough to be afflicted with it
and to demand that they abandon the practice on penalty of exclusion from the kingdom of God? This is one
of those perilous points where we stand in danger of
being killed by the letter of the law, denying the life-
giving Spirit. For it is perfectly clear that modern
psychotherapy, operating on purely secular presupposi-

tions, is able to heal, to redeem, and to restore without condemnation or judgment, without moralistic legalism. Must the church admit that the medical profession has a balm not found in the pharmacopoeia of the gospel? Clearly the physician can minister to bodily illnesses that pure preaching cannot reach, though Christian Scientists would deny even that. Most within the church, however, gratefully welcome the surgeon's services when an appendix ruptures or a limb is fractured, seeing no contradiction between one's faith and one's recourse to the therapies of medicine. In some circles it used to be—and still is—regarded as a reflection on a man's faith if he fell physically ill. Happily, that day is almost done. Still very much with us, however, is the notion that mental or emotional disease ought somehow to be banished by belief in God and ought not to require the services of the medical practitioner. Neuroses represent a question mark beside one's trust in divine grace. Especially is this true in the area of sexual deviation. How can a man be both a Christian and a homosexual? At the very least, such a man must suppress or sublimate his desires. Such is God's suppress or sublimate his desires. Such is God's command!

But the psychotherapist is able to go beyond mere restraint. He can trace the malady to its roots and cure it. He does not deal only with external behavior but with internal motivation. He transforms the "soul," though he does not, for the most part, either like or use that term. But regardless of the words one uses, which after all only point to things and must never be confused with the things themselves, the reality of the inner, conscious, willing self is there. It matters little whether one calls it soul or ego or personality, the psychiatrist or psychoanalyst can bring healing and new life. What of the pastor? What can he do? Under present circumstances, at least, he is severely limited both by his own lack of skills and by the public image which he projects. He is not trained to probe beneath the surface, to plumb the depths of the unconscious, to trace maladies to their roots, nor should he be. It is not his function to compete with the specialist in nervous and mental disorders. He should have sufficient know-how to be able to recognize a serious disturbance which is beyond his competence as a counselor, so that he can refer the person to the proper therapist. He should know his own limitations.

His more serious handicap, however, is the picture he presents to the community. He is the guardian of the conscience, the bastion of morality, the paragon of all moral virtues. Whatever he may be in fact, this is what is expected of him. It is one of the curious anomalies of history that Luther's doctrine of the spiritual priesthood of all believers, which was intended to bridge the gulf between pulpit and pew, has in fact widened the breach. The Reformation sought to make of every man a priest, insisting that there was no distinction in the eyes of God between "sacred" and "secular" vocations. The maid sweeping a room was as pleasing in the divine sight as the monk in his cell. The sanctity of all work went hand in hand with the priesthood of all believers; and the priest became pastor, one especially fitted by training and disposition to preach the gospel and administer the sacraments, but without special spiritual status conferred upon him by ordination. As the years rolled on, however, the Protestant minister became more and more set apart from his congregation, not by virtue of sacramental power, which he does not possess, but because of his moral superiority, in status if not in fact.

The homosexual, then, sees the plaster saint denouncing from the pulpit the sins of a wicked and adulterous generation. How can the sexual deviant go to his pastor with his problem? The Catholic confessor has the triple virtue of anonymity in the booth, a genuine sacramental power to forgive sins, and a proclaimed irrelevancy of his own moral status. He need not be a saint to absolve a sinner. But the non-Catholic Christian must face his minister in person and in fear that he will be judged and condemned, with no guarantee that he will receive absolution or assistance. Consequently, he turns to the secular priesthood, the psychotherapist, of whatever school. To be sure, he must pay fancy prices to be so shriven, but the cost is small beside the risk of the personal rejection of his pastor. The therapist will neither reject nor judge; he will listen and understand. No therapist will, if he can help it, leave the homosexuality undisturbed. Every effort will be made to discover the source of the distorted sexual orientation and to turn the patient toward relationships more acceptable to himself and to society. But this will involve no discussion of sin or guilt or shame. The sexual deviation is seen as a symptom of a deeper disturbance in the personality, and no wise doctor contents himself with treating symptoms. The source of the disease must be discovered and dealt with, and then the symptoms will vanish of their own accord.

The difficulty with most pastors, apart from the handicap they carry on their lofty pedestal, is their inclination to deal with symptoms rather than with causes, with "sins" rather than with sin. Jesus wasted little time belaboring harlots and libertines, because he knew that they knew they were warped and miserable. They needed not threats and condemnation but forgiveness and acceptance. What was then and is now called for is an inner transformation, not a mere external restraint. The pastor who urges the homosexual to forego his way of life ignores the inner wounds and wants which make the homosexuality necessary. The deviant who seeks help, whether from pastor, priest, or psychiatrist, has already struggled against his problem to the limits of his own strength. If he *could* give it up, he *would* have done so long ago. This is what Alcoholics Anonymous has discovered about drunkards. To blame them only drives them more deeply into guilt and self-loathing, which only makes drinking the more imperative. No one hates his drunkenness more than the alcoholic, and the homosexual, at least in his early years, yearns passionately for normalcy. However, he cannot do it alone, any more than the alcoholic can stop drinking alone. He requires help in the form of sympathy, understanding, and support.

Clearly, the pastor should not try to replace the psychotherapist. This is one of the dangers of the programs of training now spreading through the theological seminaries. The minister abandons the function proper to his office and plays the amateur psychologist, a role he may play very badly. He may be gifted with the all too rare ability to listen; he may have a capacity for empathy and even a natural insight. All of these will stand him in good stead as a counselor, but they do not license him to probe deeply into his parishioners' unconscious minds, nor does his at best superficial seminary training. No course in first aid enables one to perform an appendectomy. The minister is not a medical practitioner. His task is to mediate the forgiving grace of God, a task he is apt to forget if he becomes preoccupied with psychological jargon. The Catholic Church, with the Mass where Christ's death for the sins of men is shown forth, and with the confessional where those sins are personally and directly absolved, provides a constant flow of healing grace to those who can avail themselves of it. The Protestant churches have become platforms for moralistic exhortations or pseudo-psychological advice—social clubs complete with tea parties and ping-pong tables. But where is the

gospel? Where is the good news that God loves the
sinner and comes forth to seek and to save him? A
profound sense of the divine love and acceptance has
delivered men in the past from sins and sorrows as
deep and complex as any we face today. Why should
we doubt that they still have their power?

If the Protestant clergy began once more to preach
the gospel, to derive their message from the Bible instead of from current literature and events, it is just
possible that they might transform the public image
they now project. Instead of appearing as paragons of
virtue, stiff and stern to the sinner as well as the sin,
they might become approachable by the sexual deviant,
as ministers of the mercy of God. This is not to say
that the clergyman can heal the homosexual. He cannot, nor should he be under any illusion about that.
But he can receive him graciously, listen to him sym-
pathetically, and support him compassionately. The
minister may wish to direct his troubled parishioner
to psychiatric channels, but he has not then done with
it. He can offer continued friendship, interest, and concern through the troubled days of the therapy. Above
all, he can offer assurance to the homosexual that God
loves him in spite of his problem, that none of us is
without sin and that we all need forgiveness and grace.
Above all, the minister can make the Word become
flesh in his own attitude toward and treatment of the
homosexual. The love of God means little unless it is
mediated through personality. The pastor cannot heal

the homosexual, but the love of God can. With him all things are possible.

And what of the Christian community? What face does it present to the world, more especially to the sexual deviant? Is it a fellowship of reconciliation, of love and accepting forgiveness; or is it made up of self-righteous Pharisees, gossiping and judging and rejecting? Does it surround the sinner with hostility and threaten him with harm; or does it welcome him into a community of those who know themselves to stand in need of forgiveness, who cannot cast the first stone because they, too, fall short of the demands of a righteous God? This is the strength of Alcoholics Anonymous. The *group* is responsible, not simply its leader, and each member has his tasks to perform in the reclamation of some other alcoholic. Here is truly a place where every man is his neighbor's priest, assuring him that there is a power higher than himself that can help him, and offering himself as an agent of that power. And if it be argued that the homosexual in the Christian community represents a danger to children, the Wolfenden Report in Britain properly replies that no one holds any brief for the seduction of minors, either homosexually or heterosexually. But between two responsible and willing adults, why should homosexual relations be regarded as a serious crime? Those sexually attracted to the young and immature represent a special problem in themselves, whether they are homosexual or heterosexual. The homosexual per se is no threat to children, unless his deviation is further complicated by *paedo-philia*, which may apply to both sexes.

Until such time as the church, clergy and people, take seriously once more the gospel of Jesus Christ, reconciling the world, then the homosexual and the harlot, the adulterer and those caught in the perils and the problems of premarital relations, will turn elsewhere for help. Once before, long ago, God rejected his covenanted people because they turned their backs upon their mission to be a light to lighten the Gentiles. He broke through the old community and established a new one. The fact that his Holy Spirit clearly speaks and works through channels outside the church, redeeming and restoring, should serve as a warning to the Christian community in its self-righteous pride. The church, after all, is not a club for saints; it is a hospital for sick souls. And all those who are sick in any way should find there the healing they so desperately need.

11

OTHER

SEXUAL

DEVIATIONS

❧

W HAT WAS SAID in the preceding chapter about homosexuality applies with equal force to all other forms of
sexual aberration. They represent essentially reparative patterns of behavior, attempts to repair damaged
egos. They are for the most part the only means of
sexual satisfaction open to the individuals concerned,
and they are compulsive and rigid in character. The

373

Bible knows nothing of the sadism-masochism complex. Nor does it speak of such perversions as *necrophilia,* sexual acts with corpses; *coprophilia,* playing with excrement; or *paedophilia,* sex with young children. But incest, rape, *zoophilia* (sexual intercourse with animals), masturbation, immodesty (known to psychotherapy as exhibitionism or voyeurism, the desire to show one's body or to see the bodies of others)—all these find mention in the Scriptures. And once again it is worth noting that the mention does not mince words; it speaks clearly and without blush. Perhaps it would be well to proceed from the milder forms of sexual deviation to the more bizarre aspects, beginning with masturbation and ending with bestiality, sexual relations with animals.

MASTURBATION

The only reference to masturbation in the Bible is a questionable one: the familiar story of Onan. By this time the reader should be well acquainted with the tale of this man whose brother died, leaving a childless widow, Tamar. According to the law of the Levirate marriage, it was Onan's duty to take Tamar to bed and get her with child, a child who should be reared as the son of Onan's dead brother. Onan was unwilling to do his duty in this respect and spilled his seed upon the ground. Whether his act was masturbation or *coitus interruptus* is not clear from the narrative itself (Genesis 38:1–11). The Roman Catholic Church has traditionally interpreted the story as applicable to either or both acts, condemning them as unnatural and as mortal sins. Protestant interpreters have been inclined, on the whole, to regard Onan's sin as his failure to fulfill his responsibilities to his dead brother's memory and posterity, and therefore find no biblical basis for objection to either *coitus interruptus* or masturbation. However, despite the lack of biblical prohibition, Protestantism has been traditionally in agreement with Rome in general opposition to both acts. In recent times, psychology, especially under Freudian influence, has declared that *coitus interruptus* is productive of neuroses and therefore is dangerous on empirical grounds. The case of masturbation is not so clear.

Folklore is rich in dire warnings as to the consequences of masturbation: weakened health, feeblemindedness, insanity, loss of potency in later life. Many a youth has been severely frightened about the terrible things which might result from his self-stimulated orgasms. Modern medicine and modern psychology have together exploded all of these myths about masturbation. There is no physical damage done by the practice, as common sense should have indicated long ago. In societies where very early marriage is the custom, the young couple just beyond puberty experience numerous orgasms in their normal marital coitus without harm to either man or woman. And if, as Gertrude Stein might have put it, an orgasm is an orgasm is an orgasm, what is the physiological difference between a sexual climax achieved by intercourse and one produced by one's self? The body has its own wisdom, and after a period of indulgence in sexual activity of whatever kind, the sources simply dry up, rendering further activity impossible. As the Latin proverb has it, "After intercourse, all animals feel sad, or tired." And there is a certain fatigue produced by orgasm, however it is originated, but the lassitude passes quickly and the body recovers. The semen-producing reflex is closely akin to the mechanism manufacturing spittle. One can spit himself dry, but the supply is soon replenished and no real harm is done. Female masturbation follows a similar pattern; the body inhibits sexual activity after a period of over-indulgence. All stories of the physical dangers of masturbation are old wives' tales to be dismissed.

The real perils of the practice are rather psychological, stemming not from the act itself but from the guilt and anxiety associated with it. If an adolescent worries about his "self-abuse" and its potential consequences, he may develop neurotic symptoms; but these are produced by the worry, not by the masturbation. Thus, parents should beware of passing on to their children obsolete nonsense, lest they do real damage. Virtually every father has had some boyhood experience with masturbation. He was frightened by his own father and learned the essential falsehood of the predictions of doom, yet he persists in frightening his own sons! But despite the lack of physiological danger and the presence of psychological peril, is the Christian attitude toward masturbation to be determined purely on prudential grounds? Are we to say that it is morally indifferent? Some object to the imaginary visions conjured up to accompany masturbation, regarding them as lewd and lascivious. Some find fault with the attempt to achieve sexual satisfaction alone, insisting that sex is for two, not one, the means of creating "one flesh" between man and wife. In any case, masturbation is a poor substitute for sexual intercourse. But as in all acts, the crucial question is motivational. There is considerable difference between the adolescent youth who experiments briefly with his potentialities and then abandons the practice as lacking in real satisfaction, and the individual who compulsively masturbates habitually as a means of expressing defiance or allaying anxiety. The former seems to be a "normal" stage of development which should be treated casually, while the latter represents a neurosis requiring psychotherapy. In neither case is anything gained by accusations of sinfulness and iniquity. Those are far more dangerous than the acts of masturbation themselves. Jesus' concern for motivation is underlined by current psychology. We must learn from both to deal with whys rather than whats, with causes instead of symptoms.

IMMODESTY

There is a pair of sexual deviations which are known to psychopathology as exhibitionism (the desire to show one's sexual organs or naked body to others) and voyeurism (the desire to see the sexual organs or naked bodies of others). The latter, particularly, is found partially in many normal persons without indicating neurosis. It supports all burlesque shows, strip-tease dancers, and many modern magazines. Nor is Hollywood unaware of its presence and power. Whether the desire is pathological or normal depends upon two factors. If sexual satisfaction is in some sense dependent upon seeing, so that the orgasm cannot be achieved without it, and if the urge to see is so strong that it breaks the bonds of rational prudence, resulting in the peeping Tom, then a verdict of neurotic voyeurism must be returned. A pleasure in sexual sights of various sorts is perfectly normal, from the psychological point of view, providing that it is not the *sine qua non* of satisfaction and that it is obtained under more or less acceptable circumstances.

The Old Testament, however, takes a sterner view. From the myth of Adam and Eve onward, nakedness was a questionable state in Israel. The first parents of the race were ashamed when they discovered their nudity, "and they sewed fig leaves together and made themselves aprons" (Genesis 3:7). That this shame was a result of their sin is perfectly clear from the text. "And the man and his wife were both naked, and were not ashamed" (Genesis 2:25). When God confronted Adam after the disobedient act of eating the fruit of the forbidden tree, Adam said, " 'I heard the sound of thee in the garden, and I was afraid, because I was naked; and I hid myself.' He said, 'Who told you that you were naked? Have you eaten of the tree of which I commanded you not to eat?' " (Genesis 3:10–11). So long as Adam and Eve were innocent they were totally unaware of their nakedness. Only their guilt brought it to their attention, and God knew at once, as soon as Adam confessed his fear at his nudity, that he had disobeyed. Just why they should have been ashamed of being naked is not altogether clear. Augustine, who knew full well that the original sin was not sex, produced an ingenious explanation. Why was it, he asked, that they covered their genitals when they had sinned with hands and mouth? Why should not these bodily organs have been covered? Because, he answered, man's disobedience to God resulted in his own body's disobedience to himself in his sexual organs. No longer are these subject to rational control but are excited or placid independently of volition. Sometimes tumescence occurs unbidden, and sometimes it refuses to respond when desired. Thus, man was ashamed and covered himself.

This is neat, but it stems from Augustine's view of concupiscence or insatiable desire as one of the chief consequences of sin, which in turn was the fruit of his own deep-seated suspicion of sex in general. A more plausible explanation seems to lie in the suggestion that the disruption between man and God produced a disruption between man and man, or in this case between man and woman. No longer were they completely open to one another in innocence. Having done what they knew to be wrong, they hid from each other and from God the symbols of their identity. The small child is marvelously ingenuous and open in his innocence, and utterly lacking in modesty. When he has wittingly done wrong, however, he hides—sometimes literally, under the bed or in a closet; sometimes by lowering his eyes or looking away. It is as clear to a parent as it was to God that his child is lying. Innocence is banished by the terrible knowledge of good and evil. Adam is in truth every man.

But since the Genesis narrative is a myth, it is the effect of Israel's distaste for nakedness, not its cause. The Yahwist obviously borrowed the story from another culture and transformed it to make it carry his own message. Doubtless the nakedness and the shame were already present in the original, and the Yahwist passed them along as he had found them. He clearly had no disapproval of sex as such, but he seems to have been concerned for modesty. This becomes clear in the curious tale of Noah's drunken sleep in Genesis 9: "Noah was the first tiller of the soil. He planted a vineyard; and he drank of the wine, and became drunk, and lay uncovered in his tent. And Ham, the father of Canaan, saw the nakedness of his father, and told his two brothers outside. Then Shem and Japheth took a garment, laid it upon both their shoulders, and walked backward and covered the nakedness of their father;

their faces were turned away, and they did not see their father's nakedness. When Noah awoke from his wine and knew what his youngest son had done to him, he said, 'Cursed be Canaan; a slave of slaves shall he be to his brothers.' He also said, 'Blessed by Yahweh my God be Shem; and let Canaan be his slave. God enlarge Japheth, and let him dwell in the tents of Shem; and let Canaan be his slave' " (Genesis 9:20–27). This story combines several factors, but it carries unmistakably a judgment on three things the Israelites found among the inhabitants in their new homeland: drunkenness, sexual perversion, and filial impiety. "Noah was the first tiller of the soil." Here speaks the prejudice of the nomad, the shepherd, which speaks also in God's preference for Abel's sacrifice over Cain's. Cain was a farmer, Abel a shepherd. Yahweh found many things questionable about agriculture, so intimately connected was it with idolatry, with Baal worship. "He planted a vineyard; and he drank of the wine, and became drunk, and lay uncovered in his tent." So it happens with farmers who plant vineyards. They become drunk, something no good nomad would do. Why Noah should not have lain uncovered in his own tent is unclear except on the basis of a prior prejudice against nudity. It was a symbol of his loss of self-control and modesty. A son, however, must not look upon his father's nakedness, although there is a suggestion that there was more here than mere looking. "In the primary, popular form of the story there probably occurred here—as shown by the reference in vs. 24 to 'what his younger son had done to him'—an account of an indecent attack by Canaan on his father. This J-1 [the Yahwist] omitted from motives of delicacy."[1] It would appear, then, that a revulsion against both sexual perversion and filial impiety lay behind this story.

The law itself placed the strongest ban on "uncovering nakedness," usually associated with near relatives, which connected the prohibition with incest. There are two references, however, which once again point to the fear of pagan fertility cults. In Exodus 20, which provided instructions for the building of the altar, the section concludes, "And you shall not go up by steps to my altar, that your nakedness be not exposed on it" (Exodus 20:26). This presupposed that the head of the household served as priest, and that he wore the usual short skirt. An elevated position on steps would expose his genitals. Therefore, the precautions were extended in Exodus 28:42–43: "And you shall make for them [the priests] linen breeches to cover their naked flesh; from the loins to the thighs shall they reach; and they shall be upon Aaron, and upon his sons, when they go into the tent of meeting, or when they come near the altar to minister in the holy place; lest they bring guilt upon themselves and die." The sacred sexual cults of Canaan had considerable display of sexual organs and of nudity. The worship of Yahweh was to be absolutely pure of such contamination.

---

[1] *The Interpreter's Bible,* Vol. I, p. 556.

So concerned was the Law for modest decorum in the wives of Israel that the severest penalties were decreed. For example, "When men fight with one another, and the wife of the one draws near to rescue her husband from the hand of him who is beating him, and puts out her hand and seizes him by the private parts, then you shall cut off her hand; your eye shall have no pity" (Deuteronomy 25:11–12). This served as a warning to any and all women that the private parts of a man were taboo. No sexual relations were to take place, either, during menstruation, though this seemed due to the awe of blood rather than mere modesty (Leviticus 18:19, 20:18).

The prohibitions in Leviticus all deal with incest, and we shall consider those in that connection. There is one curious reference to nakedness in 1 Samuel, when Saul blurted out his wrath at his son Jonathan, for his defense of David. "Then Saul's anger was kindled against Jonathan, and he said to him, 'You son of a perverse, rebellious woman, do I not know that you have chosen the son of Jesse to your own shame, and to the shame of your mother's nakedness?' " (1 Samuel 20:30). This verse has been variously interpreted. Some have seen in it a suggestion of homosexual relations between David and Jonathan, which would be to the shame of Jonathan's mother's nakedness. They buttress their argument by citing the verse in David's lament over Saul and Jonathan: "I am distressed for you, my brother Jonathan; very pleasant have you been to me; your love

to me was wonderful, passing the love of women"
(2 Samuel 1:26). There are other indications, such as,
"The soul of Jonathan was knit to the soul of David, and
Jonathan loved him as his own soul" (1 Samuel 18:1).
These few verses, however, are very flimsy hooks on
which to hang such a theory. The suspicion is strong
that this interpretation comes from those whose own
angle of vision finds homosexuality in every possible
area. The more usual rendering of the verse is to read
Saul's meaning as simply, "You are no son of mine! If
you were, you would be more concerned to preserve
my dynasty upon the throne of Israel. You are playing
directly into the hands of David's ambition. This is to
the shame of your mother's nakedness."

The New Testament also reveals its concern for modesty, more particularly of women. Paul expressed the
dictum that women ought not to appear outside the
house with uncovered head. "Any man who prays or
prophesies with his head covered dishonors his head,
but any woman who prays or prophesies with her head
unveiled dishonors her head—it is the same as if her
head were shaven. For if a woman will not veil herself,
then she should cut off her hair; but if it is disgraceful
for a woman to be shorn or shaven, let her wear a veil.
. . . Judge for yourselves; is it proper for a woman to
pray to God with her head uncovered? Does not nature
itself teach you that for a man to wear long hair is de-
grading to him, but if a woman has long hair, it is her
pride? For her hair is given to her for a covering"

(1 Corinthians 11:4–6, 13–15). This passage reflects the mores of the Graeco-Roman world, where decent women wore long hair and a covering over the head (sometimes a veiled face) when going out of doors. Courtesans and prostitutes went about with bare heads, and bold women and women in disgrace sometimes had their hair cropped short. Thus any woman who appeared in public with uncovered head was patently immodest, and this Paul could not tolerate in the churches. The reader familiar with orthodox Jewish practice in the synagogue may be puzzled by the reference to the man's uncovered head in worship. The custom of wearing prayer shawls, originally a sign of mourning, dates from the fourth century A.D. and was not yet a Jewish practice.

The Pastoral Epistles also reflect concern for the modesty of women. "I desire that . . . women should adorn themselves modestly and sensibly in seemly apparel, not with braided hair or gold or pearls or costly attire" (1 Timothy 2:8–9). This sort of ostentation was to tempt men to look at them lustfully and to incur sin. Christian women were not to emulate their pagan sisters in this respect. Younger widows were to remarry, lest they get into trouble. "Refuse to enrol younger widows; for when they grow wanton against Christ they desire to marry, and so they incur condemnation for having violated their first pledge. Besides that, they learn to be idlers, gadding about from house to house, and not only idlers but gossips and busybodies, saying

what they should not. So I would have younger widows
marry, bear children, rule their households, and give
the enemy no occasion to revile us. For some have already strayed after Satan" (1 Timothy 5:11–15). And
not only is the New Testament concerned for modesty
of dress and apparel, but of speech. "Take no part in
the unfruitful works of darkness, but instead expose
them. For it is a shame even to speak of the things
that they do in secret" (Ephesians 5:11–12). It is perhaps on these grounds that the New Testament is silent
on the other sexual sins. Paul had a brief reference to
incest, as we shall see, evoked by a specific case within
the church at Corinth. But beyond that, there is no reference to incest, to rape, or to sexual relations with
animals. The Old Testament is less reticent.

RAPE

The first account of rape in the Bible occurs in Genesis 34. "Now Dinah the daughter of Leah, whom she
had borne to Jacob, went out to visit the women of the
land; and when Shechem the son of Hamor the Hivite,
the prince of the land, saw her, he seized her and lay
with her and humbled her. And his soul was drawn to
Dinah the daughter of Jacob; he loved the maiden and
spoke tenderly to her." The narrative goes on to re-
count how Shechem besought his father to get Dinah
for his wife, surely an honorable request. "And Hamor
the father of Shechem went out to Jacob to speak with

him. The sons of Jacob came in from the field when they heard of it; and the men were indignant and very angry, because he had wrought folly in Israel by lying with Jacob's daughter, for such a thing ought not to be done." But Hamor and Shechem pleaded with Jacob and his sons, offering to make a tribal alliance, sealed not only by the marriage of Dinah and Shechem but by others as well. "Make marriages with us; give your daughters to us, and take our daughters for yourselves." Shechem offered anything Jacob might ask "as marriage present and gift." Then the sons of Jacob dissembled. They could not agree to marriages with a tribe of uncircumcised males. If the Hivites would agree to be circumcised, the treaty might be concluded. So eager was Shechem for Dinah and so eager was Hamor to please his son that they persuaded the men of their city to agree. Then "on the third day, when they were sore," the sons of Jacob came into the city and slew Shechem and Hamor and took Dinah home, killing all the males and plundering the city "because their sister had been defiled." Everything was captured and taken as booty: flocks, herds, wealth, little ones, wives. Jacob rebuked his sons, saying that his neighbors might band together against him. "But they said, 'Should he treat our sister as a harlot?'" (Genesis 34). A terrible vengeance for what Israel regarded as a terrible deed.

A similar vengeance was visited upon the men of Gibeah in the tribe of Benjamin, who violated the concubine of the man from the remote hill country of

Ephraim. They preferred, apparently, homosexuality, but were satisfied with the concubine as a substitute. Theirs was a mass rape, which resulted in the exhaustion and ultimately the death of the woman (Judges 19). Israel came forth en masse to punish the Benjaminites for this abomination. The nation as a whole could not simply exterminate one of its own units, however. "The people came to Bethel, and sat there till evening before God, and they lifted up their voices and wept bitterly. And they said, 'O Yahweh, the God of Israel, why has this come to pass in Israel, that there should be today one tribe lacking in Israel?' " They could not go back on the solemn oath they had sworn not to marry their daughters to the tribe of Benjamin, but they could co-operate in providing women from other sources. "So the congregation sent thither [to Jabesh-Gilead] twelve thousand of their bravest men, and commanded them, 'Go and smite the inhabitants of Jabesh-Gilead with the edge of the sword; also the women and the little ones. This is what you shall do; every male and every woman that has lain with a male you shall utterly destroy.' And they found among the inhabitants of Jabesh-Gilead four hundred young virgins who had not known man by lying with him; and they brought them to the camp at Shiloh, which is in the land of Canaan."

But this supply was insufficient to make up for the loss of women suffered by the Benjaminites in the war between them and the rest of Israel. "Then the elders of the congregation said, 'What shall we do for wives for those who are left, since the women are destroyed out of Benjamin?' And they said, 'There must be an inheritance for the survivors of Benjamin, that a tribe be not blotted out from Israel. Yet we cannot give them wives of our daughters.'" So they laid further plans. "They said, 'Behold, there is a yearly feast of Yahweh at Shiloh, which is north of Bethel, on the east of the highway that goes up from Bethel to Shechem, and south of Lebonah.' And they commanded the Benjaminites, saying 'Go and lie in wait in the vineyards, and watch; if the daughters of Shiloh come out to dance in the dances, then come out of the vineyards and seize each man his wife from the daughters of Shiloh, and go to the land of Benjamin. And when their fathers or brothers come to complain to us, we will say to them, "Grant them graciously to us; because we did not take for each man of them his wife in battle, neither did you give them to them, else you would now be guilty."' And the Benjaminites did so, and took their wives, according to their number, from the dancers whom they carried off; then they went and returned to their inheritance, and rebuilt the towns and dwelt in them" (Judges 21). Thus, what began as the rape of one concubine by a mob of men ended with a battle, a slaughter, and a double rape—of the virgins of Jabesh-Gilead and of the daughters of Shiloh. This is strongly reminiscent of the Roman rape of the Sabine women. Necessity sometimes gives birth to strange inventions.

The other celebrated case of rape in the Old Testament is Amnon's violation of Tamar, which was half-incestuous. We have already noted the curious touch in this story of Tamar's suggestion that King David would permit the marriage of two of his children because they had different mothers. "Now therefore, I pray you," said Tamar, "speak to the king; for he will not withhold me from you" (2 Samuel 13:13). Was this merely a clever stratagem on her part to avoid rape, or was incest permissible for the royal family of Israel, as it was for the ruling house of Egypt? Absalom's comforting of his twin sister would seem to indicate that the incest was not so heinous. "Has Amnon your brother been with you?" he asked her. "Now hold your peace, my sister; he is your brother; do not take this to heart." And we are told "Absalom hated Amnon, because he had forced his sister Tamar" (2 Samuel 13:20, 22). It was the rape that rankled, not the incest. After Amnon's murder two full years later, it was said that "by the command of Absalom this has been determined from the day he forced his sister Tamar" (2 Samuel 13:32). Once again, rape was rewarded by death.

The law provided death to the rapist of a betrothed young woman. "If in the open country a man meets a young woman who is betrothed, and the man seizes her and lies with her, then only the man who lay with her shall die. But to the young woman you shall do nothing; in the young woman there is no offense punishable by death, for this case is like that of a man attacking and murdering his neighbor; because he came upon her in the open country, and though the betrothed young woman cried for help, there was no one to rescue her" (Deuteronomy 22:25–27). A different fate was decreed for the man forcing a woman unengaged. "If a man meets a virgin who is not betrothed, and seizes her and lies with her, and they are found, then the man who lay with her shall give to the father of the young woman fifty shekels of silver, and she shall be his wife, because he has violated her; he may not put her away all his days" (Deuteronomy 22:28). The rape itself was not so serious. It was the violation of another man's rights which was of concern. The rape of a betrothed woman was tantamount to adultery, and therefore merited death. But the rape of an unbetrothed girl could be expiated by marriage, though the husband had forfeited his right to divorce. Once more, the rights of the male asserted themselves.

INCEST

The most widespread sexual taboo, found in tribes all over the earth, is that against incest. In the ancient Middle East, there was a strong prejudice against it, but there were exceptions, as in Egypt and among the Hittites. So Israel was in general opposed to all incestuous relationships, even where no actual blood-kinship was involved, as in relations established by marriage. But there were also some curious exceptions to the broad rules. We first encounter the practice in the Old Testament after the destruction of Sodom and Gomorrah. Lot and his family, being warned by God, escaped early in the morning and made their way up into the hills. Lot's wife disobeyed the strict instructions not to look back and was changed to a pillar of salt. "Now Lot went up out of Zoar and dwelt in the hills with his two daughters. . . . And the first-born said to the younger, 'Our father is old, and there is not a man on earth to come in to us after the manner of all the earth. Come, let us make our father drink wine, and we will lie with him, that we may preserve offspring through our father.' So they made their father drink wine that night; and the first-born went in, and lay with her father; he did not know when she lay down or when she arose. And on the next day, the first-born said to the younger, 'Behold, I lay last night with my father; let us make him drink wine tonight also; then you go in and lie with him, that we may preserve offspring through our father.' So they made their father drink wine that night also; and the younger arose, and lay with him; and he did not know when she lay down or when she arose. Thus both the daughters of Lot were with child by their father. The first-born bore a son, and called his name Moab; he is the father of the Moabites to this day. The younger also bore a son, and called his name Ben-ammi; he is the father of the Ammonites to this day" (Genesis 19:30–38).

This whole narrative appears to be an early one taken

over by the Yahwist and adapted to his own purposes. The original form of the story probably followed upon a flood or other world-wide catastrophe, as the daughters' words would indicate, saying, "There is not a man on earth to come in to us after the manner of all the earth." Their action in this setting would be praiseworthy, and doubtless this was the original intention of the story, although the namelessness of the daughters suggests that the heroism and initiative lay with their father. The Yahwist, however, had an interest in Lot's reputation, as the nephew of Abraham, and so absolved him of blame by making him drunk and unaware. The fact that the Moabites and Ammonites were traced to this incestuous union indicates the Yahwist's disapproval, for both of these peoples were enemies of Israel. Moab was traced to the Hebrew *me'abh,* "from my father," and the Ammonites to *Ben-Ammi,* meaning "son of my kinsman." The true etymology of both terms is uncertain, but it is hinted that incest was still going on among them at the time of the Yahwist.

The Law was quite specific as to the degrees of relationship within which sexual relations were forbidden. The phrase "to uncover the nakedness of" was used again and again. The "nakedness" of a woman belonged to her husband; it was his exclusive right. "None of you shall approach any one near of kin to him to uncover nakedness. I am Yahweh. You shall not uncover the nakedness of your father, which is the nakedness

of your mother; she is your mother, you shall not uncover her nakedness. You shall not uncover the nakedness of your father's wife; it is your father's nakedness.
You shall not uncover the nakedness of your sister, the
daughter of your father or the daughter of your mother,
whether born at home or born abroad. You shall not
uncover the nakedness of your son's daughter or of
your daughter's daughter, for their nakedness is your
own nakedness. You shall not uncover the nakedness
of your father's wife's daughter, begotten by your
father, since she is your sister. You shall not uncover
the nakedness of your father's sister; she is your father's
near kinswoman. You shall not uncover the nakedness
of your mother's sister, for she is your mother's near
kinswoman. You shall not uncover the nakedness of
your father's brother, that is, you shall not approach
his wife; she is your aunt. You shall not uncover the
nakedness of your daughter-in-law; she is your son's
wife, you shall not uncover her nakedness. You shall
not uncover the nakedness of your brother's wife; she
is your brother's nakedness. You shall not uncover the
nakedness of a woman and of her daughter, and you
shall not take her son's daughter or her daughter's
daughter to uncover her nakedness; they are your near
kinswomen; it is wickedness. And you shall not take a
woman as a rival wife to her sister, uncovering her
nakedness while her sister is yet alive" (Leviticus
18:6–18).

The forbidden degrees were, then, mother, stepmother, sister or half sister, granddaughter, aunt whether by blood or by marriage, daughter-in-law. No man could marry two sisters while both were alive, nor could one marry a woman and her daughter or her granddaughter. Curiously, the father was not specifically forbidden his own daughter, though clearly the general "any one of near kin" covered that also. The punishments appropriate to the violations of the various degrees were laid down in Leviticus 20: "The man who lies with his father's wife has uncovered his father's nakedness; both of them shall be put to death, their blood is upon them. If a man lies with his daughter-in-law, both of them shall be put to death; they have committed incest, their blood is upon them. . . . If a man takes a wife and her mother also, it is wickedness; they shall be burned with fire, both he and they, that there may be no wickedness among you. . . . If a man takes his sister, a daughter of his father or a daughter of his mother, and sees her nakedness, and she sees his nakedness, it is a shameful thing, and they shall be cut off in the sight of the children of their people; he has uncovered his sister's nakedness, he shall bear his iniquity. . . . You shall not uncover the nakedness of your mother's sister or of your father's sister, for that is to make naked one's near kin; they shall bear their iniquity. If a man lies with his uncle's wife, he has uncovered his uncle's nakedness; they shall bear their sin, they shall die childless. If a man takes his brother's wife, it is impurity; he has uncovered his brother's nakedness, they shall be childless" (Leviticus 20:11–21). Presumably the Levirate marriage was excluded from the last of these provisions.

Death was the penalty for relations between son and mother or stepmother, between father-in-law and daughter-in-law; death by burning for coitus between a man and two women, mother and daughter; death before the assembled community for brother and sister or half sister; childlessness for a nephew and uncle's wife, and for brother and sister-in-law. The punishment for aunt and nephew is unclear. The silence of Leviticus 18 on relations between father and daughter was more than compensated for by Leviticus 20, where burning was the prescribed penalty. Deuteronomy repeated these laws against incest: "A man shall not take his father's wife, nor shall he uncover her who is his father's" (Deuteronomy 22:30). "Cursed be he who lies with his father's wife, because he has uncovered her who is his father's. . . . Cursed be he who lies with his sister, whether the daughter of his father or the daughter of his mother. . . . Cursed be he who lies with his mother-in-law" (Deuteronomy 27:20, 22, 23).

Despite these laws, there were violations. "While Israel [Jacob] dwelt in that land [beyond the tower of Eder] Reuben [his son] went and lay with Bilhah, his father's concubine; and Israel heard of it" (Genesis 35:22). This accounts for the curse the dying father placed upon him. "Reuben, you are my first-born, my might and the first fruits of my strength, pre-eminent in pride and pre-eminent in power. Unstable as water, you shall not have pre-eminence because you went up to your father's bed; then you defiled it—you went up to my couch!" (Genesis 49:3–4). Abraham's brother Nahor married the daughter of their other brother, Haran (Genesis 11:27–29). Esau married the daughter of Ishmael, the half brother of his father (Genesis 28:9). Rehoboam, a grandson of David, married two of his first cousins, Mahalath, the daughter of Jerimoth the son of David, and of Abihail the daughter of Eliab the son of Jesse (Rehoboam's great-uncle) and also Maacah the daughter of Absalom, whom he loved "above all his wives and concubines (he took eighteen wives and sixty concubines, and had twenty-eight sons and sixty daughters)" (2 Chronicles 11:18–21). In 1 Kings 2 Adonijah, the eldest son of David, who rightfully should have succeeded his father but lost out to Solomon, asked that Abishag the Shunammite be given him as his wife, an innocent enough request on the surface. But in 1 Kings 1 we read, "Now King David was old and advanced in years; and although they covered him with clothes, he could not get warm. Therefore his servants said to him, 'Let a young maiden be sought for my lord the king, and let her wait upon the king, and be his nurse; let her lie in your bosom, that my lord the king may be warm.' So they sought for a beautiful maiden throughout all the territory of Israel, and found Abishag the Shunammite, and brought her to the king. The maiden was very beautiful; and she became the king's nurse and ministered to him; but the king knew her not" (1 Kings 1:1–4).

Adonijah was asking for the late king's last bedfellow, which was not only a violation of the law against taking one's father's wife; it was a claim to the throne. Adonijah persuaded Bathsheba, Solomon's mother, to make his request to the new monarch. Solomon asked in rage, "Why do you ask Abishag the Shunammite for Adonijah? Ask for him the kingdom also; for he is my elder brother. . . . Adonijah shall be put to death this day!" (1 Kings 2:13–25). It is significant that the Song of Songs depicts its sensuous love scenes as taking place between Solomon and the Shunammite.

Incest, then, was taboo in Israel, but never absolutely. The Levirate marriage set aside the law against brother's and sister-in-law's coitus. There were various exceptions and violations. But Israel did not, like many primitive tribes, ban even the sight of near relatives of the opposite sex. The solidarity of the family as a unit was preserved. Close association was to be expected, but temptation could be resisted because of a carefully cultivated horror and a severe penal code. Again, the prohibition is by no means peculiar to the Hebrews; it is well-nigh universal in human society, not so much because of genetic considerations, which are dubious, as because of its destructive effect on families. Therefore children are to be reared to regard such possibilities with disgust and loathing, with guilt and shame. Extramarital sexual relations are likely to occur, by virtue of sheer proximity, with other members of the same household. To hold the family together in unity and without suspicion or jealousy, the incest taboo is made a fearful and dreadful barrier.

The apostle Paul had a brief reference to a semi-incestuous relationship in his correspondence with the Corinthian Church. "It is actually reported that there is immorality among you, and of a kind that is not found even among the pagans; for a man is living with his father's wife. And you are arrogant! Ought you not rather to mourn? Let him who has done this be removed from among you. For though absent in body I am present in spirit, and as if present, I have already pronounced judgment in the name of the Lord Jesus on the man who has done such a thing. When you are assembled, and my spirit is present, with the power of our Lord Jesus, you are to deliver this man to Satan for the destruction of the flesh, that his spirit may be saved in the day of the Lord Jesus" (1 Corinthians 5:1–5). Here the incest was spoken of with genuine horror; it was "not even found among the pagans." So strongly did the apostle feel about this that he asked for deliverance of the man to "Satan" (apparently a curse unto death, as in the case of Ananias and Sapphira).

BESTIALITY

One can learn a great deal about a culture by studying its law codes. It is never necessary to prohibit

something which nobody does. Laws against certain
acts are always indications that these things have been
done and that they have a certain appeal. The act
which horrifies the entire populace, one which no one
would dream of doing, rarely finds expression in law.
The Middle East in ancient times had an economy
based largely on pastoral activity. Agriculture and trade
played an increasing role as the centuries passed, but
always there were the flocks—sheep and goats and cattle.
The Hebrews apparently did not have much acquaintance with the camel. Their language contains no word
for the female of that species, which would be unac-
countable if they had bred camels at all. They did,
however, have considerable experience with the other
grazing beasts. The Old Testament is filled with references to sheep and goats and cattle. They were regarded by the law as "clean," fit to be eaten provided
that the blood was drained from them.

Wherever there are shepherds and goatherds, keep-
ers of grazing animals, there are always jokes and sug-
gestive remarks about sexual relations between the
beasts and the men responsible for their care, the men
using the animals as a means of sexual release. This is
the more true because the pastoral life frequently involves long periods out on the grazing lands away from
home. That such a thing was not entirely unknown in
Israel is clear from the Law, although there is no
narrative in the Old Testament about the practice.
"Whoever lies with a beast," warned Exodus, "shall be

put to death" (Exodus 22:19), a law which also was found in ancient Babylon, though there the king could, if he chose, pardon the offender. Leviticus repeated the prohibition twice, stating the ban in chapter 18 and the penalty in chapter 20, as with incest. "And you shall not lie with any beast and defile yourself with it" (Leviticus 18:23). "If a man lies with a beast, he shall be put to death; and you shall kill the beast" (Leviticus 20:15). Deuteronomy included the act among the curses which it leveled upon the more serious sins. "Cursed be he who lies with any kind of beast" (Deuteronomy 27:21). This multiple reference indicates that bestiality was practiced among the Hebrews and that they regarded it as a grossly unnatural act, since even the innocent animal was to be killed also.

Somewhat more difficult to account for, on the grounds of nomadic economy, is the prohibition against women's sexual relations with animals. This more possibly points to the practices of a pagan fertility cult. "Neither shall any woman give herself to a beast to lie with it: it is perversion" (Leviticus 18:23). "If a woman approaches any beast and lies with it, you shall kill the woman and the beast; they shall be put to death, their blood is upon them" (Leviticus 20:16). The bull and the ram were both important symbols in cults of sacred sexuality, obviously because of the impressive phallus they carry. The prohibition against women cohabiting with animals had a double indemnity: both the unnatural character of the act, as with the man-beast relationship; and its idolatrous nature as well. Certainly, few persons would care to defend bestiality or *zoophilia* as either "natural" or "normal," although many of the studies of animal sexuality show sexual activity across species lines. What may be true of other animals, however, has little relevance for man at this point. Purely aesthetic considerations, those of sensibility, render the practice entirely questionable and even revolting, moral considerations aside.

The Bible, then, treats of the full range of human sexuality: premarital intercourse, sex in marriage, prostitution, adultery, divorce, homosexuality, masturbation, immodesty, rape, incest, and bestiality. It permits and it prohibits, as do all codes of law and systems of ethics. What it does, though, has usually sound thinking and sound reasons behind it. One cannot point the finger of prudery at the Bible; it is astonishingly frank. Nor can it be accused of an unrealistic idealism. It faces the depths of human nature as well as its heights, and takes both dimensions into account. Perversion is no stranger to the Scriptures. We have tried to see the various biblical attitudes against the backdrop of history, to understand them in the context of their own times. What remains to be done is to see whether the Bible has anything to say to us today in a world so vastly changed.

12

THE BIBLE

AND

THE WORLD

OF

DR. KINSEY

❦

THERE IS A WIDESPREAD misunderstanding about the
Bible, about what it is and what it does. The most extravagant claims are made for it on the one hand; while
on the other it is summarily dismissed as full of contra-
dictions and errors, a collection of old wives' tales and
folklore that is dated and irrelevant. The Bible has
joined that noble company of martyrs which includes

the writings of Darwin, Marx, and Freud: books that everybody talks about but nobody reads! In the circles of ignorance, experts multiply. Unhappily, Hollywood has contributed its share to the general confusion by its cinematic treatment of biblical stories, a treatment which almost invariably stresses the miraculous, the extraordinary, and the spectacular. Before we can properly assess what the Bible has to say to the world of Messrs. Freud and Kinsey, we must understand what kind of book it is.

THE BIBLE AND THE WORD OF GOD

There is a vague impression abroad that the Reformation somehow or other substituted the authority of the Bible for the authority of the church. An infallible book replaced an infallible pope. The Bible is supposed to be the word of God, inerrant in every detail, or so at least Protestants are presumed to believe. And if one starts picking and choosing what he will and will not accept, where does the process end? Isn't it really a choice between all or nothing? If only *some* of it is the word of God, then who is to decide? To answer, "The Church," is to land in the lap of Rome, while to respond, "Each individual," is not only to invite chaos but also to welcome it. Confusion is wedded to confounding.

Perhaps a few swift gusts of fact will dispel the mists and reveal the blue sky of clarity. To begin with, the Protestant Reformers did not say that the Bible is the

word of God, did not substitute the authority of the
Holy Book for that of Holy Church, did not leave every
individual free to believe as he chose. The attempt to
give a status of sanctity to the Bible as pure printed
word is a relatively recent one, centered in a movement
known as Fundamentalism. Neither Luther nor Calvin
equated the dead, flat print of the page with the living
word of God. They said the Bible *becomes* the word of
God as its contents are illumined by the operation of
the Holy Spirit in the heart and mind of the believing
reader. Of course the Bible is not the word of God to an
unbeliever! It may be great literature or interesting
history or dull mythology, but God does not speak to
one whose ears are stopped with the wax of atheism.
Nor is the Bible the word of God in every jot and tittle
at every moment to every Christian. The devout may
read for hours and days in uneventful routine. The
words lie still upon the page without life or power. And
then suddenly, unpredictably, something leaps out at
the reader and addresses him personally, directly, so
that he feels unmistakably that God has spoken to him.
The Holy Spirit has made of those words *The* Word.

The Bible is a story of encounters, personal dialogues
between God and man. God speaks to individuals in
the midst of their concrete situations and he speaks with
a relevant precision. Each man is addressed where he
lives and stands. It is not a collection of abstract philosophical truths, eternally valid under all circumstances.
It is a book rooted in and related to history, not only

the history of nations but the history of individual men
and women. So it speaks to those who read it, not in
timeless aphorisms but in pointed directness. A passage
read this month may be lifeless and without voice because the reader's situation is such as to render him
deaf. Next month, however, his circumstances may have
changed, and the same passage will speak a word direct
from God. Similarly a verse eloquent today may tomorrow be silent. The Holy Spirit deals with persons where
they are, not with spirits lifted out of their involvements
in experience into some ideal vacuum.

The Bible is not, then, the word of God apart from
the work of the divine Spirit. It becomes the word of
God in the lives of individuals. This is not to say that
each man is "left free" to believe as he may choose. No
man seized by the word of God is free. He is bound by
a sense of commitment, of obligation, of responsibility.
Seek to escape as he may (and who has not so sought?)
he is nonetheless claimed and commanded. Knowing
himself to be a finite mortal, he ought not to fall into
the error of assuming that God's word to him is necessarily God's word to every man. He is saved from the
chaos of subjectivism by the fact that what he hears
comes to him from the tradition, from the record of
revelation which was centuries in the making. He must
always ask himself whether he may not be isolating a
single verse or chapter, distorting it and interpreting it
in a way that is inconsistent with the totality of the

biblical message. There is, to be sure, variety in the Bible, as one should expect, since the divine word is filtered through a variety of individual human beings. But diversity is not discord. There is a consensus, a unity to the various strands, as recent biblical scholarship has been insisting. The varieties of the viewpoints and sources of both Testaments were explored and exploited by the nineteenth century students of the Bible. The twentieth century has witnessed the discovery of harmony and unity. So the individual to whom God speaks through Scripture always finds himself in a community of believers, a community of those who have also heard the divine word. And he must live in responsible relation to that community and to its tradition.

That is why it is false to say that the Reformation represents a controversy between Bible and church. Medieval Catholicism had a very high doctrine of Scripture and its authority, and the Reformers were by no means oblivious to the claims of the tradition, or to the importance of the Holy Catholic Church. The real struggle between Rome on the one hand and Wittenberg and Geneva on the other was not over a doctrine of the Bible but over biblical doctrine. The crucial question was, "What does the Bible say?" Luther and Calvin felt that the medieval penitential system had obscured the clear scriptural proclamation of justification by faith, and they sought to free that message from its obscurity. There is no essential quarrel between Protestantism and

Roman Catholicism about the Bible as the word of God. Both agree that it contains the truth from on high. The difference lies in how that truth is to be discerned and of what it consists. Rome claims, rightly, that the church antedated the New Testament, a book which grew out of the life of the church and whose contents were determined by the church. Therefore the Book must be interpreted by the tradition. Protestantism insists that there is no substitute for the operation of the Holy Spirit in the mind and heart of the individual believer, that all else is mere ecclesiastical window-dressing. But on either side, the citation of a proof-text, out of context, in contradiction to the whole of the biblical point of view, is illegitimate. What must be sought carefully and prayerfully is the true word of God, as distinguished from the word of man, which the Bible may contain or convey.

This means, then, that the Roman Catholic must seek the guidance of his Church in his reading and interpretation of Scripture. The Protestant must listen for the word of God made manifest in his heart by the illumination of the Holy Spirit. In neither case is the mere printed word on the page necessarily to be taken literally and authoritatively. The Word must become flesh. It must be relevant in its speaking and in its being heard. Therefore, if we would encourage a dialogue between the present world and the biblical faith, we must have some knowledge of where that world stands.

THE WORLD OF DR. KINSEY

Whatever one may think of the reports of the late Dr. Kinsey and his associates (and all sorts of valid critiques have been made of them, by statisticians, psychoanalysts, sociologists, and others), there can be little doubt that they represent an important symptom of our culture. The exactitude of the statistics may be called into question, but the general picture they paint is probably a reasonable facsimile of the sexual behavior of men and women in American society. The second volume (on the female) is based, by Kinsey's own admission, on a sample of the population which is too small and too unrepresentative, and therefore it must be approached with even greater caution than the first. But any attempt to assess the sexual behavior and attitudes of Americans in the middle of the twentieth century must begin with the Kinsey reports, though such an assessment may very well end elsewhere.

One real service rendered by these studies is their careful attention to the diversities produced by the different socio-economic-educational levels of society. There is constantly the danger, particularly among the upper middle class, of assuming that the standards of one's own subcultural group are universally held. Dr. Kinsey divided the population as to levels of education completed and as to economic status. In the first volume, on the male, he used three categories under schooling:

those who never went beyond the eighth grade, those
who have stopped at high school, and those who have
had at least one year of higher education. The volume
on the female adds a fourth category: those who went
beyond college to graduate school. The economic categories distinguish nine subgroups, ranged according to
occupation. At the top are persons of great wealth, exec-
utives of large corporations, and professional men. In
the middle are upper white-collar workers, lower white-
collar workers, and skilled laborers. The bottom third
is occupied by semiskilled workers, unskilled laborers,
and members of the underworld. Those who are de-
pendents, unable to support themselves, form a special
group of their own. Both the educational and the economic status of an individual exert considerable influence on his sexual behavior, although this seems to be
more true of men than of women.

Looking at some of the kinds of sexual activity with
which we have been concerned in this volume, what
do the Kinsey reports tell us about what is going on
today? Among males, 98 per cent of the group who left
school at or before the eighth grade experience premarital intercourse with orgasm before marriage, and
during their late teens they average three such orgasms
a week. Only 67 per cent of those who go on to college
have premarital intercourse, and their average number
of orgasms per week achieved in this way is 0.3. With
females, the situation is apparently reversed. The higher
figure, 60 per cent, characterizes women with college

training, while the grade-school group only produces 30 per cent having engaged in coitus before marriage. Almost 50 per cent of all women, however, were not virgins at their weddings, although an impressive number had confined their sexual relations to the men they subsequently married and to the time just before they were married.

Masturbation follows a somewhat different pattern. At least 92 per cent of all males, according to the report, at some time or another masturbate, and Kinsey regarded this figure as conservatively low. Only 62 per cent of the women have so stimulated themselves, with 58 per cent going on to orgasm; the other 4 per cent stopped short of climax. But if the higher levels of education serve to restrain premarital coitus in males and stimulate it in females, that longer educational experience increases the incidence of masturbation in both sexes. Kinsey pointed out, however, that the earlier age at which the grade-school, high-school groups tend to marry is probably an important factor here.

There are strong inhibiting cultural restraints on the upper educational and economic levels against premarital intercourse, restraints relatively weaker in the lower groups. But a reverse trend is apparent regarding heavy petting. The very factors which produce guilt and anxiety about coitus before marriage tend, in the upper groups, to encourage petting, the manual stimulation of the genitals with strong erotic arousal. Their moral standards tend to inhibit premarital intercourse, but to permit all sexual activity short of that. The grade-school males, on the other hand, who engage in premarital coitus in such large numbers, look upon petting as immoral and disgusting. To them, soul-kissing—or the French kiss, as it is sometimes called—is unhygienic and revolting, while they think nothing of drinking from a common cup at the factory. The college group looks with extreme distaste upon sharing a drinking cup with colleagues, shuddering inwardly at the germs thus spread, yet engages with little thought in soul-kissing, even with a blind date. Another curious relation between the two groups is in their attitude toward nudity, which is in the upper levels so desirable as a state for sexual relations as to be almost a *sine qua non*, while the grade-school group are exceedingly modest and even in marital coitus rarely are naked.

Extramarital relations follow similar channels of cultural conditioning. The grade-school level male has widespread premarital experience, marries early, and diminishes but does not eliminate coitus with women other than his wife. His adultery, however, gradually decreases until he is about forty, at which time his interest in sex reaches a low point. Not only does he become faithful to his wife, but also he virtually loses his desire for her as well. He would rather play cards or pool, or bowl with his friends. The college-level male, by contrast, tends to be technically a virgin at marriage, though he has petted heavily and extensively. He is also remarkably faithful to his wife until somewhere between thirty-five and forty-five, when he begins a pattern of extramarital relations which provides him by the age of fifty-four with 38 per cent of his total orgasms.

Perhaps the most shocking aspect of the Kinsey reports were his findings on homosexuality, which he defined simply as sexual contacts between persons of the same sex. He recognized that this is a term very loosely used and sought to make some contribution to its clarification. He distinguished seven different categories. In the middle, he placed the bisexual, who apparently has no preference for either sex but enjoys relations with both equally. At the two ends of the spectrum are to be found the exclusively heterosexual and exclusively homosexual, each of whom regards relations with the same or opposite sex with extreme repugnance. Then come the two groups, one of which is basically heterosexual but with an occasional homosexual experience in their background; the other is primarily homosexual but not utterly incapable of heterosexual relations. Flanking the middle bisexual group are the final two categories, still with one marked preference or the other but with a pattern of repeated contacts with members of the opposite or same sex. The percentage of males Kinsey found occupying the extreme outpost of exclusive homosexuality was small, only 4 per cent, but even this is larger than previous estimates. For single women, the corresponding figure is 1 to 3 per cent, and very much smaller than that for females who are married. The surprising statistic in Kinsey's report on males was his finding that 37 per cent of all men have had some homosexual experience during their lives. Kinsey himself admitted that he was surprised at his own discovery, having been totally unprepared for it, but his subsequent studies continued to confirm his original data. The cumulative homosexual experience among women is apparently very much smaller, amounting to only 13 per cent.

All sorts of critics have compared the Kinsey portraits with their own experience of the models used, and have found the paintings grossly inaccurate, distorted, and ugly. But no one can claim to have studied the models more carefully than Dr. Kinsey and his associates, who calmly request the critics themselves to produce truer portraits if they can. Whatever one may say about the statistics—that they are exaggerated, unreliable, deliberately manipulated—no serious student of contemporary mores can deny that a large gap exists between the sexual behavior of men and women in our society and the moral standards to which that society pays lip service. Those standards are largely rooted in the Bible, more especially in the New Testament, which condemns all sexual activity outside of marriage. We have an apparent impasse. On the one hand, we frown upon masturbation, petting, premarital relations, adultery, and homosexuality; while on the other hand, we engage in these prohibited activities in considerable numbers. It has been suggested that in this respect, at least, we are biblical, obedient to the injunction, "Do not let your left hand know what your right hand is doing." Both churchmen and secularists seek resolution of the impasse by closing the gap between preachment and practice, but with a difference. The churchman wants to change the latter so that it conforms to the former; while the secularists, or many of them, seek the precise reverse. Kinsey himself insisted that he was merely a reporter and not a moralist, though he was less careful about letting his biases show in the second volume than he was in the first. But whatever may have been true of Kinsey, his reports produced essays and editorial comment galore to the effect that outmoded ethical standards should be updated to conform to present practice. This would leave small room for the Bible—or for its attitudes and teachings about sex, at any rate. Our final task, then, is to examine the biblical outlook and to see whether it does in fact have anything at all to say to the contemporary world about its problems with sexual behavior.

SEX IS GOOD

The first thing that must be done is to make a concession. For a variety of reasons, the Western world, under Christian influence, has all too often been inclined to view man's sexuality somewhat negatively. It must be remembered that the New Testament and the writings of the early church fathers were produced in a Roman Empire grown increasingly decadent, and that the Protestant Reformers wrote against the background of the degeneracy of much of the clergy in the late Middle Ages. Somehow the notion has got around that the original sin of Adam and Eve was the sexual act, and while the church may not have been guilty of positively creating such an impression, it must be confessed that little has been done to counteract or correct it. The unhappy fact of the matter is that the modern church has rather ignored sex altogether, save for an occasional veiled reference to lewd behavior or obscene literature. It was a misguided understanding of Christian morality which produced the pruderies of the Victorian era, so that propriety and Christianity became virtually synonymous. Against such a repressive atmosphere, which served as a cloak of hypocrisy for many a bourgeois citizen, the protests of Sigmund Freud and Havelock Ellis were profoundly just. The insistence of the secular mind upon the essential goodness of sex as a fact of nature must be underlined and strengthened by a biblically oriented viewpoint rather than attacked or refuted.

The Bible begins with the story of creation, and creation includes the fact of sexuality. Man's bodily nature is not, according to the Bible, an occasion for regret, a prison house of sensuality from which we must seek to escape. However true such an understanding may be of certain Oriental cults, it is not characteristic of biblical thinking. It is perfectly clear that the Old Testament sees man as a psychophysical unity, as a creature made to enjoy the material world, including his own body. Hebrew man was granted a remarkable sexual freedom. He could not violate his own humanity or masculinity in relations with animals or members of his own sex. He was to respect the rights of others, refraining from coitus with women betrothed or married; and he was barred from using sex idolatrously, in the worship of nature deities. But there was no limit placed upon the number of wives or concubines he might have in his household, nor was there any serious ban upon his sexual relations with any woman not under the protection of husband or father, including secular prostitutes, although this freedom was slowly curtailed as the centuries passed. If he was newly wed, he was specifically exempted from military service for a year. Every man and woman was expected to marry and rear children. The love of husband and wife was seen as a symbol of the love of God for Israel. This scarcely sounds like a people suspicious or fearful of sex! Beside our own standards, the Old Testament is lusty and free. Its contents would be banned in Boston were they published under less sacred auspices.

The New Testament is somewhat more confining, to be sure, bringing to an end the era of polygamy, divorce, and prostitution, as the Judaism of the first century A.D. had virtually already done. But still, sex is good. The apostle Paul's remarks about the flesh and the spirit, made originally in a context thoroughly Jewish, have, unfortunately, been interpreted in Hellenistic terms, so that it appears that the New Testament is prejudiced against the body. But modern scholarship has delivered us from such misinterpretation and misunderstanding, and we know that there is no important difference between the two biblical covenants in their view of the material world and man's physical nature. Paul's concept of the freedom of the Christian man is radical, indeed, beside the moralistic legalism of our own times. No one who regarded sex as evil could counsel married couples to practice coitus regularly, without dangerously prolonged intervals for purposes of prayer. Nor could a community ashamed and afraid of human sexuality see in it a "mystery" analogous to Christ's love for his Church.

There can be no quarrel with the secular world at this point. It is right and the church has been wrong. Sex is natural and good. There are those who argue that sex is morally neutral, neither good nor bad in itself, but dependent for its ethical significance on its particular use. They claim no special niche of sanctity for sex, ranking it simply with all the things of the world which derive whatever morality or immorality they may possess from their use or abuse. Against this must be placed the doctrine of creation, which affirms that "God looked upon everything that he had made and saw that it was good." Of course, everything that he made can be misused, and the person who does so becomes then a wrongdoer, but the things themselves remain good. The New Testament significantly does not regard money as the root of all evil, but rather the love of money. It is attitudes which are good or evil, never things. These are the creation of God and therefore good. Man from his narrow vantage point may wonder why God chose to create such things as mosquitoes, poisonous snakes, or the tubercular bacillus, though curiously it does not occur to him to ask whether the cow or sheep or pig might wonder why God created man. The venomous serpent stings to protect himself, the mosquito to feed itself; the bacillus, like all living organisms, merely flourishes in a receptive environment. Are they so different from *homo sapiens?* Man may be the lord of creation, a status he believes God himself has bestowed upon him, but he is not the Creator, as Job painfully learned. The "balance of nature" is a given fact which man finds and does not make, and he tampers with it at his peril. Augustine was profoundly biblical in his view that everything that exists is good precisely because it is the creation of God. It is only the intrusion of nonbeing, of what Augustine called *de-gradatio*, which is evil. All things are good, and sex is no exception.

Concretely, this means that those who take the Bible seriously must stop apologizing for sex. Under present circumstances, children are raised with an emotional scar, a wound received early in life. They manifest an insatiable curiosity about themselves and the wondrous world about them, and insofar as parents are able, the endless questions receive honest answers. Let the child trespass, however, onto the tabooed grounds of sex, and one of three responses is forthcoming, any one of which is damaging. The parents lie, using pious fictions about storks or rosebushes or doctor's little black bags; the parents scold, condemning the child for being "dirty" or "nasty" to raise such dreadful queries; or the parents, enlightened and "modern," try to answer honestly but stumble over their own embarrassment, delivering the little speech about birds and bees and flowers, liberally interspersed with hesitations and awkward pauses. Eugene O'Neill produced a painfully hilarious scene of this kind in *Ah, Wilderness!* in Nat Miller's attempt to educate his teen-age son. That play is set in the early twentieth century, but that scene is re-enacted still in many a household. Any of these three parental responses to childhood questions sooner or later makes it apparent to the growing child that sex is an area best approached with considerable caution and even shame. A similar principle operates in the more active aspects of youthful exploration. The baby boy or girl is fascinated by the body—fingers, toes, eyes, ears, nose, mouth—and plays with the possibilities and combinations to the accompaniment of delighted exclamations of parents and relatives. But when the genitals become the source of curiosity and experimentation, the delight quickly flees before horror, and hands are spanked to the background of loud noises clearly expressing disapproval.

The sex education of children is primarily a matter

of attitudes, and only secondarily of facts. This is why the Roman Catholic Church is right in its insistence that such education is the province of the home and not the school. Nonetheless, this is an area where the churches can be of genuine help to their families, not in trying to educate the children but in the training of parents. Most fathers and mothers are acutely aware of their inadequacies in the best methods of initiating their children into the mysteries of life's facts. That is why they buy books in such quantities and pore over magazine articles with such avidity. It is a problem they face, and yet the church is for the most part silent and apparently indifferent. If the pastor cannot speak freely to his "children" in the faith, how are parents to overcome their own uneasiness and shame? This is one of the greatest challenges facing the church today, the challenge to take the doctrine of creation seriously and to implement that doctrine practically in its program.

SEX IS PERSONAL

If the churches take the biblical viewpoint seriously, they must begin with a concession to the secular mind, granting that sex is natural. This does not mean, however, as some representatives of that mind are suggesting, that "anything goes." One of the more disturbing aspects of the Kinsey reports and their reception has been the tendency to refer to sexual relations as "contacts" and to assume that almost all sexual acts are "natural." This is to ignore the personal quality of sex and to reduce man to mere animality. No one will deny that humans are members of the animal kingdom, that they share common kinship with other forms of life. But there are levels of existence to which man aspires and which he sometimes reaches that are, so far as we know, denied to the "lower" species. The entire realm of self-conscious morality is uniquely human. One cannot speak meaningfully of a "good" tiger or a "bad" lion. The behavior of animals is regulated by the timeless laws of instinct; and it is entirely misleading to draw parallels between the sexual behavior of other mammals, which are utterly devoid of either personal or moral significance, and human behavior, which is never without such significance.

Those who argue that almost all sexual acts are "natural" point to the evidence amassed by observers of animal sexuality and to the findings of anthropologists about the sex life of other cultures. In both sets of data are to be found all of the phenomena regarded by our society not simply as deviations but as perversions: masturbation, homosexuality, mouth-genital contacts, even sexual relations across the lines of species (or "bestiality"). Incest is common among animals and not unknown to humanity. This evidence is used to demonstrate that Freud was right, that humans are "polymorphous perverse," often biologically predetermined to seek sexual satisfaction in deviant ways. Society, then, must stop condemning such behavior and learn to be tolerant of it. No responsible student would condone violence or the subversion of small children. Obviously any society must protect itself against this kind of deviant. But so long as the partners are responsible and willing, no crime is committed against humanity if their tastes are different from the majority, if they choose to pursue sexual pleasure in bizarre and devious ways. This point of view is implicit throughout Kinsey's studies, and it became very explicit in many comments on those studies.

If this assumption is correct—that biological factors produce diverse sexual types—then there is literally nothing that society can do to change the situation. It can only repress these tendencies and drive them underground with threats of severe punishment—punishment which may restrain but can never heal. And since society is not really harmed by those persons who are discreet and responsible, all that the threat of severe punishment accomplishes is an invitation to real crime, in the form of blackmail. This is why the Federal Government is so cautious about homosexuals in sensitive positions, not only out of concern for the example set by people in high places, but also because they are susceptible to blackmail. If society changed its basic attitude and learned to accept sexual deviation with equanimity, then the dangers would vanish. Thus argue the "sexual naturalists." This was the way of fifth century Athens, after all, where bisexual love was taken for granted.

Against this point of view is arrayed the contention of those who see sexual deviations as the products not of biology but of culture. In its efforts to prevent irresponsible procreation, Western civilization has used the device of what Freud called the walls of loathing, guilt, and shame. On the whole this method of social control has worked reasonably well, but a price has been paid for its success—the price of sexual perversion, which is the product of fear and anxiety. Reparative patterns of sexual behavior have been the inevitable consequence of the West's repressive attitudes and practices. The removal of these repressions, the adoption of less ego-damaging methods of social control, would sharply reduce if not eliminate the incidence of sexual deviation. Therefore, we are not reduced to the passive acceptance of perversion as an inexorable biological fact. The removal of anxiety-producing factors in the sexual education and training of children would free them to pursue the "natural" methods of sexual activity, indicated by society and nature alike.

The etiology of perversion is essentially a scientific question, one in which the Bible claims no special competence. It cannot play the referee in this dispute. What it can contribute to the discussion, however, is a steady insistence upon the personal qualities involved in all sexuality. There is no sexual act which does not have its source in and its effect upon the center of selfhood. Or, to put it another way, there is no sexual act which is morally neutral, a merely instinctual contact.

Every "contact" involves a relationship, and every relationship is characterized by certain qualities. These may be exploitative, protective, tender, casual, or commercial. Whatever they are, they affect both persons involved and their attitudes toward themselves and toward others. Recent studies, thus far unpublished, being carried on by Professor Lester A. Kirkendall of the Oregon State Teachers College, concentrating on the premarital sexual experience of college men, indicate a close correlation between the attitudes of these men toward their sexual partners and their attitudes toward other persons in general. This we should expect from the perspectives both of the psychology of personality and of biblical thinking. All discussions of sex which would cut it off from the dynamic centers of personality, making it a thing apart, a separate area of existence, must be steadfastly resisted by all who take the Bible seriously. Sex involves relationships, and the Bible is centered in relationships.

Not only does sex relate to the individuals concerned, in their inner, psychic lives, but also to the nexus of community in which those persons are involved. No parent is indifferent to the sexual experiences of his child; no married person regards the activities of his or her spouse casually; no close friend is uninvolved in the risks and problems of those bound to him by the ties of affection. These lines of community, of relatedness, are obscured by much current discussion of sex, which centers only on those immediately concerned, or the couple *in vacuo*. But no couple is ever isolated. The inescapably interpersonal character of all life is a note the Bible strikes again and again, from the Old Testament stress on the family and its demands, the community and its concerns, to the New Testament assertion that "we are members one of another." We are caught in a network of mutual responsibility, in the biblical affirmative to Cain's ancient question, "Am I my brother's keeper?" Every sexual act, therefore, draws into itself the total personalities of the two human beings participating, and also those to whom they are bound in kinship and affection. If the act is perverse, frowned upon by society, or if it lies beyond the boundaries of propriety, the risk of censure and punishment is not confined to those committing the act. The act is like a stone cast into a pool of water; its ripples move out to touch areas far removed from the center. The Bible, then, insists that sex is personal and therefore must be responsible.

The Old Testament seeks to delineate the areas of responsibility in a legal code, and the Roman Catholic Church follows suit, with its careful distinctions between what is permissible and prohibited, sins that are mortal and venial. This is clearly one way to promote responsible personal relatedness. It may turn out that this is the only way or at least the best way to advance social responsibility. The apostle Paul, however, disagreed, and so did the Reformers. They insisted on a highly dangerous commodity—what they called Chris-

tian liberty. They believed that the gospel had set them
free from the Law, whether Jewish or Catholic. They
saw the way of legalism as in fact emphasizing mere outward conformity, whatever its intention to involve the
inner springs of motivation. Jesus appeared to them to
be protesting against the external character of Jewish
moralism, seeking an avenue into the centers of personal
existence. "It was said to the men of old . . . But I say
to you." This whole series of sayings plunges inward, as
do the harsh words about polishing the outside of the
cup while leaving the inside greasy with filth, about the
sepulchres whited with limestone yet filled with decay
and rot. Jesus himself apparently thought of his work
as fulfilling the Law, not destroying it; and Paul and the
Reformers saw Christ as precisely that fulfillment, rendering the Law superfluous.

What they sought was not mere outward conformity
to a sterile moralism, against which the inner self strug-
gles constantly, but rather a transformation, a radical
reversal of direction, so that one recognizes and gratefully affirms the claims laid upon him by a gracious God.
But those claims are not spelled out in a detailed legal
code. They are rather stated in the principle of love.
He who loves God loves also his neighbor, and in so
doing he fulfills the Law. He needs no external instru-
ment to direct his behavior in each concrete situation.
He can be trusted to work out his own salvation in fear
and trembling as a free man. He will make mistakes; he
will err in judgment and in act. This is why Christian

liberty is so dangerous. The Law is far safer, erecting
barriers to protect pilgrims from straying from the paths
of rectitude. But the pilgrim so protected may long for
the courage to leap the barrier and gambol in the prim-
roses, restrained only by his fears. Neither way is without its perils and its problems. Legalism keeps its
adherents proper in behavior, but, according to Paul,
cultivates inner rebellion. Christian liberty establishes
internal freedom, but runs the risk of rationalization and
miscalculation.

One cannot, however, have it both ways. To set up a
series of "Thou shalt nots," clearly labeled as sins, either
mortal or venial, is plainly to rob men of their freedom.
And such a series, while it may control behavior, cannot
control inner attitudes and desires. To emphasize spontaneity and freedom in an individual motivated by love
of God and neighbor, on the other hand, is to invite the
possibility of misdemeanors and misdeeds, no matter
how pure the spirit involved. The issue squarely before
the world of Dr. Kinsey is a crucial question of policy.
Given the gross violations of society's legal codes, what
shall be done? Should the laws be strengthened, the
sanctions increased, an even sterner morality enjoined?
Or, is a radically new direction indicated, an entirely different method called for? To the present writer, the indications point inescapably to the latter. The method of
moralism has been weighed in the balance and found
wanting, partly because it moves in the wrong direction
and partly because it has based its case on fear. The

three "bogeymen" used to frighten the young into a decorous conformity have been shame about sex in general, the dangers of venereal disease, and the perils of conception. The first has been destroyed by a new conviction that sex is good, a happy victory on all counts. The second and third, while still threatening, are rapidly retreating before the advance of modern technology. The miracle drugs have all but banished the twin specters of syphilis and gonorrhea, and the progress in contraception has driven back if not dispelled the haunting threats of pregnancy. The new pills now in early stages of experimentation may exorcise this spook entirely. Already, moralism is breaking down, as the Kinsey reports make abundantly clear. To attempt to repair and restore the old method of social control is to live under a nostalgic illusion.

What seems required is a new approach, based squarely upon a biblical understanding of Christian freedom. We must, to begin with, abandon all efforts to frighten children and young people about sex, seeking rather to emphasize its positive God-given possibilities and promises. We must also abandon all attempts to deal with sex in terms of proscription, indicating social approval or disapproval of acts on the basis of externals. What society has been saying is that sex is proper if the couple are married and improper if they are not, ignoring all qualitative considerations entirely. A married couple may be wholly selfish and sensual in their sexual relations, while an engaged pair, deeply in love, may be using their bodies to express a genuine unity of spirit. To approve the one and to condemn the other on moralistic grounds is the sheerest hypocrisy, especially when so many of these very engaged couples marry and live together happily afterward.

The emphasis must be exactly where the New Testament places it, on the inner motivation and not the outer act. It is never enough to concentrate narrowly on what people do. That is the method of Kinsey and company: to deal with sexual relations as contacts. We must always ask the deeper questions: "What does the act mean?" "Why are they acting as they do?" Holding hands or a good-night kiss may, from this perspective, be harmful and evil if persons are being treated as things, as mere bodies to be exploited for personal pleasure. The central importance must be given to love —not romantic, erotic love, as the modern world understands it, an ephemeral, highly unstable motion of the feelings, but *agape,* which means respect, reverence, and concern for persons as channels through whom Christ confronts us, saying, "Inasmuch as ye have done it unto one of the least of these my brethren, ye have done it unto me." To abuse another human being is to do violence to God and to self. The law of love means that we cannot allow our personal whims to dictate our treatment of others. Every man lays claim to our compassion and our concern. This is the measuring rod which must be set beside our sexual acts and attitudes, rather than a law outside of ourselves declaring arbitrarily what we

may or may not do. It is not this or that act which is right
or wrong, but the inner meaning of the act, the motivation it represents and the attitude it carries. Those who
are fearful of reliance on love and therefore retreat to
law are thinking of romantic love, rather than of love
as the New Testament understands it. *Agape* is responsible love, not selfish, unstable emotion.

Given, then, the centrality of the law of love, the
Christian man can say with Paul, "All things are lawful
for me." The question so frequently asked by young
people, "How far is it all right to go?" becomes meaningless because it focuses entirely on external behavior.
It may not be "all right" to go anywhere at all if selfish
sensuality is being expressed. On the other hand, it may
be "all right" to go quite a way if one is operating in a
context of mutual love, respect, and reverence. But no
one outside can determine the limits. This is a decision
each couple must make in fear and trembling, recognizing that there are risks involved at every step and that
the risks increase, the more steps are taken. But life itself is filled with risks, and no one can avoid them. The
moralistic law seeks to deliver us from responsibility for
our acts, guaranteeing us objective certainty from outside ourselves. But no law can deliver us from responsibility or risk, for we must take the responsibility for accepting its claim upon us and run the risk that it may
be wrong. Kipling's line is singularly pertinent in this
connection, where St. Peter says, "May the God that

you took from a printed book be good to you, Tomlinson!" We cannot evade the necessity of answering for our acts; we cannot shift the burden to an infallible Book, to an infallible Church, or to an infallible Law. For we are the ones who agree to the infallibility, and we may be wrong!

It is this freedom and its risks which must be stressed by the biblical approach to the world of Dr. Kinsey, this centrality of *agape* in our every approach to other human beings. This is not to say that love justifies all, that young people are set free to follow their inner feelings wherever they may lead. The principle, "All things are lawful for me," is limited first of all by the statement, "But not all things are wholesome." This means that the Christian must constantly guard against those things which rob him of the very freedom he has gained through Christ. He has been liberated from every bondage in the world. Nothing is his master, because the meaning of his life is not bound up in it. He can endure the loss of all things, persuaded that he cannot be separated from the love of God in Christ Jesus. His ultimate concern, his "treasure" is not in the world at all, and therefore he can count everything in the world as refuse. But he must be cautious. Prior to his liberation he was a slave. The meaning of his life was bound to something: sex, money, power, or prestige. Whatever that something was must be regarded as "not wholesome," because he is endangered by it. If it were sex, he had best be careful in his freedom, lest he fall back once more ensnared.

The statement, "All things are lawful for me," is limited also by the recognition that "not all things build up," which is to say that not all things contribute to community. The Christian is one who is free to renounce his freedom, for the sake of his neighbor. He does not need to insist upon his liberty compulsively and defiantly. He can allow his concern for the conscience of another to determine his actions. His own conscience remains free, responsible only to God; but his acts are guided by his respect and reverence for those around him. His liberty is thus not license, not libertinism. It is responsible, which is another way of saying, "able to respond" to the claims of his neighbor. But no minutely detailed code of behavior guides him in his relationships. He is to "prove all things," seeking to find what is the will of God for him in each encounter. And again he risks being wrong.

The biblical conception of responsible freedom seems the only viable alternative in the present parlous situation of sexual anarchy. Some express fear that the young under such guidance might go astray, misunderstanding or rationalizing. That such a possibility exists clearly cannot be denied. But it is painfully apparent that the young are certainly "going astray" anyhow, despite the specific prohibitions and dire warnings from moralistic legalism. Perhaps a new approach might prove more effective. If young people are going to misbehave, all of the external restrictions in the world cannot keep them from it. The only practical barriers to misbehavior are internal ones, built into the self and therefore willingly affirmed and accepted.

What has been said earlier about responsibility to the wider circle of family, friends, and community must be placed beside these remarks concerning liberty; but that responsibility must be accepted, not imposed. A wide experience with the college youth of today on many campuses indicates that this segment of our society, at any rate, is seriously searching for moral guidance in the area of sexuality. They are not looking for excuses, for rationalizations of selfish and irresponsible behavior, but for ethical principles that make sense. Fearful warnings of the evils of sex and its dangers do not make sense to college students. They have been liberated already from such notions, but their freedom is only *from* something and not *for* anything. It is precisely that freedom for which they seek; and an emphasis upon the quality of interpersonal relatedness, together with a mature re- sponsibility to family and community, receives an un- failingly positive response.

If it be objected that such an approach to college stu- dents who are relatively mature might be exceedingly dangerous with junior or senior high-school boys and girls, who are less capable of responsible freedom, the answer is that this is an outlook which ought to begin

from earliest childhood. And it is by no means confined to sex. It extends to all areas of personal encounter
and relatedness. To be sure, one does not expect responsible freedom from a small child, who needs considerable guidance and protection both from himself and his
world. But the wise parent does not withhold all freedom and responsibility or all information about sex
from the child until a certain age, and then suddenly
bestow it *in toto*. How can the youth handle something
for which he is wholly unprepared? There is a gradually
increased giving of freedom and a corresponding expectation of responsibility, as the youth is prepared to
receive it and use it wisely. Thus, the early teen-ager is
quite prepared to deal with his puberty and its problems
because he knows its promises and possibilities. He is
not independent yet, any more than the college student.
He still needs sympathetic help and guidance, and he
welcomes it from those who understand and accept him.
He cherishes Paul's word to Timothy, "Let no man
despise your youth," and responds maturely to expectations of maturity.

CONCLUSION

What all of this adds up to is an appeal for what Tin
Pan Alley some years ago called "accentuating the positive" rather than the negative. Essentially, this is what
the Bible does, despite all of the Old Testament prohibitions and all of Paul's diatribes against immorality.

Curiously enough, this is also the approach of contemporary psychotherapy, in spite of its microscopic
examination of sexual perversion and abnormality. What
the therapist does is to try to use the counseling situation as a protected area where the client can work
through his problems without the necessity of "acting
out," of taking out his conflicts and anxieties on those
around him. The therapist recognizes the risks involved
in the freedom of "the fifty-minute hour," but he is less
concerned about any specific act of his client than about
the direction in which the total personality is moving.
If the individual finally wins his way to responsible freedom, an isolated incident of sexual immorality may
prove in the long run to be of minor importance. He
will be a fuller and more creative person than the paragon of virtue whose stern moralistic repressions keep
him free of moral taint, but may also bar him from genuine selfhood and thus from genuine relatedness.

The title of this volume is no accident. Sex and love
belong together—in life no less than in the Bible. Where
the one flows from the other, the experience is creative,
releasing, and enlarging. It is even rooted in eternity, in
God himself and his love for his covenanted people.
Hosea understood this, as did the rabbis who included
the Song of Songs in the biblical canon, and the author
of the Epistle to the Ephesians. Separated from love,
sex becomes distorted and demonic, descending to the
realm of mere instinct and sensual lust, transforming
men into something subhuman. When this relationship

is properly grasped, it may be that the world of Dr. Kinsey will gladly forfeit its shallow pleasures for the sake of a "more excellent way," not fearfully restraining lustful desires for forbidden fruits, but gratefully reserving the divine gift of sexuality for its highest possibilities.

INDEX

Aaron, 313, 382
Abel, 381
Abishag, 397, 398
Abner, 36
Abortion, 170, 179, 208
Abraham, 23, 24, 26, 27, 31, 57,
    81, 83, 113, 184, 237, 345,
    393, 397
Absalom, 39f., 80, 83, 390
Achan, 352
Acts of the Apostles, 117, 249
Adam, 31, 188, 189, 274, 286,
    301, 378, 379, 416
Adonijah, 397, 398
Adonis, 174
Adultery, 83, 138, 177, 207, 225,
    260, 261, 278, 291, 294, 306,
    318ff., 412f.
Agag, 34
Ahab, 38, 179
Ahimelech, 284
Ai, 31
Alcoholics Anonymous, 145, 368f.,
    371
Alexander the Great, 43, 200,
    215, 217
Amalekites, 34
Amaziah, 64
Amazons, 195f.
Amenhotep IV; see Ikhnaton
Ammonites, 179, 392, 393
Amnon, 39, 55, 85, 86, 190, 390
Amon-Ra, 168, 170, 171, 178
Amorites, 32
Amos, 23, 25, 64, 73f., 107, 109,
    183, 309
Antiochus III, 43
Antiochus IV, 43
Aphasia, 200
Aphrodite, 201, 317
Apocalypse, 100ff.
Aquinas, Thomas, 298
Aralu, 173

Arameans, 23
Aristophanes, 199, 205, 271
Aristotle, 204, 215
Ark of the Covenant, 37, 58
Asa, 350
Asceticism, 222, 227, 229
Asherah, 180
Ashur, 178, 179
Assyria, 42, 44, 76, 178f., 308
Astarte; see Ishtar
Athaliah, 42
Athens, 199, 200, 201, 210, 343,
    423
Aton, 38, 171, 172, 185
Attis, 217f., 219
Augustine, 55, 91, 144, 295, 379,
    419
Augustus, 208, 209, 212

Baals, 17ff., 32, 60, 72, 82, 179ff.,
    217, 241
Babel, Tower of, 25, 27, 162
Babylon, 28, 42, 44, 48, 50, 63,
    163, 165, 172ff., 178, 215
Babylonian Exile, 42, 43, 47, 48,
    245, 270, 352
Bacchus, 60, 63
Barnabas, 248, 249
Barrenness, 237
Bathsheba, 37, 40, 73, 85, 190,
    284, 398
Beatitudes, 94
"Beatniks," 233
Beelzebub, 180
Bel, 172, 173
Benjamin, son of Jacob, 80
Benjamin, tribe of, 37, 349,
    387ff.
Bestiality, 399ff.
Betrothal, 239
Bible, doctrine of, 404ff.
Bilhah, 396
Birth control, 294ff.

438

Bisexuality, 197ff., 349
Blood, 282f., 383
Bride-price (mohar), 240, 243, 275, 332
Bultmann, Rudolph, 108, 137, 138

Cain, 70, 245, 381, 426
Calvin, John, 243, 336, 405, 407
Canaan, 17ff., 27, 31, 60, 61, 63, 71, 72, 162, 241, 309, 323, 382, 388
Canaanites, 17ff., 27, 61ff., 179ff.
Canticles; see Song of Solomon
Cato the Censor, 210
Celibacy, 222, 228, 286, 295, 302
Chemosh, 179
Church (ecclesia), 123ff., 256ff.
Cicero, 210
Circumcision, 249, 250, 387
Coitus interruptus, 208, 281, 296ff., 374f.
Cole, William Graham, 232, 354f.
Colossians, 121
Constantine, 338
Contraception, 285, 295ff.
Coprophilia, 374
Corinna, 212
Corinth, 146, 201, 226, 229, 251, 252, 293, 294, 316, 317, 363, 386, 398
Corinthians, 125, 251, 252, 258, 289, 295, 297, 298, 301
Cornelius, 116
Covenant, 17, 26ff., 40, 125
Creation, 27, 270ff.
Crete, 197
Criticism, higher, 29
Criticism, lower, 29
Crusoe, Robinson, 274
Cybele, 217f., 219, 220
Cyrus, 44, 49

Dagon, 179
Daniel, book of, 44
Darwin, Charles, 404
David, 27, 28, 34ff., 38, 39, 40, 41, 42, 49, 73, 76, 80, 81, 83, 85, 113, 114, 190, 274, 284, 285, 352, 383f., 390, 397
Deborah, 19
Decalogue, 58, 83, 318
Demeter, 168, 174

Deuteronomy, 45f., 60, 75, 300, 301, 313, 314, 319, 331, 332, 334, 350, 396, 401
Dinah, 386f.
Diodorus, 170
Dionysus, 60, 211, 217
Divorce, 82, 169, 177, 205, 207, 225, 307, 330, 331ff.
Dodd, C. H., 112
Domitian, 121
Dowry, 176f., 207, 243
DuMaurier, George, 94

Edomites, 27
Egypt, 23, 26, 29, 30, 37, 43, 48, 63, 80, 163, 166ff., 175, 215, 308, 390, 391
Ekron, 180
Eli, 80, 309
Elijah, 38, 60, 73, 179
Elisha, 63, 65
Ellis, Havelock, 416
Elohist (E), 28, 345
Emasculation, 218
Ephesians, 98, 287, 436
Er, 297
Ereshkigal, 173, 174
Esau, 397
Eschatology, 110ff., 118, 120ff., 156
Essenes, 122
Ethbaal, 38
Ethiopians, 25
Eucharist, 125, 220
Eve, 188, 189, 274, 301, 378, 379, 416
Exhibitionism, 374, 377ff.
Exodus, book of, 28, 318, 382, 400
Ezekiel, 52, 76, 109, 245, 307, 326ff.
Ezra, 43

Family, Hebrew concept of, 244ff.
Flesh (sarx), 95, 258ff., 417f.
Fornication (porneia), 247ff.
Fosbroke, Hughell E. W., 61, 63f.
Fourth Gospel, 97, 98, 121, 131, 143, 147f.
Freedom from the Law, 95f., 143ff., 250, 263ff., 363f., 426f.

Freud, Sigmund, 203, 263, 277, 354, 355, 358, 375, 404, 416, 422, 423
Fromm, Erich, 151, 244

Galatians, 95, 96, 218, 249, 258, 264
Gehazi, 65
Genesis, 26, 55, 162, 187, 188, 189, 270f., 297, 298, 301, 333, 344, 349, 380, 386
Gibeah, 345f., 387ff.
Gideon, 19, 24, 61, 181
Gilgal, 30
Gilgamesh Epic, 161, 173
Gnosticism, 221ff., 227, 228, 292
Goliath, 35
Gomer, 16ff., 157, 322
Graves, Robert, 196
Greece, 28, 195ff., 210, 214, 344

Habbakuk, 52
Hagar, 83, 237
Ham, 381f.
Hammurabi, 177
Hamor, 386f.
Hannah, 80
Harlotry, 83, 310
Harlots, 93, 94, 225, 239, 241, 248, 257, 307, 315, 366
Heilsgeschicte, 30
Hera, 197
Hermaphroditus, 198
Herodotus, 175f., 177, 215
Hetairae, 200f.
Hillel, 332
Hiltner, Seward, 263
History, Hebrew understanding of, 48ff., 184f.
Homer, 28, 32
Homosexuality, 35, 177, 194, 197ff., 201ff., 205, 212f., 225, 294, 342ff., 383f., 413f.
Hophni, 80
Horace, 211, 213
Horney, Karen, 355
Horus, 168, 170, 218
Hosea, 15ff., 25, 52, 64, 69, 74, 76, 89, 107, 129, 157, 182, 277, 287, 307, 309, 310, 322
Hyksos, 169

Idolatry, 55, 146, 194, 317, 361
Ikhnaton, 171f., 185

Immodesty, 377ff.
Incest, 169, 289, 382, 386, 390, 391ff.
India, 215, 269
Infatuation, 85
Infidelity, test for, 320ff.
Irenaeus, 222ff.
Isaac, 26, 27
Isaiah, 29, 45, 49, 58, 74, 101, 107, 109, 309, 324
Ish-bosheth, or Ishbaal, 36, 182
Ishmael, 397
Ishtar, 168, 173, 174, 177, 178, 180
Isis, 167, 217, 218, 219

Jabesh-Gilead, 388
Jacob, 26, 27, 57, 79, 80, 81, 83, 84, 85, 237, 241, 275, 386f., 396
James, Epistle of, 148f.
James of Jerusalem, 249
James, son of Zebedee, 98
Jamnia, Council of, 86
Japheth, 381f.
Jason, 196
Jehoshaphat, 350
Jepthah, 19, 61, 79, 182, 314
Jeremiah, 38, 45, 54, 64, 74, 107, 109, 180, 187, 274, 309, 324f., 333
Jericho, 31
Jeroboam I, 28
Jeroboam II, 74
Jerome, 288, 296n.
Jerusalem, 28, 37, 39, 42, 43, 44, 45, 58, 83, 112, 117, 118, 180, 248, 249, 250, 326, 338
Jesse, 41, 275, 397
Jesus, 51, 79, 90, 93, 95, 96, 97, 99, 100, 101, 102, 103, 104, 105, 106, 107, 108, 109, 110, 111, 112, 113, 114, 115, 116, 117, 118, 119, 120, 121, 122, 123, 124n., 125, 128, 131, 134, 136, 137, 138, 141, 142, 143, 150, 152, 153, 154, 155, 156, 160, 220, 221, 225, 227, 228, 251, 257, 260, 261, 262, 263, 265, 286, 291, 315, 334, 335, 337, 338, 339, 360, 368, 372, 377, 398, 427
Jethro, 162
Jezebel, 38, 73, 179

Joab, 39f., 285
Job, 54, 68, 419
Joel, 112
Johannine literature, 118f., 132, 147f., 227f.
John the Baptist, 100, 101, 117
John, son of Zebedee, 98, 249
Jonah, 54, 76f., 100
Jonathan, 34, 35, 36, 80, 383f.
Jordan river, 30, 31
Joseph, son of Jacob, 26, 79, 80, 274
Joshua, 30, 31, 352
Josiah, 45, 60, 242, 301, 350
Jotham, 182
Judah, son of Jacob, 80, 241, 297, 314
Judah, tribe of, 37
Judaism, 107, 108, 110, 134ff., 140, 156, 220, 250, 260, 295, 341, 417
Judas, 98
Judges, book of, 19, 33, 181, 182, 309, 348, 349
Justice (mishpat), 21
Juvenal, 213

Kali, 168
Kamsutra, 269
Karnak, 171
Kenites, 162
Kerouac, Jack, 233
Kerygma, 111ff.
Kinsey, Alfred, 203, 232, 233, 266, 341, 358, 359, 404, 409ff.
Kipling, Rudyard, 431
Kirkendall, Lester A., 425
Knossos, 197
Know (yada), 188f., 276ff.
Krafft-Ebing, Baron Richard von, 353f.

Laban, 84
Leah, 83, 85, 237, 386
Lesbianism, 194, 203f., 358
Levirate marriage, 237f., 283, 298, 375, 396, 398
Leviticus, 319, 351, 383, 395, 396, 401
Lewinsohn, Richard, 197, 202
Lewis, C. S., 91, 111, 123, 255
Libertinism, 222, 229, 233f., 265ff.

Liberty, Christian, 143ff.
Lincoln, Abraham, 26, 79
Lingam, 180
Livy, 211
Lot, 345, 346, 347, 392, 393
Love (agape), 67f., 91, 92, 129, 131ff., 143f., 147f., 430ff.
Love (aheb), 21, 53ff., 67, 75
Love (eros), 91, 92, 129, 131f.
Love (philia), 68, 91, 92
Love
    filial, 78f., 152f.
    neighborly, 66f., 141ff., 149
    parental, 78f., 152f., 299
    romantic, 53, 84f.
    self, 67, 149ff.
Lucretia, 207
Luke, 95n., 131, 334, 335
Lust, 138, 256
Luther, Martin, 91, 144, 145, 264, 336, 366, 405, 407
Lyciscus, 213
Lysistrata, 205

Maacah, 350, 397
Maccabees, 44
MacMurray, John, 231
Malachi, 55, 333
Man (ish), 272ff., 300
Marduk, 172, 173, 178
Mark, 95n., 117, 329, 334, 335
Marriage, as sacrament, 288
Marriage ceremony, 237, 275f.
Martial, 213
Marx, Karl, 404
Masculine freedom, 240f.
Masturbation, 297, 374ff., 411
Matriarchy, 168f., 195
Matthew, 95n., 124, 129, 139, 334, 335, 336
Medea, 196
Mehl-Koehnlein, H., 160
Melchizedek, 346
Melkart, 179
Menstruation, 280ff., 383
Meretrices, 210
Mesopotamia, 38, 162, 166, 178, 188, 215
Micah, 64, 74, 310
Michal, 35
Midianites, 32
Milkom, 179
Minear, Paul, 120
Mithras, 217, 219f.

Moabites, 27, 32, 179, 310, 392, 393
Mohammed, 60
Monogamy, 248, 288f.
Montefiore, Claude, 90
Moralism, 233f., 260, 265ff.
Moses, 17, 24, 28, 58, 81, 107, 162, 172, 281, 312, 314, 334
Motherhood, 82f.
Mylitta, 175
Mystery cults, 217ff.

Naaman, 65
Naboth, 38, 73
Nahum, 76, 309
Nakedness, 189, 377ff., 393ff.
Naomi, 80, 275
Nathan, 37, 38, 40, 73
Nature cults, 163ff., 174, 184ff.
Nazirites, 72, 74, 183
Necking, 235, 267
Necrophilia, 374
Nehemiah, 43
Niebuhr, Reinhold, 261
Noah, 162, 380f.
Nob, 284
Nonresistance, 142f., 338
Nuit, 166
Numbers, book of, 312
Nygren, Anders, 91, 92

Oholah, 307, 327
Oholibah, 307, 327
Onan, 281, 297f., 300f., 374, 375
One flesh (henosis), 252f., 275f., 291, 300, 316f., 333
Orient, 215ff., 221, 271
Original sin, 188f., 379, 416
Osiris, 167, 168, 217, 218, 219, 220
Othniel, 61
Ovid, 211ff., 268

Paederasty, 202
Paedophilia, 199, 374
Palestine, 32, 43, 44, 156, 248, 360
Pascal, Blaise, 150
Pastoral counseling, 339f.
Pastoral Epistles, 289, 301f., 330, 385
Paul, 90, 91, 95, 96, 97, 98, 99, 112, 118, 120, 123, 125, 126, 130, 133, 134, 142, 143, 144, 145, 146, 147, 156, 193, 194, 199, 218, 225, 226, 228, 248, 249, 250, 251, 252, 253, 254, 255, 256, 257, 258, 259, 260, 262, 264, 265, 273, 286, 289, 290, 291, 292, 293, 294, 296, 301, 302, 315, 316, 317, 329, 330, 335, 336, 360, 362, 363, 364, 384, 385, 398, 417, 426, 427, 431, 435
Pauline privilege, 336
Pedersen, Johannes, 310, 311
Pentecost, 112f., 115, 116
Pericles, 198, 199, 200
Persephone, 174
Persia, 42, 60, 177, 217, 219
Peter, 97, 112, 113, 114, 115, 131, 148, 155, 227, 249, 431
Petrie, Sir W. Flinders, 169n.
Petting, 235, 267, 411f.
Phallic symbols, 190, 350
Pharaoh, 38, 169, 170, 178
Pharisees, 90, 93, 94, 97, 101, 108, 110, 131, 133, 134ff., 140, 143, 154, 156, 228, 259, 260, 265, 315, 334, 371
Philippians, 121
Philistines, 23, 24, 27, 32, 34ff., 37, 179
Phineas, 80
Phinehas, 311
Phoebe, 302
Pilate, 108, 220
Pilgrims, 27
Piper, Otto, 276
Planned parenthood, 299
Plato, 28, 199, 271
Plautus, 29
Pliny, 214
Polygamy, 83, 248, 283, 340
Polytheism, 164f.
Pompey, 44, 211, 219
Population explosion, 304f.
Pornography, 213
Predestination, 97f., 133
Premarital relations, 176, 230ff., 410f.
Priestly writers (P), 28, 60, 270, 313, 345
Procreation 232, 294ff.
Propertius, 211
Prophets (nebiim), 38, 45, 59ff., 64ff., 121f.

Prostitution, 168, 171, 175f., 178, 200ff., 210, 212f., 225, 239ff., 252f., 294, 306, 307ff.
Protestantism, 231, 264, 285, 288, 295, 298ff., 336, 339, 375, 407f.
Proverbs, 314, 328
Psalms, 52, 135, 185, 309
Psychotherapy, 142, 150, 234, 262f., 360, 364f., 436f.
Ptolemy, 43, 169, 219
Puritans, 27

Ra, 38, 167
Rachel, 57, 83, 84, 237
Rado, Sandor, 271, 353ff.
Rahab, 314
Rape, 83, 86, 207, 386ff.
Rechabites, 72, 183
Rehoboam, 28, 41, 349, 350, 397
Renaissance, 28
Renault, Mary, 195
Repentance (metanoia), 105
Reuben, 396
Revelation, 121, 317f.
Rhythm method, 296f., 303
Roman Catholicism, 231, 264, 281, 285, 288, 295, 296, 297, 298, 336, 339, 375, 408, 421, 426
Romans, 98, 99, 126, 193, 225, 329, 360
Rome, 28, 44, 204, 205ff., 318
Rosenzweig, Franz, 124n.
Royden, Maude, 337
Russell, Jane, 67
Ruth, 76, 80

Sabine women, 208, 389
Sadducees, 135, 136
Sahu, 166
Samson, 61, 81, 183
Samuel, 33, 34, 36, 59, 64, 65, 73, 80, 113, 183, 284
Sapirstein, Milton, 269
Sappho, 203
Sarah, 57, 83, 237
Satan, 100, 101, 108, 386
Saul, 24, 27, 33ff., 37, 40, 59, 63, 64, 80, 182, 284, 383f.
Second Isaiah, 47ff., 89
Seleucids, 43
Semen, 280ff.
Seneca, 210, 213, 214
Sennacherib, 44, 49

Septuagint, 92
Serapis, 219
Sermon on the Mount, 94, 118, 338
Sex education, 419ff.
Sex in marriage, 268ff.
Shechem, 31, 180
Shechem, son of Hamor, 386f.
Sheen, Fulton J., 341
Shem, 380f.
Shiloh, 37, 80, 182, 309, 388, 389
Shiva, 180
Sibu, 166
Silas, 249
Sinai, Mount, 17, 24, 26, 27, 30, 55, 125
Slaves, sexual treatment of, 242f.
Socrates, 202
Sodom, 344ff., 392
Sodomite, 239, 351
Solomon, 28, 40, 41, 81, 83, 86, 103, 349, 397, 398
Solon, 202
Song of Songs, 22, 55, 86f., 307, 398, 436
Sophocles, 29
Stein, Gertrude, 375
Stoicism, 260
Strabo, 201
Svengali, 94
Synoptic Gospels, 95n., 99, 143
Syrians, 23, 24

Tacitus, 209
Tamar, daughter of David, 39, 55, 85, 190, 390
Tamar, wife of Er, 314, 375
Tammuz, 173, 174, 180
Tarquins, 207
Tarzan of the Apes, 274
Taurobolium, 218, 219
Temple, William, 21
Ten Commandments; *see* Decalogue
Terence, 29
Thebes, 168
Theseus, 196
Thessalonians, 120, 251
Thomas, 98
Thurber, James, 103
Tillich, Paul, 55, 138, 139, 151
Titus, Emperor, 136
Tolstoi, Leo, 140
Totemism, 282
Toynbee, Arnold, 27

Transvestism, 351ff.
Tribades, 203
Trojan war, 32
Tutankhamen, 172
Tutunus, Mutuus, 206
Tyre, 179

Uriah, 37, 73, 85, 284, 285
Uzzah, 58

Veblen, Thorsten, 84
Venus, 174, 175, 180
Virgil, 28, 211
Virginity, 176, 206, 222, 228,
    235, 286, 295
Virginity, tokens of, 236f.
von Allmen, J. J., 228
Voyeurism, 374, 377ff.

Washington, D.C., 37
Washington, George, 26
Wifehood, 82f.
Wolfe, Thomas, 123
Wolfenden Report, 371
Woman (ishshah), 272ff., 300
Word of God, 29, 404ff.
Wright, George Ernest, 166n.,
    186n.
Wylie, Philip, 279

Yahwist (J), 28, 313, 345, 380,
    382

Zealots, 101
Zedekiah, 38
Zeus, 43, 196, 197
Zoophilia, 374, 399ff.

INDEX OF BIBLICAL REFERENCES

The books are listed in their order in the English versions.

OLD TESTAMENT

Genesis

1	187
1:1-2	270
1:4a	270
1:26-28	270-271
2	28, 187, 333
2:4b	272
2:18	273
2:23	273
2:24	244
2:25	378
3:7	378
3:10-11	378-379
4:14	70
9:20-27	380-381
11:27-29	397
12:1-2	184
13:8-9	345
13:13	345
14	345
14:21	346
18:20	346
19	344
19:1-11	346-347
19:30-38	392

22:17-18	25
27	78
28:9	397
29	85
34	386-387
35:22	396
37:34-35	79
38	314
38:1-10	281
38:1-11	297, 374-375
38:12-19	241
44:30-31	80
49:3-4	396-397

Exodus

3	28
15:1	185
19:14-15	281
20:14	318
20:17	82
20:26	382
21:7-11	242
21:15	78
21:17	78
22:16-17	238
22:19	400-401

28:42-43	382	27:22	396
33:18-23	58	27:23	396
34:15-16	241-242	31:16	314
Leviticus		*Joshua*	
12:2-5	283	4:21-23	30-31
15:16-18	280	7—8	31
15:19-24	280	7:24-26	352
15:25-30	282	24	31
17:14	282	24:2	23
18	396		
18:6-18	393-394	*Judges*	
18:19	383	2:16-17	309
18:22	351	3:10	61
18:23	401	6:34	61
19:29	239, 312	7:1	181
20	396	8:33	180
20:10	319	9:8-15	182
20:11-21	395-396	11	314
20:15	401	11:29	61
20:16	401	11:39-40	182
20:18	280, 383	15:14	61
21:7	312	19	388
21:9	239, 312	19:22-26	348
21:10	319	21	388-389
21:10-15	239, 240	21:19-23	182
21:13-14	312	21:25	33
21:14	333		
		Ruth	
Numbers		1:16	81
5:11-31	320-322		
25:6-9	312, 313	*1 Samuel*	
		2:22	309
Deuteronomy		8	33
1:16-17	46	9:1—10:16	33
5:18	319	9:7-9	64-65
7:7-8	24	10:5	59
20:7	284	13	34
22:5	351	15	34
22:13-19	332	15:22	65
22:13-21	236-237	16:14 ff.	34-35
22:23-27	235	17	35
22:25-27	391	18:1	384
22:28	391	19:24	59
22:28-29	238, 332	20:30	383
22:30	396	21	284
23:17-18	239, 313, 351		
24:1	82,307	*2 Samuel*	
24:1-4	331, 334	1:26	383-384
24:5	284	6:6-7	58
25:11-12	383	11—12	37
26:5	23	11:2-4	85
27:20	396	11:11-13	284-285
27:21	401	13:2	85
		13:13	85, 390

13:15	86
13:16	190
13:20	390
13:22	390
13:32	390
15:4	39
18	40, 80

1 Kings
1:1-4	397-398
2	397
2:13-25	398
3:16-28	40, 81
12:14	41
14:22-24	349-350
15:12-14	350
18:28-29	60
21	38
22:46	350

2 Kings
5	65
23	350
23:7	242

2 Chronicles
11:18-21	397

Psalms
106	313
119	135

Proverbs
6:23-32	328
6:24-26	241
7	314-315
23:27-28	241
29:3	241

Song of Solomon
1:2	86
4	86-87
5	87

Isaiah
1:18-19	47
5:1-7	45
6	58
35:5-6	101
40	48
43:25	47
44:22	49
49:14-15	48
51:22	47
53:4-6	50
54:6-8	47

55:3	49
55:11	78
57:3-5	324
57:7-8	324

Jeremiah
1:12	187
2:1-37	45
3:1	333
3:1-2	325
3:6-9	325
4:1-2	45
5:7-9	325
7:9	325
7:16-20	180
9:2	326
13:26	326
13:27	326
23:11	326
23:14	326
29:23	326
44:15-30	180

Ezekiel
8:14	180
16:7-8	307
16:31-34	326-327
18	109
23:5-8	308
23:16-17	308
23:19-21	308
23:37-45	327

Hosea
1:2	16
2:2-3	322
2:14-15	21
3:1	323
4:1-2	323
4:11-14	310
4:12-14	323
7:4	323
11:8-9	20

Amos
2:7-8	309
2:12	74, 184
3:2	25
5:10	74
5:21-24	74
5:25	74
7:14-15	64
9:7	23, 25

Jonah
4:2	46

Micah
1:7   310

Malachi
2:13-16   333

NEW TESTAMENT

Matthew
5:17   136-137
5:18-19   137
5:21-28   138
5:27-28   260, 291, 329
5:32   330, 335
5:45   93
6:5   131
6:32   104
10:35-36   152
10:37   131, 152
11:4-5   101
13:57   153
15:11-20   227
15:19   291, 329
19:1-9   334
19:9   335
19:10-11   291
19:12   286
20:1-16   93
21:31   225
22:14   98
22:40   129
23:6-7   131
23:29-33   90
25   189
25:41   90-91

Mark
1:15   100
1:22   136
3:21   153
3:31-35   102-103
7:23   329
10:2-10   334
10:9   291
12:29-31   129

Luke
6:32   132
9:59-62   102
10:18   101
11:43   132
12:16-21   103
14:16-20   104
14:26   102, 152
16:18   330, 334
17:21   106

John
1:14   227
6:44   98
6:64-65   98
7:5   154
8:11   225
15:15   138
21:15-17   131

Acts of the Apostles
2:15-21   112-113
2:22-24   113-114
2:25-36   114-115
2:37-39   116
3:18   113
3:20-21   116
3:24   113
3:25   113
4:11-12   115
5:30-31   115
5:32   115
10:9-16   227
10:36-43   116-117
15:19-20   249

Romans
1:18-28   361
1:19-27   193-194
1:26 ff.   294
2:1   329
2:21-22   329
3:23   95
3:27   133-134
5:5   129
5:8   95
7:2-3   288-289
8:28-29   99
9-11   99
12:10   131
13:8   144
13:8-10   329
13:9-10   144
16:1   302

1 Corinthians
1:27-31   97
1:29   134
4:7   97
5:1   289
5:1-5   399
5:9-11   257-258
5:9-15   225-226
6   317
6:9-11   258, 294, 362

6:12 | 144, 364
6:13 | 364
6:15-20 | 252, 294, 316
7 | 156, 228, 301
7:1-9 | 291-292
7:2-6 | 297, 298
7:2-9 | 251-252
7:6 | 296
7:7 | 286
7:10-11 | 335
7:12-16 | 335-336
7:26-31 | 293
7:36 | 255-256
7:39 | 157, 288, 289
7:39-40 | 289, 330
10:23 | 145
10:24 | 147
11 | 125
11:4-6 | 384-385
11:5 | 302
11:8-9 | 158-159, 273
11:13-15 | 384-385
13:8 | 149
14:34 | 290

2 Corinthians
2:5-8 | 226
12:14 | 158

Galatians
2:9 | 249
2:10 | 249
3:3 | 258
5:12 | 218
5:19-21 | 226-227

Ephesians
1:4 | 98
3:15 | 158
5 | 317
5:1-13 | 256-257
5:5 | 227, 317
5:11-12 | 386
5:22-32 | 287
5:25 | 157
5:28-33 | 157
6:4 | 158
6:9 | 158

Philippians
2:6-8 | 149
2:8 | 290

Colossians
3:5 | 258
3:5-8 | 226

3:17 | 288
3:18 | 158
3:18-19 | 290

1 Thessalonians
4:2-8 | 251

1 Timothy
2:8-9 | 385
2:9-15 | 301
3:2 | 289
3:12 | 289
4:1-5 | 228
5:10 | 158
5:11-15 | 385-386
5:14 | 158
6:10 | 131

Titus
1:6 | 289

Hebrews
13:1 | 131
13:4 | 290-291, 330

James
2:1-7 | 148-149
2:8 | 148
2:14-16 | 148
3 | 148

1 Peter
3:1-6 | 158
3:8 | 131

2 Peter
2:20 | 331
2:22 | 331

1 John
1:8-9 | 99
2:15 | 132
3:1 | 147
3:16 | 147
4:2-3 | 228
4:7-11 | 147-148
4:10 | 99, 132
4:20-21 | 66, 129
5:3 | 148

Revelation
17 | 318
19:2 | 318
21:8 | 318
22:5 | 318